Focus on GRAMMAR 3B

FOURTH EDITION

Focus on GRAMMAR 3B

FOURTH EDITION

Marjorie Fuchs
Margaret Bonner
Miriam Westheimer

ALWAYS LEARNING

PEARSON

To the memory of my parents, Edith and Joseph Fuchs—MF
To my parents, Marie and Joseph Maus, and to my son, Luke Frances—MB
To my husband, Joel Einleger, and my children, Ari and Leora—MW

FOCUS ON GRAMMAR 3B: An Integrated Skills Approach, Fourth Edition

Pearson Education, 10 Bank Street, White Plains, NY 10606

Staff credits: The people who made up the *Focus on Grammar 3B, Fourth Edition,*
team, representing editorial, production, design, and manufacturing, are Elizabeth Carlson,
Tracey Cataldo, Aerin Csigay, Dave Dickey, Christine Edmonds, Nancy Flaggman, Ann France,
Françoise Leffler, Lise Minovitz, Barbara Perez, Robert Ruvo, and Debbie Sistino.

Cover image: Shutterstock.com
Text composition: ElectraGraphics, Inc.
Text font: New Aster

PEARSON LONGMAN ON THE **WEB**

Pearsonlongman.com offers online
resources for teachers and students. Access
our Companion Websites, our online catalog,
and our local offices around the world.

Visit us at **pearsonlongman.com**.

Printed in the United States of America

ISBN 10: 0-13-216061-7
ISBN 13: 978-0-13-216061-2

5 6 7 8 9 10—V082—16 15

ISBN 10: 0-13-216928-2 (with MyLab)
ISBN 13: 978-0-13-216928-8 (with MyLab)

1 2 3 4 5 6 7 8 9 10—V082—16 15 14 13 12 11

CONTENTS

WELCOME TO *FOCUS ON GRAMMAR*

Now in a new edition, the popular five-level *Focus on Grammar* course continues to provide an integrated-skills approach to help students understand and practice English grammar. Centered on thematic instruction, *Focus on Grammar* combines controlled and communicative practice with critical thinking skills and ongoing assessment. Students gain the confidence they need to speak and write English accurately and fluently.

NEW for the FOURTH EDITION

VOCABULARY

Key vocabulary is highlighted, practiced, and recycled throughout the unit.

PRONUNCIATION

Now, in every unit, pronunciation points and activities help students improve spoken accuracy and fluency.

LISTENING

Expanded listening tasks allow students to develop a range of listening skills.

UPDATED CHARTS and NOTES

Target structures are presented in a clear, easy-to-read format.

NEW READINGS

High-interest readings, updated or completely new, in a variety of genres integrate grammar and vocabulary in natural contexts.

NEW UNIT REVIEWS

Students can check their understanding and monitor their progress after completing each unit.

MyFocusOnGrammarLab

An easy-to-use online learning and assessment program offers online homework and individualized instruction anywhere, anytime.

Teacher's Resource Pack One compact resource includes:

THE TEACHER'S MANUAL: General Teaching Notes, Unit Teaching Notes, the Student Book Audioscript, and the Student Book Answer Key.

TEACHER'S RESOURCE DISC: Bound into the Resource Pack, this CD-ROM contains reproducible Placement, Part, and Unit Tests, as well as customizable Test-Generating Software. It also includes reproducible Internet Activities and PowerPoint® Grammar Presentations.

THE *FOCUS ON GRAMMAR* APPROACH

The new edition follows the same successful four-step approach of previous editions. The books provide an abundance of both controlled and communicative exercises so that students can bridge the gap between identifying grammatical structures and using them. The many communicative activities in each Student Book provide opportunities for critical thinking while enabling students to personalize what they have learned.

- **STEP 1: GRAMMAR IN CONTEXT** highlights the target structures in realistic contexts, such as conversations, magazine articles, and blog posts.
- **STEP 2: GRAMMAR PRESENTATION** presents the structures in clear and accessible grammar charts and notes with multiple examples of form and usage.
- **STEP 3: FOCUSED PRACTICE** provides numerous and varied controlled exercises for both the form and meaning of the new structures.
- **STEP 4: COMMUNICATION PRACTICE** includes listening and pronunciation and allows students to use the new structures freely and creatively in motivating, open-ended speaking and writing activities.

Recycling

Underpinning the scope and sequence of the *Focus on Grammar* series is the belief that students need to use target structures and vocabulary many times, in different contexts. New grammar and vocabulary are recycled throughout the book. Students have maximum exposure and become confident using the language in speech and in writing.

Assessment

Extensive testing informs instruction and allows teachers and students to measure progress.

- **Unit Reviews** at the end of every Student Book unit assess students' understanding of the grammar and allow students to monitor their own progress.
- Easy to administer and score, **Part and Unit Tests** provide teachers with a valid and reliable means to determine how well students know the material they are about to study and to assess students' mastery after they complete the material. These tests can be found on MyFocusOnGrammarLab, where they include immediate feedback and remediation, and as reproducible tests on the Teacher's Resource Disc.
- **Test-Generating Software** on the Teacher's Resource Disc includes a bank of *additional* test items teachers can use to create customized tests.
- A reproducible **Placement Test** on the Teacher's Resource Disc is designed to help teachers place students into one of the five levels of the *Focus on Grammar* course.

COMPONENTS

In addition to the Student Books, Teacher's Resource Packs, and MyLabs, the complete *Focus on Grammar* course includes:

Workbooks   Contain additional contextualized exercises appropriate for self-study.

Audio Program   Includes all of the listening and pronunciation exercises and opening passages from the Student Book. Some Student Books are packaged with the complete audio program (mp3 files). Alternatively, the audio program is available on a classroom set of CDs and on the MyLab.

THE *FOCUS ON GRAMMAR* UNIT

Focus on Grammar introduces grammar structures in the context of unified themes. All units follow a **four-step approach**, taking learners from grammar in context to communicative practice.

STEP 1 GRAMMAR IN CONTEXT

This section presents the target structure(s) in a natural context. As students read the **high-interest texts**, they encounter the form, meaning, and use of the grammar. **Before You Read** activities create interest and elicit students' knowledge about the topic. **After You Read** activities build students' reading vocabulary and comprehension.

Vocabulary exercises improve students' command of English. Vocabulary is **recycled** throughout the unit.

Engaging **readings** present the grammar in realistic contexts such as **magazine articles** and **blog posts**.

Reading comprehension tasks focus on the meaning of the text and draw students' attention to the target structure.

This section gives students a comprehensive and explicit overview of the grammar with detailed **Grammar Charts** and **Grammar Notes** that present the form, meaning, and use of the structure(s).

Grammar Charts present the structure in a clear, easy-to-read format.

Grammar Notes give concise, simple **explanations** and **examples** to ensure students' understanding.

REDESIGNED!

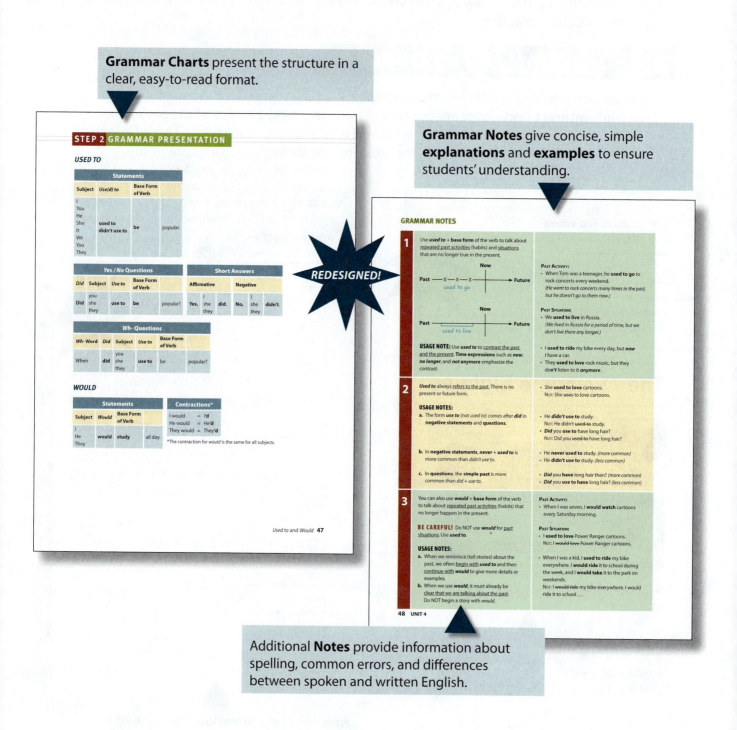

Additional **Notes** provide information about spelling, common errors, and differences between spoken and written English.

STEP 3 FOCUSED PRACTICE

Controlled practice activities in this section lead students to master form, meaning, and use of the target grammar.

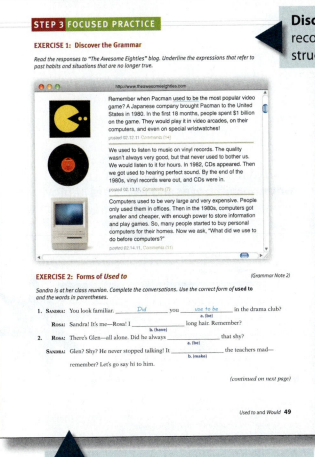

STEP 3 FOCUSED PRACTICE

EXERCISE 1: Discover the Grammar

Read the responses to "The Awesome Eighties" blog. Underline the expressions that refer to past habits and situations that are no longer true.

http://www.theawesomeeighties.com

Remember when Pacman used to be the most popular video game? A Japanese company brought Pacman to the United States in 1980. In the first 18 months, people spent $1 billion on the game. They would play it in video arcades, on their computers, and even on special wristwatches!
posted 02.12.11 Comments (14)

We used to listen to music on vinyl records. The quality wasn't always very good, but that never used to bother us. We would listen to it for hours. In 1982, CDs appeared. Then we got used to hearing perfect sound. By the end of the 1980s, vinyl records were out, and CDs were in.
posted 02.13.11 Comments (7)

Computers used to be very large and very expensive. People only used them in offices. Then in the 1980s, computers got smaller and cheaper, with enough power to store information and play games. So, many people started to buy personal computers for their homes. Now we ask, "What did we use to do before computers?"
posted 02.14.11 Comments (11)

EXERCISE 2: Forms of *Used to*   *(Grammar Note 2)*

Sandra is at her class reunion. Complete the conversations. Use the correct form of **used to** *and the words in parentheses.*

1. **SANDRA:** You look familiar. ___Did___ you ___use to be___ in the drama club?
          a. (be)
   ROSA: Sandra! It's me—Rosa! I _____ long hair. Remember?
          b. (have)
2. **ROSA:** There's Glen—all alone. Did he always _____ that shy?
          a. (be)
   SANDRA: Glen? Shy? He never stopped talking! It _____ the teachers mad—
          b. (make)
   remember? Let's go say hi to him.

(continued on next page)

Used to and Would   **49**

A **variety of exercise types** engage students and guide them from recognition and understanding to accurate production of the grammar structures.

Discover the Grammar activities develop students' recognition and understanding of the target structure before they are asked to produce it.

An **Editing** exercise ends every Focused Practice section and teaches students to find and correct typical mistakes.

EXERCISE 5: Editing

Read the journal entry about a high school reunion in Timmins, Ontario, a small town 500 miles north of Toronto. There are nine mistakes in the use of **used to** *and* **would**. *The first mistake is already corrected. Find and correct eight more.*

Shania Twain

    The high school reunion tonight was awesome! I
talked
~~used to talk~~ to Eileen Edwards for a long time. Well,
she's the famous country pop singer Shania Twain now.
In high school, she was used to be just one of us, and
tonight we all called her Eileen. She graduated in 1983,
the same year as me. Today she uses to live in a
chateau in Switzerland and has her own perfume
brand, but her life didn't use to be like that at all! She
uses to be very poor, and her grandma used to made all her clothes because her
family couldn't afford to buy them. She was always a good musician, though. In fact, she
used to earns money for her family that way. On Saturday nights, she would performed
with a local rock band, and my friends and I would go hear her. She could really sing!
Her new name, Shania, means "on my way" in Ojibwa (her stepfather's Native American
language). After she left Timmins, I would think that Timmins wasn't important to her
anymore—but I was wrong. Now that she's famous, she has a lot of power, and she
uses it to do good things for our community. And tonight she was just the way she
used be in high school—simple and friendly!

A school reunion

52   UNIT 4

STEP 4 COMMUNICATION PRACTICE

This section provides practice with the structure in **listening** and **pronunciation** exercises as well as in communicative, open-ended **speaking** and **writing** activities that move students toward fluency.

Listening activities allow students to hear the grammar in natural contexts and to practice a range of listening skills.

STEP 4 COMMUNICATION PRACTICE

EXERCISE 6: Listening

A | *Two friends are talking about their past. Listen to their conversation.*

B | *Read the statements. Then listen again to the conversation and circle the letter of the correct information.*

1. The friends are at a _____.
   a. rock concert   **(b.)** school reunion

2. Their present lives are very _____ their past lives.
   a. similar to   **b.** different from

3. They have _____ memories about their past.
   a. good   **b.** bad

4. They used to play a lot of _____.
   a. video games   **b.** music CDs

5. The friends are enjoying talking about _____.
   a. a trip   **b.** the past

C | *Listen again to the conversation. Check (✓) the things the friends used to do in the* **past** *and the things they do* **now**.

	Past	Now
1. get up very early without an alarm clock	✓	☐
2. use an alarm clock	☐	☐
3. have a big breakfast	☐	☐
4. have a cup of coffee	☐	☐
5. look at the newspaper	☐	☐
6. have endless energy	☐	☐
7. do aerobics	☐	☐
8. take car trips on weekends	☐	☐
9. meet at class reunions	☐	☐

EXPANDED!

Pronunciation Notes and **exercises** improve students' spoken fluency and accuracy.

EXERCISE 7: Pronunciation

A | *Read and listen to the Pronunciation Note.*

Pronunciation Note

We often pronounce *used to* like "usta." Notice that the pronunciation of *used to* and *use to* is the same.

EXAMPLES: I *used to* play chess.   →   "I **usta** play chess."
What games did you *use to* play?   →   "What games did you **usta** play?"

Be sure to write *used to* or *use to*, NOT "usta."

We often use the contraction of *would* (*'d*) in both **speech** and **writing**.

EXAMPLE: We *would* play for hours.   →   "We**'d** play for hours."

NEW!

B | *Listen to the sentences. Notice the pronunciation of* used to *and the contraction of* would.

1. I **used to** live in a small town.
2. I didn't **use to** have a lot of friends.
3. I**'d** spend hours alone.
4. On weekends, my sister **used to** play cards with me.
5. She**'d** always win.
6. We**'d** have a lot of fun.

C | *Listen again and repeat the sentences.*

EXERCISE 8: Picture Discussion

Work with a partner. Look at the pairs of pictures and talk about how the people have changed. Then write sentences that describe the changes. Compare your sentences with those of your classmates.

Then	Now

1. Sharifa *used to be very busy, but now she is more relaxed. She would always be in a hurry.*
   Now she takes things more slowly. She used to wear glasses, but now she doesn't . . .

C: *Everybody* used to have long hair then.

EXERCISE 10: Writing

A | *Write a two-paragraph essay. Contrast your life in the past with your life now. In the first paragraph, describe how your life used to be at some time in the past. In the second paragraph, describe your life today. Remember: We often begin with* **used to** *and then change to* **would**.

EXAMPLE: I used to live in Russia. I attended St. Petersburg University. I would ride my bike there every day. In those days I used to . . . Today I am living in Florida and attending Miami University . . .

B | *Check your work. Use the Editing Checklist.*

Editing Checklist

Did you . . . ?
☐ use *used to* correctly
☐ use *would* correctly
☐ change from *used to* to *would*

NEW!

Writing activities encourage students to produce meaningful writing that integrates the grammar structure.

An **Editing Checklist** teaches students to correct their mistakes and revise their work.

Speaking activities help students synthesize the grammar through discussions, debates, games, and problem-solving tasks, developing their fluency.

54   UNIT 4

Unit Reviews give students the opportunity to check their understanding of the target structure. **Answers** at the back of the book allow students to monitor their own progress.

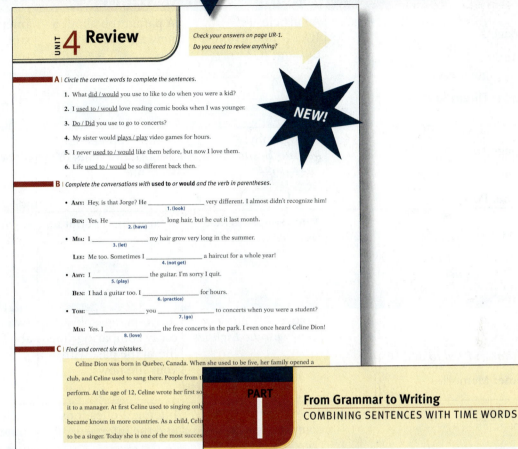

UNIT **4** Review

Check your answers on page UR-1.
Do you need to review anything?

NEW!

A | *Circle the correct words to complete the sentences.*

1. What <u>did / would</u> you use to like to do when you were a kid?

2. I <u>used to / would</u> love reading comic books when I was younger.

3. <u>Do / Did</u> you use to go to concerts?

4. My sister would <u>plays / play</u> video games for hours.

5. I never <u>used to / would</u> like them before, but now I love them.

6. Life <u>used to / would</u> be so different back then.

B | *Complete the conversations with* **used to** *or* **would** *and the verb in parentheses.*

• **AMY:** Hey, is that Jorge? He _____ very different. I almost didn't recognize him!
  1. (look)

  BEN: Yes. He _____ long hair, but he cut it last month.
  2. (have)

• **MIA:** I _____ my hair grow very long in the summer.
  3. (let)

  LEE: Me too. Sometimes I _____ a haircut for a whole year!
  4. (not get)

• **AMY:** I _____ the guitar. I'm sorry I quit.
  5. (play)

  BEN: I had a guitar too. I _____ for hours.
  6. (practice)

• **TOM:** _____ you _____ to concerts when you were a student?
  7. (go)

  MIA: Yes. I _____ the free concerts in the park. I even once heard Celine Dion!
  8. (love)

C | *Find and correct six mistakes.*

Celine Dion was born in Quebec, Canada. When she used to be five, her family opened a club, and Celine used to sang there. People from t... perform. At the age of 12, Celine wrote her first so... it to a manager. At first Celine used to singing only... became known in more countries. As a child, Celin... to be a singer. Today she is one of the most succes...

Extended writing tasks help students integrate the grammar structure as they follow the steps of the **writing process**.

PART **1**

From Grammar to Writing
COMBINING SENTENCES WITH TIME WORDS

You can often improve your writing by combining two short sentences into one longer sentence that connects the two ideas. The two sentences can be combined by using *time words* such as *while, when, as soon as, before, after,* or *until.* The new, longer sentence is made up of a main clause and a time clause.

EXAMPLE: I was shopping. I saw the perfect dress for her. →

TIME CLAUSE   MAIN CLAUSE
While I was shopping, I saw the perfect dress for her.

MAIN CLAUSE   TIME CLAUSE
I saw the perfect dress for her **while** I was shopping.

The time clause can come first or second. When it comes first, a **comma** separates the two clauses.

1 | *Read the paragraph. Underline all the sentences that are combined with a time word. Circle the time words.*

I always exchange holiday presents with my girlfriend, Shao Fen. Last year, (while) I was shopping for her, I saw an umbrella in her favorite color. As soon as I saw it, I thought of her. I bought the umbrella and a scarf in the same color. When Shao Fen opened the present, she looked really upset. She didn't say anything, and she didn't look at me. I felt hurt and confused by her reaction. Later she explained that in Chinese, the word for "umbrella" sounds like the word for "separation." When she saw the umbrella, she misunderstood. She thought I wanted to end the relationship. After I heard that, I was very upset! When we both felt calmer, we talked about our misunderstanding. At the end, we laughed about it, and I think we're better friends because of it. I discovered something new about Shao Fen's culture. Now I want to learn more about cross-cultural communication.

SCOPE AND SEQUENCE

UNIT	READING	WRITING	LISTENING
1 page 2 **Grammar:** Present Progressive and Simple Present **Theme:** Different Cultures	An article: *What's Your Cross-Cultural IQ?*	A paragraph about a new experience	Interviews of foreign students studying in the United States
2 page 16 **Grammar:** Simple Past **Theme:** Poets	A biography: *Matsuo Basho, 1644–1694*	A paragraph about important events in your life	An interview with a poet
3 page 31 **Grammar:** Past Progressive and Simple Past **Theme:** Accidents	A newspaper article: *Disaster at Sea*	A paragraph about an event you witnessed	A witness describing a traffic accident
4 page 45 **Grammar:** *Used to* and *Would* **Theme:** Memories	A blog: *The Awesome Eighties*	A two-paragraph essay comparing your life in the past with your life now	Two friends talking about their past
5 page 58 **Grammar:** *Wh-* Questions **Theme:** In Court	An excerpt from a court transcript: *State of Illinois vs. Harry M. Adams*	Interview questions and the interview	A telephone conversation about an accident
PART I **From Grammar to Writing,** page 69 **Combining Sentences with Time Words:** Write a paragraph about a misunderstanding or mistake.			
6 page 74 **Grammar:** Future **Theme:** Space Travel	A radio program transcript: *Space Tourists: Not Just Science Fiction*	A paragraph about your life five years from now	Conversations about future plans and about something happening now
7 page 91 **Grammar:** Future Time Clauses **Theme:** Setting Goals	An article: *Go For It! What are your dreams for the future?*	A goal-planning worksheet	A telephone call to an employment agency
PART II **From Grammar to Writing,** page 103 **Showing the Order of Events:** Write a blog post about your weekend plans.			

SPEAKING	PRONUNCIATION	VOCABULARY	
Find Someone Who . . . *Picture Discussion:* Understanding gestures and facial expressions *Compare and Contrast:* Appropriate cultural questions	Reduction of *What do you* and *What are you* ("Whaddaya")	abroad culture* distance	event misunderstanding native
Compare and Contrast: Two poets *Information Gap:* Celebrity Profile	*Wh-* questions with *did* ("Why'd")	admirer emotion journey	restless topic*
Game: Are You a Good Witness? *Role Play:* Alibi	Pausing after time clauses	alarmed area* calm (adj)	disaster sink (v) survivor*
Picture Discussion: Then and now *Compare and Contrast:* How you used to be and how you are now	Reduction of *used to* ("usta") and contraction of *would* ('d)	awesome collect memory	popular power weird
Role Play: On the Witness Stand *Game:* To Tell the Truth	Intonation of *Wh-* questions asking for information or asking for repetition	defendant frightened in a hurry	indicate* record (n)
Making Plans: Finding a time when you and your partner are both free *Reaching Agreement:* Deciding which events to attend	Contraction of *will* ('ll) and reduction of *going to* ("gonna")	edge experience (v) float	incredible sold out takeoff (n)
What About You? Comparing your plans with your classmates' plans *Game:* What's Next?	Intonation in sentences with time clauses	achieve* catalog degree	download goal* interview (n)

* = AWL (Academic Word List) items

SPEAKING	PRONUNCIATION	VOCABULARY	
Role Play: A Job Interview	Intonation in *yes / no* questions and *wh-* questions	consider dramatically* opportunity	positive* residence support (v)
Information Gap: Chores *What About You?* Things you've already done and things you haven't done yet	Contractions of *have* in the present perfect	available* organized professional*	specific* successful
Find Someone Who . . .	Reduction of auxiliary *have* ("books of") and *has* ("hotelz") after a noun	adventure affordable ancient	annual* survey* transportation*
Compare and Contrast: Events last year and this year *Interview:* Asking your partner about a long-distance relationship	Pronunciation of *-ed* in the simple past and past participle of regular verbs	apart arrangement manage	solution temporary* turn down
Find Someone Who . . . *Picture Discussion:* Global warming *Discussion:* Recent changes in your life	Stress in present perfect and present perfect progressive verb phrases	climate design (v)* develop	energy* expert* pollution
Information Gap: Can they do the tango? *Ask and Answer:* Finding someone who can do each task	Distinguishing unstressed *can* /kən/ and stressed *can't* /kænt/	aspiration confused dedication	integrated* perception* talent
Problem Solving: Asking permission *Role Play:* Could I . . . ?	Linking final consonants with *I* or *he:* *can I, could he, may I*	annoyed assume* establish*	guidelines* neat presentation

* = AWL (Academic Word List) items

SPEAKING	PRONUNCIATION	VOCABULARY	
Making Plans: Requesting help with things on your schedule	Reductions of *you* in requests ("couldja," "wouldja," "willya," and "canya")	appreciate* cheer up deliver	distribute* text (v)
Cross-Cultural Comparison: Advice about customs *Problem Solving:* Discussing everyday situations *Picture Discussion:* Improving a classroom	Reductions of *ought to* ("oughta") and *had better* ("'d better" or "better")	avoid behavior communication*	identity* normal* protect
Quotable Quotes: Time *Problem Solving:* Creating a time capsule	Dropping unstressed vowels ("histry")	civilization create* impressed	intentional interpret* occasion
Game: Quiz Show *Information Gap:* Story Time *Discussion:* What the morals of stories mean; tell a story that illustrates a moral	Two ways to pronounce *the*: /ði/ and /ðə/	enormous* famous immediately	struggle wonderful
What About You? Describing where you live *Compare and Contrast:* Different types of housing *Discussion:* Describing your ideal home *Game:* A Strange Story	Stressing contrasting or new information	charming convenient ideal	located* peaceful satisfied
Compare and Contrast: Pizzas from around the world *Role Play:* Your Restaurant	Reduction of *as* /əz/ and *than* /ðən/	crowded delicious fresh	relaxed* traditional* varied*

* = AWL (Academic Word List) items

SPEAKING	PRONUNCIATION	VOCABULARY	
What About You? Describing a city you have visited *Discussion:* Some cities in your country	Dropping the final -*t* sound before an initial consonant sound	dynamic* feature* financial*	multicultural public
Compare and Contrast: Famous athletes *Questionnaire:* Work and Play	Linking final consonants to beginning vowels in *as* + adverb + *as*	aggressively consistently* effectively	frequently intensely*
Survey: Opinions about smoking *For or Against:* Smoking in public and private places	Linking final -*ing* with an initial vowel sound	approve of ban (v) illegal*	in favor of permit (v) prohibit*
What About You? Describing childhood relationships *Cross-Cultural Comparison:* How do young people in your culture socialize?	Stress in infinitive phrases	focus (v)* interact* obviously*	similar* solve
Survey: Opinions about cell phones *For or Against:* Pros and cons of new technology *Problem Solving:* Other uses for everyday objects *Discussion:* New uses for a smart phone	Stress in adjective + infinitive phrases	combine device* function (n)*	major* multipurpose old-fashioned
Brainstorming: Ideas for work breaks *Information Gap:* At the Support Group *Quotable Quotes:* Procrastination *Problem Solving:* Ways of stopping clutter	Reduction of *to* /tə/, *for* /fər/, and *on* /ən/	anxious discouraging project (n)*	put off task* universal

* = AWL (Academic Word List) items

UNIT	READING	WRITING	LISTENING
27 page 376 **Grammar:** Reflexive and Reciprocal Pronouns **Theme:** Self-Talk	An article from a psychology magazine: *Self-Talk*	An advice column entitled "Help Yourself with Self-Talk"	Conversations at an office party
28 page 391 **Grammar:** Phrasal Verbs **Theme:** Animal Intelligence	An article about animal behavior expert Cesar Millan: *When He Whispers, They Tune In*	A paragraph about a pet or an animal you've read about or observed	Conversations about a college science class
PART VIII **From Grammar to Writing,** page 403 **Using pronouns for Coherence:** Write instructions to someone taking care of your home while you are away.			
29 page 408 **Grammar:** Necessity: *Have (got) to, Must, Don't have to, Must not, Can't* **Theme:** Transportation	An article: *Know Before You Go*	A paragraph about an application procedure	Short conversations about driving
30 page 422 **Grammar:** Expectations: *Be supposed to* **Theme:** Wedding Customs	A page from an etiquette book: *Wedding Wisdom*	A short essay about an important life event	Short conversations about a wedding
31 page 434 **Grammar:** Future Possibility: *May, Might, Could* **Theme:** Weather	A transcript of a TV weather report: *Weather Watch*	An email to a friend about your weekend plans	A weather forecast
32 page 446 **Grammar:** Conclusions: *Must, Have (got) to, May, Might, Could, Can't* **Theme:** Mysteries	The beginning of a Sherlock Holmes mystery: *The Red-Headed League*	Possibilities and conclusions based on a story outline	A radio play: the end of *The Red-Headed League*
PART IX **From Grammar to Writing,** page 461 **Combining Sentences with *Because, Although, Even though*:** Write a letter of complaint.			

SPEAKING	PRONUNCIATION	VOCABULARY	
Questionnaire: Are you an optimist or a pessimist? *Game:* Who Remembers More? *Picture Discussion:* Imagining people's self-talk *Problem Solving:* Feeling better in difficult situations	Stress in reflexive and reciprocal pronouns	fault finally* impact (v)*	maintain* reaction* realize
Making Plans: Organizing a class field trip *For or Against:* Owning a pet	Stress on noun and pronoun objects of phrasal verbs	figure out give up keep on	straighten out take over turn on
Picture Discussion: Traffic signs *Game:* Invent a Sign *What About You?* Describing tasks you have to and don't have to do *Discussion:* Rules and Regulations	Reductions of *have to* ("hafta" and "hasta") and *have got to* ("have gotta" and "gotta")	equipment* hassle (n) inspect*	regulation* strict valid*
Discussion: Important plans that you changed *Cross-Cultural Comparison:* Customs for important life events	Reductions of *supposed to* ("supposta") and *going to* ("gonna")	assistant* ceremony certificate	etiquette role* select*
Conversation: Your weekend plans *Problem Solving:* Predicting what two students might do in the future	Stress in short answers with modals	affect (v)* bundle up exceed*	forecast local trend*
Picture Discussion: Making guesses about a family *Problem Solving:* Giving possible explanations for several situations	Stress on modals that express conclusions	advertisement amazed encyclopedia method*	millionaire position salary

* = AWL (Academic Word List) items

ABOUT THE AUTHORS

Marjorie Fuchs has taught ESL at New York City Technical College and LaGuardia Community College of the City University of New York and EFL at the Sprach Studio Lingua Nova in Munich, Germany. She has a master's degree in Applied English Linguistics and a certificate in TESOL from the University of Wisconsin-Madison. She has authored and co-authored many widely used books and multimedia materials, notably *Crossroads, Top Twenty ESL Word Games: Beginning Vocabulary Development, Families: Ten Card Games for Language Learners, Focus on Grammar 4: An Integrated Skills Approach, Focus on Grammar 3 CD-ROM, Focus on Grammar 4 CD-ROM, Longman English Interactive 3* and *4, Grammar Express Basic, Grammar Express Basic CD-ROM, Grammar Express Intermediate, Future 1: English for Results,* and workbooks for *The Oxford Picture Dictionary High Beginning* and *Low Intermediate, Focus on Grammar 3* and *4,* and *Grammar Express Basic.*

Margaret Bonner has taught ESL at Hunter College and the Borough of Manhattan Community College of the City University of New York, at Taiwan National University in Taipei, and at Virginia Commonwealth University in Richmond. She holds a master's degree in library science from Columbia University, and she has done work toward a PhD in English literature at the Graduate Center of the City University of New York. She has authored and co-authored numerous ESL and EFL print and multimedia materials, including textbooks for the national school system of Oman, *Step into Writing: A Basic Writing Text, Focus on Grammar 4: An Integrated Skills Approach, Focus on Grammar 4 Workbook, Grammar Express Basic, Grammar Express Basic CD-ROM, Grammar Express Basic Workbook, Grammar Express Intermediate, Focus on Grammar 3 CD-ROM, Focus on Grammar 4 CD-ROM, Longman English Interactive 4,* and *The Oxford Picture Dictionary Low-Intermediate Workbook.*

Miriam Westheimer taught EFL at all levels of instruction in Haifa, Israel, for a period of six years. She has also taught ESL at Queens College, at LaGuardia Community College, and in the American Language Program of Columbia University. She holds a master's degree in TESOL and a doctorate in Curriculum and Teaching from Teachers College of Columbia University. She is the co-author of a communicative grammar program developed and widely used in Israel.

ACKNOWLEDGMENTS

Before acknowledging the many people who have contributed to the fourth edition of *Focus on Grammar,* we wish to express our gratitude to those who worked on the first, second, and third editions, and whose influence is still present in the new work. Our continuing thanks to:

- **Joanne Dresner**, who initiated the project and helped conceptualize the general approach of *Focus on Grammar*
- Our editors for the first three editions: **Nancy Perry**, **Penny Laporte**, **Louisa Hellegers**, **Joan Saslow**, **Laura Le Dréan**, and **Françoise Leffler**, for helping to bring the books to fruition
- **Sharon Hilles**, our grammar consultant, for her insight and advice on the first edition

In the fourth edition, *Focus on Grammar* has continued to evolve as we update materials and respond to the valuable feedback from teachers and students who have been using the series. We are grateful to the following editors and colleagues:

- The entire Pearson FOG team, in particular **Debbie Sistino** for overseeing the project and for her down-to-earth approach based on years of experience and knowledge of the field; **Lise Minovitz** for her enthusiasm and alacrity in answering our queries; and **Rosa Chapinal** for her courteous and competent administrative support.
- **Françoise Leffler**, our multi-talented editor, for her continued dedication to the series and for helping improve *Focus on Grammar* with each new edition. With her ear for natural language, eye for detail, analytical mind, and sense of style, she is truly an editor *extraordinaire*.
- **Robert Ruvo**, for piloting the book through its many stages of production
- **Irene Schoenberg** and **Jay Maurer** for their suggestions and support, and Irene for generously sharing her experience in teaching with the first three editions of this book
- **Ellen Shaw** for being a fan and for her insightful and thorough review of the previous edition
- **Sharon Goldstein** for her intelligent, thoughtful, and practical suggestions

Finally, we are grateful, as always, to **Rick Smith** and **Luke Frances**, for their helpful input and for standing by and supporting us as we navigated our way through our fourth *FOG*.

REVIEWERS

We are grateful to the following reviewers for their many helpful comments:

Aida Aganagic, Seneca College, Toronto, Canada; **Aftab Ahmed**, American University of Sharjah, Sharjah, United Arab Emirates; **Todd Allen**, English Language Institute, Gainesville, FL; **Anthony Anderson**, University of Texas, Austin, TX; **Anna K. Andrade**, ASA Institute, New York, NY; **Bayda Asbridge**, Worcester State College, Worcester, MA; **Raquel Ashkenasi**, American Language Institute, La Jolla, CA; **James Bakker**, Mt. San Antonio College, Walnut, CA; **Kate Baldrige-Hale**, Harper College, Palatine, IL; **Leticia S. Banks**, ALCI-SDUSM, San Marcos, CA; **Aegina Barnes**, York College CUNY, Forest Hills, NY; **Sarah Barnhardt**, Community College of Baltimore County, Reisterstown, MD; **Kimberly Becker**, Nashville State Community College, Nashville, TN; **Holly Bell**, California State University, San Marcos, CA; **Anne Bliss**, University of Colorado, Boulder, CO; **Diana Booth**, Elgin Community College, Elgin, IL; **Barbara Boyer**, South Plainfield High School, South Plainfield, NJ; **Janna Brink**, Mt. San Antonio College, Walnut, CA; **AJ Brown**, Portland State University, Portland, OR; **Amanda Burgoyne**, Worcester State College, Worcester, MA; **Brenda Burlingame**, Independence High School, Charlotte, NC; **Sandra Byrd**, Shelby County High School and Kentucky State University, Shelbyville, KY; **Edward Carlstedt**, American University of Sharjah, Sharjah, United Arab Emirates; **Sean Cochran**, American Language Institute, Fullerton, CA; **Yanely Cordero**, Miami Dade College, Miami, FL; **Lin Cui**, William Rainey Harper College, Palatine, IL; **Sheila Detweiler**, College Lake County, Libertyville, IL; **Ann Duncan**, University of Texas, Austin, TX; **Debra Edell**, Merrill Middle School, Denver, CO; **Virginia Edwards**, Chandler-Gilbert Community College, Chandler, AZ; **Kenneth Fackler**, University of Tennessee, Martin, TN; **Jennifer Farnell**, American Language Program, Stamford, CT; **Allen P. Feiste**, Suwon University, Hwaseong, South Korea; **Mina Fowler**, Mt. San Antonio Community College, Rancho Cucamonga, CA; **Rosemary Franklin**, University of Cincinnati, Cincinnati, OH; **Christiane Galvani**, Texas Southern University, Sugar Land, TX; **Chester Gates**, Community College of Baltimore County, Baltimore, MD; **Luka Gavrilovic**, Quest Language Studies, Toronto, Canada; **Sally Gearhart**, Santa Rosa Community College, Santa Rosa, CA; **Shannon Gerrity**, James Lick Middle School, San Francisco, CA; **Jeanette Gerrity Gomez**, Prince George's Community College, Largo, MD; **Carlos Gonzalez**, Miami Dade College, Miami, FL; **Therese Gormley Hirmer**, University of Guelph, Guelph, Canada; **Sudeepa Gulati**, Long Beach City College, Long Beach, CA; **Anthony Halderman**, Cuesta College, San Luis Obispo, CA; **Ann A. Hall**, University of Texas, Austin, TX; **Cora Higgins**, Boston Academy of English, Boston, MA; **Michelle Hilton**, South Lane School District, Cottage Grove, OR; **Nicole Hines**, Troy University, Atlanta, GA; **Rosemary Hiruma**, American Language Institute, Long Beach, CA; **Harriet Hoffman**, University of Texas, Austin, TX; **Leah Holck**, Michigan State University, East Lansing, MI; **Christy Hunt**, English for Internationals, Roswell, GA; **Osmany Hurtado**, Miami Dade College, Miami, FL; **Isabel Innocenti**, Miami Dade College, Miami, FL; **Donna Janian**, Oxford Intensive School of English, Medford, MA; **Scott Jenison**, Antelope Valley College, Lancaster, CA; **Grace Kim**, Mt. San Antonio College, Diamond Bar, CA; **Brian King**, ELS Language Center, Chicago, IL; **Pam Kopitzke**, Modesto Junior College, Modesto, CA; **Elena Lattarulo**, American Language Institute, San Diego, CA; **Karen Lavaty**, Mt. San Antonio College, Glendora, CA; **JJ Lee-Gilbert**, Menlo-Atherton High School, Foster City, CA; **Ruth Luman**, Modesto Junior College, Modesto, CA; **Yvette Lyons**, Tarrant County College, Fort Worth, TX; **Janet Magnoni**, Diablo Valley College, Pleasant Hill, CA; **Meg Maher**, YWCA Princeton, Princeton, NJ; **Carmen Marquez-Rivera**, Curie Metropolitan High School, Chicago, IL; **Meredith Massey**, Prince George's Community College, Hyattsville, MD; **Linda Maynard**, Coastline Community College, Westminster, CA; **Eve Mazereeuw**, University of Guelph, Guelph, Canada; **Susanne McLaughlin**, Roosevelt University, Chicago, IL; **Madeline Medeiros**, Cuesta College, San Luis Obispo, CA; **Gioconda Melendez**, Miami Dade College, Miami, FL; **Marcia Menaker**, Passaic County Community College, Morris Plains, NJ; **Seabrook Mendoza**, Cal State San Marcos University, Wildomar, CA; **Anadalia Mendoza**, Felix Varela Senior High School, Miami, FL; **Charmaine Mergulhao**, Quest Language Studies, Toronto, Canada; **Dana Miho**, Mt. San Antonio College, San Jacinto, CA; **Sonia Nelson**, Centennial Middle School, Portland, OR; **Manuel Niebla**, Miami Dade College, Miami, FL; **Alice Nitta**, Leeward Community College, Pearl City, HI; **Gabriela Oliva**, Quest Language Studies, Toronto, Canada; **Sara Packer**, Portland State University, Portland, OR; **Lesley Painter**, New School, New York, NY; **Carlos Paz-Perez**, Miami Dade College, Miami, FL; **Ileana Perez**, Miami Dade College, Miami, FL; **Barbara Pogue**, Essex County College, Newark, NJ; **Phillips Potash**, University of Texas, Austin, TX; **Jada Pothina**, University of Texas, Austin, TX; **Ewa Pratt**, Des Moines Area Community College, Des Moines, IA; **Pedro Prentt**, Hudson County Community College, Jersey City, NJ; **Maida Purdy**, Miami Dade College, Miami, FL; **Dolores Quiles**, SUNY Ulster, Stone Ridge, NY; **Mark Rau**, American River College, Sacramento, CA; **Lynne Raxlen**, Seneca College, Toronto, Canada; **Lauren Rein**, English for Internationals, Sandy Springs, GA; **Diana Rivers**, NOCCCD, Cypress, CA; **Silvia Rodriguez**, Santa Ana College, Mission Viejo, CA; **Rolando Romero**, Miami Dade College, Miami, FL; **Pedro Rosabal**, Miami Dade College, Miami, FL; **Natalie Rublik**, University of Quebec, Chicoutimi, Quebec, Canada; **Matilde Sanchez**, Oxnard College, Oxnard, CA; **Therese Sarkis-Kruse**, Wilson Commencement, Rochester, NY; **Mike Sfiropoulos**, Palm Beach Community College, Boynton Beach, FL; **Amy Shearon**, Rice University, Houston, TX; **Sara Shore**, Modesto Junior College, Modesto, CA; **Patricia Silva**, Richard Daley College, Chicago, IL; **Stephanie Solomon**, Seattle Central Community College, Vashon, WA; **Roberta Steinberg**, Mount Ida College, Newton, MA; **Teresa Szymula**, Curie Metropolitan High School, Chicago, IL; **Hui-Lien Tang**, Jasper High School, Plano, TX; **Christine Tierney**, Houston Community College, Sugar Land, TX; **Ileana Torres**, Miami Dade College, Miami, FL; **Michelle Van Slyke**, Western Washington University, Bellingham, WA; **Melissa Villamil**, Houston Community College, Sugar Land, TX; **Elizabeth Wagenheim**, Prince George's Community College, Lago, MD; **Mark Wagner**, Worcester State College, Worcester, MA; **Angela Waigand**, American University of Sharjah, Sharjah, United Arab Emirates; **Merari Weber**, Metropolitan Skills Center, Los Angeles, CA; **Sonia Wei**, Seneca College, Toronto, Canada; and **Vicki Woodward**, Indiana University, Bloomington, IN.

NOUNS, QUANTIFIERS, AND ARTICLES

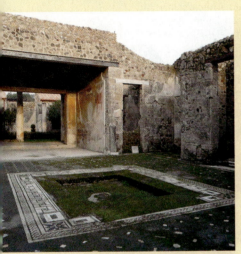

STEP 1 GRAMMAR IN CONTEXT

Before You Read

Look at the illustration of a time capsule. Discuss the questions.

1. What things can you name in the capsule?
2. What is a time capsule?
3. Why is the article called "Time in a Bottle"?

Read

Read the article on time capsules.

TIME IN A BOTTLE

An **alarm clock, lipstick**, a **toy car**, *some* **fabrics** made out of **cotton** and **wool**. A **picture** of a **baseball, money** (a **dollar bill** and *a few* **coins**). **Seeds** (such as **rice** and **corn**). The **Bible**, a written **message** from **Albert Einstein**, and hundreds of **books** and **newspapers** on **microfilm.**[1]

What do these **items** have in common? They all went into a **capsule** 50 **feet** underground in **Flushing Meadows Park**, in **New York City**. The **year** was 1939; the **occasion**, the **New York World's Fair**; and the **instructions** were not to open the **capsule** for 5,000 **years**!

The **Westinghouse Time Capsule** is just one of *many* **capsules** all over the **world**. They hold hundreds of everyday **objects**, but they have just one **purpose**: to tell **people** of the **future** about **life** in the **past**. To help make this happen, **Westinghouse** published a **book**, printed on special **paper** with **ink** that will not fade over **time**. The **book** tells how to find and open the **capsule**. It even explains how to interpret the **capsule's English**, which will be very different from **languages** 5,000 **years** from now!

The **Westinghouse Time Capsule** is an **example** of an intentional **time capsule**, but **history** has given

us unintentional **time capsules** too. The most famous is the ancient Roman **city** of **Pompeii**, in **Italy**. In the **year** 79, **Vesuvius**, a nearby **volcano**, erupted.[2] It buried the **city** under 60 **feet** of **ash** and created an instant **time capsule**. **Archeologists**[3] are still studying it today.

Intentional or unintentional, **time capsules** give us the **chance** to "communicate" with **people** from other **times**. What will **people** think of us when they open the **Westinghouse Time Capsule** in 5,000 **years**? Will they be as impressed with our **civilization** as we are with ancient **Pompeii**? Only **time** will tell—although we certainly won't be there to find out!

---

[1] *microfilm:* a special type of film used for making very small photos of important papers

[2] *erupt:* to explode and send out smoke, fire, and rocks into the sky

[3] *archeologist:* someone who studies ancient cultures by examining their buildings and objects

After You Read

A | Vocabulary: *Circle the letter of the word or phrase closest in meaning to the word in* **blue.**

1. I hear that Emily is having a big party tomorrow night. What's the **occasion**?

   a. starting time

   b. location

   c. reason for the event

2. Some of her friends **created** a birthday "time capsule" for her.

   a. bought

   b. found

   c. made

3. Emily was really **impressed**.

   a. unhappy

   b. full of respect

   c. important

4. James arrived late, but it wasn't **intentional**.

   a. on purpose

   b. very important

   c. too annoying

5. I couldn't **interpret** her email. Was she sad or angry?

   a. exactly describe

   b. completely remember

   c. decide on the meaning of

6. This semester, we're studying the **civilization** of ancient Rome.

   a. government

   b. society

   c. manners

B | Comprehension: *Check (✓)* **True** *or* **False.** *Correct the false statements.*

	True	False
1. Time capsules contain unusual items.	☐	☐
2. There are time capsules all over the world.	☐	☐
3. The Westinghouse Time Capsule is in Italy.	☐	☐
4. The ancient city of Pompeii is an unintentional time capsule.	☐	☐
5. Time capsules teach us about different civilizations.	☐	☐
6. People will soon be able to see the contents of the Westinghouse Time Capsule.	☐	☐

NOUNS AND QUANTIFIERS

Count Nouns			
	Noun	**Verb**	
One	**capsule**	is	in New York.
Two	**capsules**	are	

Non-Count Nouns		
Noun	**Verb**	
Money	is	inside.

Quantifiers and Count Nouns		
	Quantifier	**Noun**
It holds	*some* *enough* *a lot of* *a few* *several* *many*	fabrics. seeds. coins.
It doesn't hold	*any* *enough* *a lot of* *many*	
Does it hold	*any* *enough* *a lot of* *many*	coins?

Quantifiers and Non-Count Nouns		
	Quantifier	**Noun**
It holds	*some* *enough* *a lot of* *a little* *a great deal of*	wool. rice. money.
It doesn't hold	*any* *enough* *a lot of* *much*	
Does it hold	*any* *enough* *a lot of* *much*	money?

GRAMMAR NOTES

1 There are two categories of nouns: **proper nouns** and **common nouns**.

a. Proper nouns are the <u>names</u> of particular people, places, or things. They are usually unique (there is only one).

People	Albert Einstein, Emily Lee
Places	New York, Italy
Things	Coca Cola, *Time* magazine
Months	September, October
Nationalities	American, Italian

<u>Capitalize</u> the first letter of proper nouns.

• Have you ever visited **Pompeii**?

b. Common nouns refer to people, places, and things, but <u>not by their names</u>. For example, *scientist* is a common noun, but *Einstein* is a proper noun.

People	scientist, teacher, archeologist
Places	city, country, continent
Things	soda, newspapers, wool

<u>Do NOT capitalize</u> the first letter of a common noun unless the noun is the first word in a sentence.

• Einstein was a **scientist**.
  NOT: Einstein was a ~~Scientist~~.

2 **Common nouns** can be **count** or **non-count**.

a. Count nouns are people, places, or things that you can <u>count separately</u>: *one book, two books, three books* . . .

• Count nouns can be <u>singular or plural</u>.
• They take <u>singular or plural verbs</u>.
• You can use *a, an* or *the* before them.

• He read one **book**. She read two **books**.
• The **book** *is* new, but the **newspapers** *are* old.
• There's **a toy** in **the box**.

b. Non-count nouns are things that you <u>cannot count separately</u>. For example, you can say *rice*, but you cannot say ~~one rice~~ or ~~two rices~~. To the right are some categories of non-count nouns.

Abstract words	education, love, time
Activities	exploring, farming, sailing
Courses of study	archeology, history, math
Foods	corn, milk, rice
Fabrics	cotton, silk, wool

Some common non-count nouns do not fit into categories.

equipment	homework	news
furniture	information	work

• Non-count nouns have <u>NO plural</u> forms.
• They take <u>singular verbs and pronouns</u>.

• She bought a lot of **wool**. NOT: ~~wools~~
• **Archeology** *is* an interesting subject. **It** *was* his favorite subject.
  NOT: ~~An archeology~~ is an interesting subject.

• We usually do NOT use *a* or *an* with them.

(continued on next page)

3 Use **quantifiers** with nouns to talk about *how many* or *how much*. Some quantifiers go only with count or with non-count nouns. Other quantifiers can go with both.

a. In **affirmative statements**, use:

- *many*, *a lot of*, *a great many*, and *a great deal of* for a large quantity

- *some* and *several* for a smaller quantity

- *enough* for *the* necessary quantity

- *few / a few* and *little / a little* for a small quantity

BE CAREFUL! The meaning of *few* and *little* is different from *a few* and *a little*. *Few* and *little* usually mean *not enough*.

b. In **negative statements** and in **questions** use:

- *many*, *a lot of*, *any*, and *enough* with count nouns

- *much*, *a lot of*, *any*, and *enough* with non-count nouns

USAGE NOTE: Sometimes, people use *much* instead of *a lot of* in affirmative sentences. This is very formal and not common.

- ***Many* people** worked on the capsule.
- They did **a great deal of work**.
- It took **a few years** to finish.
- That wasn't **much time**.

Count Nouns	Non-Count Nouns
many / a lot of coins	***a lot of*** money
a great many jobs	***a great deal of*** work
some toys	***some*** wool
several books	***some*** paper
enough apples	***enough*** rice
a few years	***a little*** time

- We had **a little time** to complete the project. *(We had some time, but not a lot.)*
- We had **little time** to complete the project. *(We almost didn't have enough time.)*

- There weren't **many students** in class.
- Did you put **any seeds** in the capsule?
- There weren't **enough books**.

- We didn't have **much rice**.
- Does he have **any homework**?
- There was never **enough time**.

VERY COMMON: They spent **a lot of money**.
NOT COMMON: They spent **much money**.

REFERENCE NOTES

For a list of **irregular plural nouns**, see Appendix 6 on page A-4.
For a list of **non-count nouns**, see Appendix 7 on page A-4.
For **categories of proper nouns**, see Appendix 8 on page A-5.
For **spelling rules** for **regular plural nouns**, see Appendix 25 on page A-11.
For **capitalization rules**, see Appendix 27 on page A-13.

EXERCISE 1: Discover the Grammar

A | *Read the article about Pompeii. Underline the nouns.*

Pompeii: A Window to Ancient History

Pompeii was a rich and lively city on the bay of Naples, south of Rome. Wealthy Romans came to spend the summer there in large and beautiful villas.[1] Then, on August 24 in the year 79, Vesuvius erupted. The volcano buried the city under 60 feet of ash and killed thousands of people. It also destroyed a great many of the buildings. But not all of them. The ash preserved many houses, roads, theaters, statues, and a lot of beautiful art.

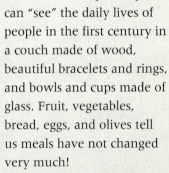

Pompeii's ruins stayed buried for almost 2,000 years. Then one day in 1748, a Spanish engineer discovered them. Since that time, archeologists have dug up many everyday objects from this ancient civilization.

Furniture, jewelry, money, and even a little food remain from that terrible day. Today we can "see" the daily lives of people in the first century in a couch made of wood, beautiful bracelets and rings, and bowls and cups made of glass. Fruit, vegetables, bread, eggs, and olives tell us meals have not changed very much!

Today Pompeii is "alive" again. Millions of tourists walk its roads each year. This amazing unintentional time capsule shows them what everyday life in ancient Rome was like. It is their window to ancient history.

_____

[1] *villa:* an ancient Roman house or farm with land surrounding it

B | *Put nouns from the article into the correct columns. Choose only 16 count nouns.*

Proper Nouns	Common Nouns			
	Count Nouns		**Non-Count Nouns**	
1. _Pompeii_	1. _window_	9. _____	1. _history_	8. _____
2. _____	2. _____	10. _____	2. _____	9. _____
3. _____	3. _____	11. _____	3. _____	10. _____
4. _____	4. _____	12. _____	4. _____	11. _____
5. _____	5. _____	13. _____	5. _____	12. _____
6. _____	6. _____	14. _____	6. _____	13. _____
	7. _____	15. _____	7. _____	
	8. _____	16. _____		

EXERCISE 2: Noun and Verb Agreement

(Grammar Note 2)

Emily and James are planning a trip to Pompeii. They are checking a travel website for some tips on packing. Complete the tips. Use the correct form of the words in parentheses. Go to Appendix 7 on page A-4 for help with non-count nouns.

Pompeii Packing Posts

On the Road

Your ___*feet need*___ your help! Good _____ a must! You'll be walking
    1. (foot / need)   **2. (shoe / be)**

for _____ among the _____ of this ancient civilization. And, remember, those
  3. (hour)   **4. (ruin)**

_____ very, very old—almost 2,000 _____!
  5. (street / be)   **6. (year)**

Hey, it's hot out there!

_____ essential. You can't buy it once you're inside, so don't forget to take
  7. (water / be)

several _____ with you. The _____ VERY hot, so _____ very
  8. (bottle)   **9. (sun / be)**   **10. (sunblock / be)**

important too. And don't forget your _____! Both these _____ protect
              11. (hat)   **12. (thing / help)**

you from the sun.

Pompeii—It's picture perfect!

Pompeii is amazing, and you'll want to take a lot of _____. So bring a camera and
         13. (picture)

an extra memory card. Extra _____ important too!
    14. (battery / be)

What to wear

The right _____ a big difference. Pompeii often _____ cool at night, so
  15. (clothing / make)   **16. (get)**

bring a sweater.

Tempus fugit

That's Latin for _____. Most _____ a whole day at Pompeii.
    17. (time / fly)   **18. (people / spend)**

The _____ huge. Take a map, and take your time!
  19. (ruin / be)

EXERCISE 3: Quantifiers

(Grammar Note 3)

Circle the correct words to complete the conversations.

1. **EMILY:** There were so (many) / much people at the ruins today. Was it some kind of special
   a.

   occasion or something?

   JAMES: I don't think so. I heard the guide say it's the most popular tourist attraction in Italy.

   EMILY: And I can understand why. I've never seen so much / many fascinating things.
   b.

2. **EMILY:** My feet hurt! We did a lot of / much walking today!
   a.

   JAMES: Tell me about it! But it sure was amazing.

   EMILY: How many / much pictures did you take?
   b.

   JAMES: I took a few / a lot of pictures—over 200!
   c.

3. **JAMES:** It sure was hot. I'm glad we took some /any water with us. I really drank a lot / much.
   a.   **b.**

   EMILY: Me too. And I used several / a great deal of sunblock. The sun was *really* strong.
   c.

   JAMES: Do we have some / any water left? I'm still thirsty.
   d.

4. **EMILY:** Are you hungry? I saw a little / a few nice-looking restaurants nearby.
   a.

   JAMES: OK. But we need to stop at an ATM first. We only have a little / a few money left.
   b.

   EMILY: That's not a problem. Very little / few restaurants don't accept credit cards these days.
   c.

5. **JAMES:** You know, we should spend some / any time in Naples. Our guidebook says they have
   a.

   a lot of / much art from Pompeii at the Archeological Museum.
   b.

   EMILY: Do we have little / enough time to do that? Tomorrow is our last day.
   c.

   JAMES: True. But I think we can spend few / a few hours there. We don't need enough / much
   d.   **e.**

   time to pack, do we?

   EMILY: I haven't bought some / any souvenirs yet, and I feel like we're running out of time.
   f.

   JAMES: Don't worry. We can do some / a few shopping before dinner. How much / many gifts
   g.   **h.**

   do you need to buy?

   EMILY: Not much / many, I guess. Just some / any things for the family.
   i.   **j.**

(continued on next page)

6. **EMILY:** I'm impressed with our guidebook. It does a great job of interpreting the art.

   JAMES: Yes. It has <u>a lot of / many</u> useful information. Maybe it can recommend a restaurant.
   a.

   EMILY: What do you feel like eating?

   JAMES: I'd love <u>some / any</u> pasta. What about you?
   b.

   EMILY: Sounds good. And <u>a little / a few</u> dessert would be nice too. Maybe they have that
   c.

   Roman apple cake.

EXERCISE 4: Editing

Read Emily's email to her family. There are fifteen mistakes in the use of nouns and in the use of verb and pronoun agreement. The first mistake is already corrected. Find and correct fourteen more.

Hi Everyone!

James and I got back from Pompeii *a* few days ago. We bought a little souvenirs, which I'll

mail to you all very soon. We're still unpacking and looking over the many, many

photograph (hundreds!) we took of this amazing place. Our Guidebook calls the Pompeii

a "time capsule," and I truly felt that we were somehow communicating with this rich and

vibrant cultures. There are never enough times for everything on vacation, but that's

especially true of Pompeii. Really, there are few places in the world this amazing. You

should all try to go. I was so impressed!

   I plan to do a several blog posts and put up a lot photos to show you what I mean.

Speaking of time capsules, I was just in the attic putting away any suitcases, and I

discovered a trunk with much old stuff. The old clothing were still in great shape—I might

wear some of the skirts and blouses. Oh, and I found a great deal of letters that Grandpa

wrote to grandma when he was working in Italy on an archeological dig. A few of them

made me cry, and one of them had a recipe for Roman apple cake! I think we'll try to make

it, and we'll let you know how it turns out.

Love,

Emily

EXERCISE 5: Listening

A | *Emily and James are discussing a recipe. Look at the list of ingredients. Then listen to the conversation. Listen again and complete the list of ingredients. (You'll complete the shopping list later.)*

Roman Apple Cake

✓ 1 ½ cups _____sugar_____
½ cup vegetable _____
2 _____
2 _____ flour
1 teaspoon baking powder
1 _____ baking soda
¼ teaspoon _____
½ teaspoon cinnamon
1 cup _____
½ cup _____
½ cup _____
3 _____

Shopping List

eggs

B | *Listen to the rest of the conversation between Emily and James and check (✓) the items on the list of ingredients that they have enough of.*

C | *Listen again to Emily and James's conversation. Complete the shopping list of ingredients they need to buy.*

EXERCISE 6: Pronunciation

A | *Read and listen to the Pronunciation Note.*

> **Pronunciation Note**
>
> In **conversation** we sometimes **do not pronounce unstressed vowels**. For example, in the word *history*, we drop the vowel in the second syllable, *histⱷry*, and say "histry."
>
> EXAMPLES: history → "histry"
> family → "famly"
> camera → "camra"

B | *Read the sentences. Which vowels do you think are dropped? Draw a slash (/) through them. Then listen to the sentences and check your answers.*

1. Pompeii is very interesting.

2. We saw several wall paintings.

3. Don't forget your camera!

4. It makes a big difference.

5. I'm studying history.

6. We ate at my favorite restaurant.

7. The vegetables are delicious.

8. I bought some jewelry for my family.

C | *Listen again and repeat the sentences.*

EXERCISE 7: Quotable Quotes

Read the quotes about time. Discuss them with a partner. What do they mean? Do you agree with them?

1. It takes time to build castles. Rome wasn't built in a day.
   —*Irish proverb*

   EXAMPLE: **A:** I think this proverb means that you can't do something important quickly.
   B: I agree. Success isn't instant.

2. Time gives good advice.
   —*Maltese proverb*

3. Be happy while you're living for you're a long time dead.
   —*Scottish proverb*

4. There's no time like the present.
   —*English proverb*

5. Tomorrow is nothing; today is too late; the good lived yesterday.
   —*Marcus Aurelius (121–180, Roman emperor, historian, philosopher)*

6. Time stays long enough for anyone who will use it.
   —*Leonardo da Vinci (1452–1519, Italian painter, sculptor, architect, engineer)*

7. Time is money.
   —*Benjamin Franklin (1706–1790, U.S. statesman, scientist, writer)*

8. Time you enjoyed wasting is not wasted time.
   —*T. S. Eliot (1888–1965, U.S.-British poet)*

9. When you sit with a nice girl for two hours, you think it's only a minute. But when you sit on a hot stove for a minute, you think it's two hours. That's relativity.
   —*Albert Einstein (1879–1955, German-U.S. physicist)*

EXERCISE 8: Problem Solving

A | *Work with a group. Imagine that you are going to create a time capsule to tell people in the future about your present life. You have room in your capsule for only 10 things. Try to use both count and non-count nouns.*

Some categories to consider:

- books
- clothing
- food
- games
- money
- music
- technology
- tools

Answer the questions:

1. Which 10 items will you put in your time capsule? (Give the reasons for your choices.)

    EXAMPLE: **A:** Let's put in some fast food.
    B: A hamburger will go bad in less than a day!
    A: We could put *pictures* of popular kinds of fast food.

2. When do you want people to open it?

    EXAMPLE: **A:** I think people should open it 50 years from now. Then we can see their reactions.
    B: Good. It's enough time for a lot of things to change.

3. Where will you put your time capsule?

    EXAMPLE: **A:** Let's put it in the school basement.
    B: I don't know about that. Maybe the school won't still be here 50 years from now. How about . . . ?

4. What will you call your time capsule? Give it a name.

    EXAMPLE: **A:** Let's just name it after the year.
    B: Good idea. We'll call it Capsule 2011.

B | *Compare your choices with other groups' choices. Have other groups made any of the same choices as your group?*

EXERCISE 9: Writing

A | *Write a note to put in a time capsule. Use information from Exercise 8 or choose at least five items to put in the capsule. Your note is to the people who will open the capsule. Answer the questions:*

1. When did you create the capsule?
2. Where did you put it?
3. What is inside and why did you choose those items? How many or how much did you include?

EXAMPLE: On October 4, 2010, my classmates and I created a time capsule. We buried it under the oldest tree in Lincoln Park. The capsule contains 10 items. Each item tells something about the lives we live today. For example, we put a few sales receipts inside to show . . .

B | *Check your work. Use the Editing Checklist.*

Editing Checklist

Did you . . . ?
- ☐ capitalize proper nouns
- ☐ use non-count nouns with singular verbs and pronouns
- ☐ use the correct verb (singular or plural) after count nouns
- ☐ use correct quantifiers

A | *Circle the letter of the correct answer to complete each sentence.*

1. Where would you like to go today? We only have a _____ time.
   a. little   **b.** few   **c.** great deal of

2. Do we have _____ time for the photography museum?
   a. several   **b.** enough   **c.** few

3. Sure! They have _____ old photographs of the city, and I'd love to see them.
   a. any   **b.** much   **c.** a lot of

4. The museum is _____ miles from here. Let's take our bikes.
   a. few   **b.** a great deal of   **c.** several

5. OK. And we should remember to bring _____ water. It's hot today.
   a. some   **b.** a few   **c.** little

B | *Complete the suggestions for items to put in a time capsule. Use the correct form of the words in parentheses.*

1. _____ essential. Include different kinds.
   (music / be)

2. Family _____ relationships, personalities, and a lot more.
   (photograph / show)

3. _____ a great item. Include bills and coins.
   (money / make)

4. _____ the popular styles and the fabrics of the time.
   (clothing / show)

5. _____ bad fast, so put in pictures of food instead.
   (food / go)

C | *Find and correct ten mistakes.*

One night in june, 1,400 Years ago, a volcano erupted in today's El Salvador and buried a village of the great Mayan civilization. Archeologists have already found many large building from this time, but only a little homes of farmers and workers. The village of El Ceren contains perfect examples of a great deal of everyday objects. The archeologists have found some knives (with foods still on them), much pots made of clays, a lot garden tools, a little fabric, and a book. On the wall of one room, they found a few word in an unknown language. There is still a lot to learn from this time capsule, called "the Pompeii of Latin America."

Articles: Indefinite and Definite
STORIES

STEP 1 GRAMMAR IN CONTEXT

Before You Read

Look at the pictures on this page and the next. Read the title of each story. Discuss the questions.

1. What kind of a story is a fable?
2. Are fables only for children?
3. Do you know a fable in your first language?

Read

Read the two fables.

Two Fables

Aesop was **a famous storyteller** in Greece more than 2,000 years ago. **The fables** he told are still famous all over **the world**. Here are two of Aesop's fables.

The Ant and the Dove

Help!

An ant lived next to **a river**. One day, **the ant** went to **the river** to drink, and he fell into **the water**. **A dove** was sitting in **a tree** next to **the river**. **The dove** saw **the ant** struggling in **the water**. She picked **a leaf** from **the tree** and dropped it into **the river**. **The ant** climbed onto **the leaf** and floated safely to **the shore**.

An hour later, **a hunter** came to **the river** to catch **birds**. He was **the best hunter** in that part of **the country**, and all **the animals** feared him. When **the ant** saw **the hunter**, he wanted to save his friend, but he thought, "How can **a tiny ant** stop **a big man**?" Then he had **an idea**. He climbed on **the hunter's foot** and bit him hard. **The hunter** shouted in pain, and **the noise** made **the dove** fly away.

The Town Mouse and the Country Mouse

A town mouse went to visit his cousin in **the country**. **The country cousin** was poor, but he gladly served his town cousin **the only food** he had—**some beans** and **some bread**. **The town mouse** ate **the bread** and laughed. He said, "What **simple food** you **country mice** eat! Come home with me. I'll show you how to live." **The moon** was shining brightly that night, so **the mice** left immediately.

As soon as they arrived at **the town mouse's house**, they went into **the dining room**. There they found **the leftovers** of **a wonderful dinner**. **The mice** were soon eating **jelly** and **cake** and many nice things. Suddenly, **the door** flew open, and **an enormous dog** ran in. **The mice** ran away quickly. "Good-bye, Cousin," said **the country mouse**. "Are you leaving so soon?" asked **the town mouse**. "Yes," his honest cousin replied. "This has been **a great adventure**, but I'd rather eat **bread** in peace than **cake** in fear."

After You Read

A | Vocabulary: *Complete the sentences from another fable with the words from the box.*

enormous	famous	immediately	struggled	wonderful

1. A long time ago, a smart cat lived with a very poor master. The cat _____

   to help his master, but it wasn't easy.

2. One day, he had an adventure with a(n) _____ giant. The giant was 10 feet tall.

3. To show his magic powers, the giant became a tiny mouse, and the clever cat ate him. He and

   his master didn't wait. They _____ moved into the giant's castle.

4. The cat and his master became _____. Everyone knew about the man and his

   clever cat. People even wrote stories about them.

5. The cat's master married a princess, and they lived a(n) _____ life in the castle.

   The cat became rich and powerful and wore beautiful clothes. He only chased mice for fun.

B | Comprehension: *Number the sentences in each group in the correct order (1–5).*

"The Ant and the Dove"

_____ An hour later, a hunter came to the river to catch birds.

_____ She picked a leaf from the tree and dropped it into the river.

_____ The dove saw the ant struggling in the water.

_____ A dove was sitting in a tree next to the river.

_____ The ant climbed onto the leaf and floated safely to the shore.

"The Town Mouse and the Country Mouse"

_____ The town mouse ate the bread and laughed.

_____ The mice ran away quickly.

_____ The country cousin was poor, but he gladly served his town cousin the only food he had.

_____ This has been a great adventure.

_____ A town mouse went to visit his cousin in the country.

STEP 2 GRAMMAR PRESENTATION

ARTICLES: INDEFINITE AND DEFINITE

Indefinite

Singular Count Nouns		
	A / An	**(Adjective) Noun**
Let's read	**a**	**story.**
This is	**an**	**old story.**

Plural Count Nouns / Non-Count Nouns		
	(Some)	**(Adjective) Noun**
Let's listen to	**(some)**	**stories** on this CD.
This CD has		**nice music** too.

Definite

Singular Count Nouns		
	The	**(Adjective) Noun**
Let's read	**the**	**story** by Aesop.
It's		**oldest story.**

Plural Count Nouns / Non-Count Nouns		
	The	**(Adjective) Noun**
Let's listen to	**the**	**stories** by Aesop.
I like		**old music** on this CD.

GRAMMAR NOTES

1 We can use **nouns** in two ways:

a. A noun is **indefinite** when you and your listener <u>do not have a specific person, place, or thing in mind</u>.

A: Let's buy **a book**.
B: Good idea. Which one should we buy?
(A and B are not talking about a specific book.)

b. A noun is **definite** when you and your listener both <u>know which person, place, or thing</u> you are talking about.

A: I bought **the book** yesterday.
B: Good. You've wanted it for a while.
(A and B are talking about a specific book.)

2 To show that a noun is **indefinite**, use the **indefinite article** *a / an*, or **no article**, or *some*.

a. Use the **indefinite article** *a / an* with <u>singular count nouns</u> that are **indefinite**.

A: I'm reading *a* **fable**.
B: Oh really? Which one?

- Use *a* before <u>consonant sounds</u>.
- Use *an* before <u>vowel sounds</u>.

- *a* **r**iver, *a* **t**iny ant
- *an* **i**dea, *an* **e**xciting story

BE CAREFUL! It is the <u>sound</u>, not the letter, that determines whether you use *a* or *an*.

- *a* **E**uropean writer (a "Yuropean")
- *an* **h**onest relative (an "ahnest")

b. Use **no article** or *some* with <u>plural count nouns</u> and with <u>non-count nouns</u> that are **indefinite**. *Some* means an indefinite number.

PLURAL COUNT
- I had (*some*) **leftovers** for dinner.

NON-COUNT
- I should buy (*some*) **food**.

3 Notice these uses of *a / an*, **no article**, and *some*:

a. To **identify** (say what someone or something is), use:

- *a / an* with <u>singular count nouns</u>

A: What do you do?
SINGULAR COUNT
B: I'm *a* **chef**. NOT: I'm chef.

- **no article** with <u>plural count nouns</u> and <u>non-count nouns</u>

A: What's in the pot?
PLURAL COUNT   NON-COUNT
B: They're **beans**. I'm making **soup**.

b. To make **general statements**, use **no article** with <u>plural count nouns</u> and <u>non-count nouns</u>.

PLURAL COUNT   NON-COUNT
- Ava loves **stories** and **music**.
(stories and music in general)
NOT: Ava loves the stories and the music.

c. *Some* in general statements means "several, but not all."

- I like *some* **stories**, but a lot of them are boring.

(continued on next page)

4   Use the **definite article *the*** with most <u>common nouns</u> (count and non-count, singular and plural) that are **definite**.

Use ***the*** when:

a. a person, place, or thing is <u>unique</u>—there is only one

- Aesop is famous all over ***the* world**.
- ***The* moon** was shining brightly.

b. the <u>context</u> makes it clear which person, place, or thing you mean

A: Who is she?
B: She's ***the* teacher**.
    (A and B are students in a classroom.
    A is a new student.)

c. the noun is mentioned for the <u>second time</u> (it is often indefinite the first time it is mentioned)

- ***An* ant** lived next to ***a* river**. One day, ***the* ant** went to ***the* river** to drink.
- They ate **cake**. ***The* cake** was delicious.

d. a <u>phrase or adjective</u> such as ***first***, ***best***, ***right***, ***wrong***, or ***only*** identifies the noun

- He was ***the best* hunter** in the country.
- He served ***the only* food** he had.

Use the **definite article** with some <u>proper nouns</u>, for example, the names of:
- certain books and documents
- countries and geographical features

- ***the*** Koran, ***the*** U.S. Constitution
- ***the*** United Arab Emirates, ***the*** Alps

5   **Adjectives** often go <u>directly before a noun</u>. When you use an article or *some*, the adjective goes between the article or *some* and the noun.

- ***Old* fables** are great.
- We read ***the first* story** in the book.
- He has **some *wonderful old*** books.

REFERENCE NOTES
For a list of **non-count nouns**, see Appendix 7 on page A-4.
For more information about the use of ***the*** with **proper nouns**, see Appendix 8 on page A-5.
For more information about the **word order of adjectives**, see Appendix 12 on page A-6.

STEP 3   FOCUSED PRACTICE

EXERCISE 1: Discover the Grammar

Read the conversations. Circle the letter of the statement that best describes each conversation.

1. **CORA:** Dad, could you read me a story?

    DAD: Sure, I'd love to.

      a. Dad knows which story Cora wants him to read.

      b. Cora isn't talking about a particular story.

2. Fred: Mom, where's the new book?

   Mom: Sorry, I haven't seen it.

      a. Mom knows that Fred bought a new book.

      b. Mom doesn't know that Fred bought a new book.

3. Dad: I'll bet it's in the hall. You always drop your things there.

   Fred: I'll go look.

      a. There are several halls in the house.

      b. There is only one hall in the house.

4. Dad: Was I right?

   Fred: You weren't even close. It was on a chair in the kitchen.

      a. There is only one chair in the kitchen.

      b. There are several chairs in the kitchen.

5. Dad: Wow! Look at that! The pictures are great.

   Fred: So are the stories.

      a. All books have great pictures and stories.

      b. The book Fred bought has great pictures and stories.

6. Fred: Oh, I forgot . . . I also got a video game. Do you want to play?

   Dad: Sure. I love video games.

      a. Dad is talking about video games in general.

      b. Dad is talking about a particular video game.

EXERCISE 2: Definite Article or No Article

(Grammar Notes 1, 3–5)

Ben went to a bookstore to buy books for his niece. Complete the sentences. Use **the** *where necessary. Leave a blank if you don't need an article.*

Ben: I'm looking for _____ books for my 14-year-old niece. Do you have any
1.

   recommendations?

Clerk: Let's go to _____*the*_____ young adult section. Does she like _____
2.   3.

   mysteries? Doris Duncan wrote some good ones for teenagers.

Ben: She's read all _____ mysteries by Duncan. She's _____ fastest
4.   5.

   reader in the family!

Clerk: It's hard to keep up with _____ fast readers. Here's a good one by Gillian
6.

   Cross—*Born of* _____ *Sun*. It's about finding a lost Inca city.
7.

(continued on next page)

BEN: She'll like that one. She loves _____ books about _____
8.   9.
history—and science too.

CLERK: Then how about *A Short History of* _____ *Universe*? It's in
10.

_____ science section.
11.

BEN: This is great! She likes _____ books with beautiful pictures.
12.

CLERK: Well, _____ pictures in this one are wonderful. *Nature Magazine* called this
13.

book _____ best introduction to this subject.
14.

BEN: OK, I'll take _____ mystery by Cross and _____ science book.
15.   16.
Anything else?

CLERK: Well, _____ kids have fun with _____ trivia games. Here's a
17.   18.
good one.

BEN: Great. I'll get _____ trivia game too. Thanks. You've been very helpful.
19.

EXERCISE 3: Indefinite or Definite Article

(Grammar Notes 1–5)

*Complete the information and the story about Nasreddin. Use **a, an,** or **the.***

Nasreddin lived _____ *a* _____ long time ago in Turkey. He
1.
is one of _____ most famous characters in literature.
2.
People often thought he was _____ fool, but he was
3.
_____ very wise man. Here is _____
4.   5.
funny story about him:

Nasreddin Solves _____ Difficult Problem
6.

Nasreddin had _____ little donkey. There was
7.
_____ market in _____ nearby
8.   9.
town, and Nasreddin and his grandson often went there with

_____ donkey. One day, they were traveling to
10.

_____ market when _____ group of people passed by. Someone
11.   12.
shouted, "Look! _____ old man is walking while _____ boy rides!" So
13.   14.

_____ boy got down, and Nasreddin rode. Then they passed _____
15.   16.
storyteller sitting under _____ tree. _____ storyteller called out,
17.   18.

"Why is that poor child walking in _____ hot sun?" So they both rode. Next,
                                   19.

they met _____ old woman. "_____ little donkey is tired!" she
         20.   **21.**

shouted. So Nasreddin said, "_____ best thing is for both of us to walk." Soon
                             22.

they met _____ merchant. _____ merchant's donkey was carrying
         23.   **24.**

_____ enormous bag. "Why are you two walking?" _____ merchant
   25.   **26.**

laughed. "That's _____ strong little donkey!" Nasreddin immediately picked up
                 27.

_____ donkey and carried it on his shoulders. "These people will never leave us
   28.

alone," he told his grandson. "So this is _____ only way to solve _____
                                          29.   **30.**

problem."

EXERCISE 4: Indefinite, Definite, or No Article

(Grammar Notes 1–5)

Circle the correct article to complete the paragraph. Circle Ø if you don't need an article.

People all over the / Ø world know a / the fables of Aesop, but
            1.   **2.**

there is very little information about the / Ø life of this famous
                                        3.

Greek storyteller. Scholars agree that Aesop was born around

620 B.C.E.[1] In his early years, he was a / the slave, and he lived on
                                       4.

Samos, an / a island in an / the Aegean Sea. Even as a / the slave,
       5.   **6.**   **7.**

Aesop had the / Ø wisdom and knowledge. His master respected
           8.

him so much that he freed him. When Aesop became a / Ø free
                                                  9.

man, he traveled to many countries in order to learn and to teach.

In Lydia, the / Ø king invited him to stay in that country and gave Aesop some difficult jobs in
        10.

a / the government. In his work, Aesop often struggled to convince people of his ideas. Sometimes
11.

he used a / Ø fables to help people understand what he meant. One time, a / the king sent Aesop to
       12.   **13.**

Delphi with a / Ø gold for a / the people of that city. Aesop became disgusted with the / Ø people's
        14.   **15.**   **16.**

greed, so he sent the / Ø gold back to a / the king. A / The people of Delphi were very angry at Aesop
             17.   **18.**   **19.**

for this, and they killed him. After his death, a / the famous sculptor made a / the statue of Aesop you
                                             20.   **21.**

see in a / the photo above.
      22.

---

[1] **B.C.E.:** the abbreviation for *Before Common Era*, a year-numbering system used in many parts of the world

EXERCISE 5: Indefinite, Definite, or No Article

(Grammar Notes 1–5)

This is a trivia game. Complete the clues for each item. Then, using the clues and the appropriate picture, write the answer. Use **a, an,** *or* **the** *where necessary. Leave a blank if you don't need an article. The answers to the trivia game are on page 260.*

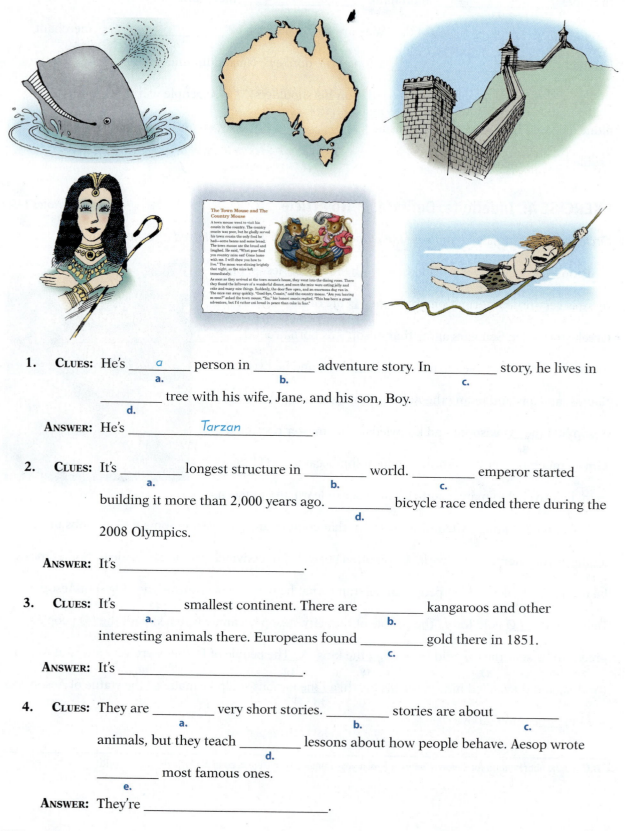

1. **CLUES:** He's _____*a*_____ person in _____ adventure story. In _____ story, he lives in
          a.   **b.**   **c.**
   _____ tree with his wife, Jane, and his son, Boy.
       d.

   ANSWER: He's _____*Tarzan*_____.

2. **CLUES:** It's _____ longest structure in _____ world. _____ emperor started
           a.   **b.**   **c.**
   building it more than 2,000 years ago. _____ bicycle race ended there during the
                                     d.
   2008 Olympics.

   ANSWER: It's _____.

3. **CLUES:** It's _____ smallest continent. There are _____ kangaroos and other
           a.   **b.**
   interesting animals there. Europeans found _____ gold there in 1851.
                                 c.

   ANSWER: It's _____.

4. **CLUES:** They are _____ very short stories. _____ stories are about _____
             a.   **b.**   **c.**
   animals, but they teach _____ lessons about how people behave. Aesop wrote
                      d.
   _____ most famous ones.
       e.

   ANSWER: They're _____.

5. **CLUES:** She was _____ intelligent and beautiful woman. She was _____ most
   a.   b.

   famous queen of Egypt. She ruled _____ country with her brother.
   c.

   ANSWER: She was _____.

6. **CLUES:** They are _____ biggest living animals on Earth. They have _____ fins, but
   a.   b.

   they aren't _____ fish.
   c.

   ANSWER: They're _____.

EXERCISE 6: Editing

Read the article about video games. There are thirteen mistakes in the use of **a, an,** *and* **the***.*
The first mistake is already corrected. Find and correct twelve more.

THE PLUMBER AND THE APE

Once there was a plumber named Mario.
The plumber
~~Plumber~~ had beautiful girlfriend. One

day, a ape fell in love with the girlfriend

and kidnapped her. The plumber chased

ape to rescue his girlfriend. This simple

tale became *Donkey Kong*, a first video

game with a story. It was invented by Shigeru Miyamoto, an artist with Nintendo,

Inc. Miyamoto loved the video games, but he wanted to make them more

interesting. He liked fairy tales, so he invented story similar to a famous fairy tale.

Story was an immediate success, and Nintendo followed it with *The Mario*

Brothers and then with *Super Mario*. The third game became popular all over a

world, and it is still most famous game in video history. Nintendo has continued

to add the new adventures and new ways to play game. Now players can follow

Mario to outer space and play the game on their Wii.[1] But success and space travel

do not change Mario. He is still brave little plumber in a red hat.

_____

[1] *Wii* (pronounced "we"): a game system in which players hold a wireless controller and
control the game by their movements and by pressing buttons

EXERCISE 7: Listening

A | *Read the sentences. Then listen to the short conversations. Listen again and circle the words that you hear.*

1. I just finished a /(the) story by Nasreddin.

2. It's a / the new video game. Do you want to try it?

3. She's a / the princess with magic powers.

4. What about Aesop? Have you read a / the fable?

5. You know, I'd like to buy a / the book of fables for Ava.

6. Let's go to a / the bookstore this weekend.

7. Why don't you have a / the sandwich?

8. I think I put it on a / the shelf above the sink.

B | *Read the statements about the conversations. Then listen again to each conversation and circle the letter of the correct statement.*

1. **a.** Ben already knows about the story.
   b. Ben and Amy haven't spoken about the story before.

2. **a.** Ben and Amy have already spoken about this video game.
   b. Ben has never mentioned this video game before.

3. **a.** The story has several princesses. One of them has magic powers.
   b. The story has just one princess.

4. **a.** Ben and Amy have already spoken about this fable.
   b. Amy has never mentioned this fable before.

5. **a.** Amy has a specific book of fables in mind.
   b. Amy isn't thinking of a particular book of fables.

6. **a.** Amy has a specific bookstore in mind.
   b. Amy isn't thinking of a particular bookstore.

7. **a.** There is only one sandwich.
   b. There are several sandwiches.

8. **a.** There is only one shelf above the sink.
   b. There is more than one shelf above the sink.

EXERCISE 8: Pronunciation

A | *Read and listen to the Pronunciation Note.*

Pronunciation Note
The can be pronounced in two ways:
1. Before a **vowel sound**, say "thee" /ði/
EXAMPLE: the ant
2. Before a **consonant sound**, say "the" /ðə/
EXAMPLE: the dove

B | *Listen to the sentences. Which pronunciation of* **the** *do you hear? Check (✓) the box.*

	/ði/	/ðə/
1. We watched **the** new quiz show last night.	☐	☐
2. My sister answered all **the** questions.	☐	☐
3. I only answered **the** easy ones.	☐	☐
4. One question was about *The Mario Brothers*.	☐	☐
5. It's **the** oldest video game with a story.	☐	☐
6. I have one of **the** earliest games.	☐	☐
7. It's **the** only one I still play.	☐	☐
8. My friends like **the** newer games.	☐	☐

C | *Listen again and repeat the sentences.*

EXERCISE 9: Game: Quiz Show

Work with a small group. Choose five interesting or famous things. Write three clues for each thing. Then join another group. Give your clues and ask the other group to guess what each thing is. Look at Exercise 5 on page 254 for ideas. You can use the Internet or a library to find information.

EXAMPLE: **A:** It's a planet. It's the closest one to the Sun. There might be water there.
                B: Does it have rings?
                C: No, it doesn't.

EXERCISE 10: Information Gap: Story Time

Work in pairs (A and B). **Student A,** *follow the instructions on this page.* **Student B,** *turn to page 260 and follow the instructions there.*

1. Look at the picture below. Ask your partner for the information you need to finish labeling the picture.

   EXAMPLE: **A:** Who's the man in the black cape?
   B: He's the magician.

2. Answer your partner's questions.

   EXAMPLE: **B:** What's the magician holding?
   A: A magic wand.

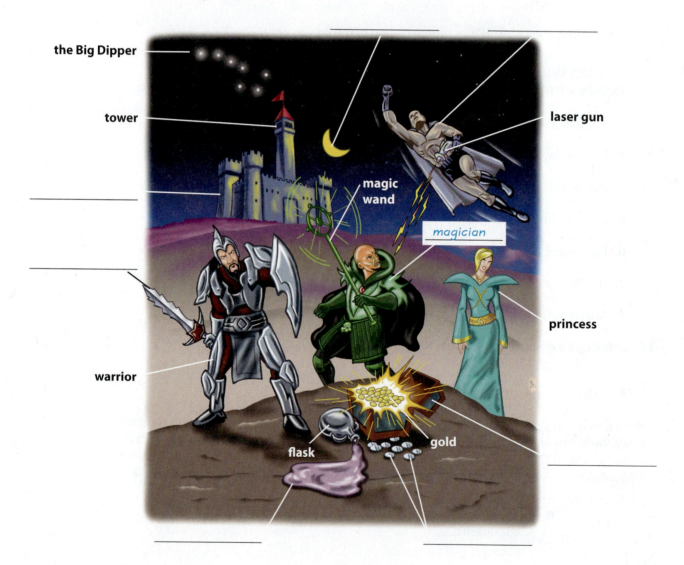

When you are finished, compare pictures. Are the labels the same?

EXERCISE 11: Discussion

A | *Fables often have a* moral—*a sentence at the end that explains the lesson of the story. Work with a small group. Read the list of morals. Answer the questions.*

- You can't please everyone.
- Sometimes a little friend is a great friend.
- Look before you leap.
- It's better to eat bread in peace than cake in fear.
- Slow and steady wins the race.
- Self-help is the best help.

1. Which ones belong to the two fables on pages 246–247?
2. Which one goes with the Nasreddin story on page 252?
3. What do you think they mean?

EXAMPLE: **A:** "It's better to eat bread in peace than cake in fear" goes with the second fable.
B: I think this means it's better to have a good life situation with poorer things than a bad life situation with better things.
C: I agree. You can't enjoy the better things if you're living in fear.

B | *Tell a story that illustrates one of the other morals. The story can be an experience you have had yourself or something you know about. The group will guess the moral.*

EXAMPLE: "When I went to college, my sister wanted to sew some curtains for my dorm room. She wanted the curtains to be really special, so she asked a friend to help her choose the material. The friend promised to help, but she didn't really have time to do it. My sister didn't start the curtains because she kept waiting for her friend . . ."

EXERCISE 12: Writing

A | *Choose one of the morals from Exercise 11. Write a paragraph about an experience that illustrates the meaning of the moral.*

EXAMPLE: "Slow and steady wins the race."
When I was in high school, I was a good student, but I always waited until the night before a test to study. I learned very fast, so I never had trouble. Then I took a class from Mr. Fox, the toughest teacher in the school . . .

B | *Check your work. Use the Editing Checklist.*

Editing Checklist

Did you use . . . ?
- [ ] *a*, *an*, *some*, or **no article** with indefinite nouns
- [ ] *the* with definite nouns
- [ ] *a*, *an*, *some*, or **no article** to identify and make general statements
- [ ] *the* when a noun is unique, or it is clear which person, place, or thing it is

1. Look at the picture below. Answer your partner's questions.

   EXAMPLE: **A:** Who's the man in the black cape?
   B: He's the magician.

2. Ask your partner for the information you need to finish labeling the picture.

   EXAMPLE: **B:** What's the magician holding?
   A: A magic wand.

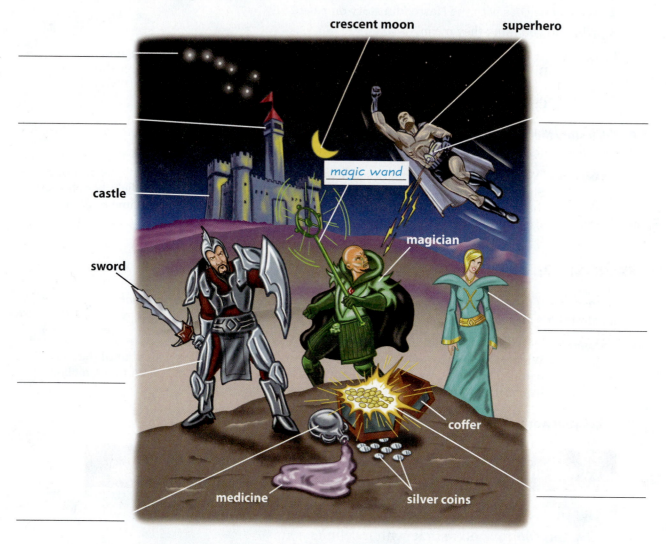

When you are finished, compare pictures. Are the labels the same?

Review

Check your answers on page UR-5.

Do you need to review anything?

A | *Circle the correct articles to complete the sentences. Circle Ø if you don't need an article.*

1. Is there <u>a / the</u> good bookstore around here?

2. I want to buy <u>a / the</u> book for my niece.

3. She really enjoys <u>the / Ø</u> fables.

4. I just read <u>a / an</u> excellent collection of fables.

5. <u>Some / Ø</u> fables have mice in them.

6. My niece is afraid of <u>Ø / the</u> mice.

7. This is <u>a / the</u> best story I've ever read.

8. It's famous all over <u>a / the</u> world.

B | *Complete the conversations with* **a, an,** *or* **the.**

* **A:** Did anyone feed _____ cat today?
  1.

  B: I did. Why?

  A: He's still hungry.

  B: Well, there's more food in _____ kitchen.
  2.

* **A:** Look at this picture of Boots.

  B: It's really cute. What kind of cat is it?

  A: It's not _____ cat. It's _____ dog.
  3.   **4.**

  B: You're kidding! What _____ unusual animal!
  5.

C | *Find and correct seven mistakes.*

Yesterday I downloaded the movies. We watched comedy and a Argentinian thriller. A comedy was very funny. I really enjoyed it. The thriller wasn't that good. There wasn't enough action in it. Tonight I think I'd rather read the book than watch a movie. I recently bought the book of fables and a mystery. I think I'll read a mystery before I go to bed.

PART V

From Grammar to Writing
DEVELOPING A PARAGRAPH WITH EXAMPLES

One way to develop a paragraph is to add **examples**. Examples give more information about the people, places, and things you are describing. They make your writing clearer and more interesting.

EXAMPLE: We celebrate with **food**. ➔
We celebrate with **food**. **For example, we bake loaves of bread we call "souls."**

1 | Read the paragraph about a holiday. Write the examples from the box in the correct place in the paragraph.

My family always hires a mariachi band	**For my sister, we offer toys.**
~~we bake loaves of bread we call "souls."~~	**We also create an altar¹ and put candy skulls² on it.**

A Happy Holiday

In Mexico we celebrate *Los Días de los Muertos* ("The Days of the Dead") on November 1 and 2. On these days, we remember our relatives who have died. We celebrate with wonderful food, special gifts for the dead, and music. For example, _____we bake loaves of bread we call "souls."_____
                                                                                    1.
They are shaped like people. _____ In addition,
                                                        2.
we remember special things our relatives liked, and we buy them gifts. For example, for my grandfather, we always put out a new hat. _____
                                                                          3.
On the second day, everyone in my family meets at the cemetery.³ This sounds like a sad occasion, but it is really a big party. _____ , and we all sing.
                                                        4.
Some people think that *Los Días de los Muertos* is like Halloween, but they are wrong. At Halloween, people pretend to be afraid of evil spirits, but during *Los Días de los Muertos*, we invite the friendly spirits of our family to visit us. It's our way of communicating with them.

---

¹ *altar:* a special table for religious ceremonies
² *skull:* the bones of a person's head
³ *cemetery:* a special area where dead people are buried

2 | *Complete the outline of the paragraph in Exercise 1.*

1. The name of the holiday and when it is celebrated: _____

2. The purpose of the holiday: _____

3. How people celebrate the holiday:

    a. _____*food*_____

        EXAMPLES: ___*loaves of bread called "souls"*___ and _____

    b. _____

        EXAMPLES: ___*a new hat for my grandfather*___ and _____

    c. _____

        EXAMPLES: _____ and _____

3 | *Before you write . . .*

1. Think about a holiday that is special to you. Develop an outline like the one in Exercise 2 for a paragraph about the holiday.

2. Work with a partner. Exchange outlines. Ask questions about your partner's holiday. Answer your partner's questions.

4 | *Write a paragraph about a special holiday. Include the information your partner asked you about.*

5 | *Exchange paragraphs with a different partner. Complete the chart.*

	Yes	No
1. Does the paragraph include examples?	☐	☐
2. Do the examples give more information about people, places, and things?	☐	☐
3. Are there more examples that you would like to see?	☐	☐
4. If yes, what would you like an example of? _____		
5. What else would you like to know about this holiday? _____		

_____

6 | *Work with your partner. Discuss each other's editing questions from Exercise 5. Then rewrite your own paragraph and make any necessary corrections.*

ADJECTIVES AND ADVERBS

Adjectives and Adverbs
HOME

STEP 1 GRAMMAR IN CONTEXT

Before You Read

Look at the house. Discuss the questions.

1. Is this a good place to live? Why or why not?
2. What is important when looking for a home?

Read

Read the ad for two apartments in the house.

WAKEFIELD HOUSE

Are you looking for a **nice** neighborhood with **safe**, **quiet** streets?
Do you love the **big sunny** rooms and **high** ceilings in **interesting old**
buildings—but want **modern** appliances[1] and **high-speed** Internet too?
Apartments in Wakefield House offer that and more. Here's your place to relax **completely** after
a **long hard** day at school or work. We are located in a **peaceful residential** area near **famous**
Lake Forest Park. And you'll still be just a **convenient** drive or bus ride from downtown and the
university. **Exciting** nightlife, shopping, and museums are only minutes away.

It sounds **very expensive**, right? But it's not! A **comfortable one-bedroom** apartment is
surprisingly affordable. We have two **beautifully furnished** apartments **available** right now.
But don't wait! Our apartments rent **very quickly**.

Call 555-1234 now for an appointment.

★ ★

Here's what some of our **satisfied** tenants[2] are saying about life at Wakefield House:

"The neighborhood is like a
small village, with **really friendly**
people and **charming** houses."
—Maggie Chang

"This place is
absolutely perfect.
It's my **ideal** home."
—Luis Rivera

"Weekends here are **so peaceful**—no **annoying**
traffic noise. I love walking through the
nearby park or just sitting on the **front** porch."
—Alice Thompson

---

[1] *appliance:* a piece of equipment, such as a washing machine or stove, that people use in their homes
[2] *tenant:* someone who lives in a house, apartment, or room and pays rent to the owner

A | **Vocabulary:** *Circle the letter of the word or phrase closest in meaning to the word in* **blue.**

1. We found an **ideal** house today.

   a. perfect
   b. expensive
   c. nearby

2. The bus to town is very **convenient**.

   a. safe
   b. easy to use
   c. comfortable

3. There's a **charming** garden behind the house.

   a. large
   b. quiet
   c. lovely

4. The house is **located in** a residential area.

   a. close to
   b. far from
   c. part of

5. It's on a **peaceful** street.

   a. dangerous
   b. quiet
   c. crowded

6. We were very **satisfied** with the neighborhood.

   a. happy
   b. unhappy
   c. relaxed

B | **Comprehension:** *Check (✓)* **True** *or* **False.** *Correct the false statements.*

	True	False
1. Wakefield House is in a dangerous neighborhood.	☐	☑
2. The apartments have a lot of light.	☑	☐
3. It's in an exciting area of the city.	☐	☑
4. You'll be surprised that the rent is so low.	☐	☑
5. There are three apartments for rent now.	☐	☑
6. One tenant likes to spend weekends at home.	☑	☐

ADJECTIVES AND ADVERBS

Adjectives	Adverbs of Manner	Degree Adverbs
They are **quiet** tenants.	They talk **quietly**.	They're **very** quiet. They talk **very** quietly.
The house is **beautiful**.	They decorated it **beautifully**.	It's **so** beautiful. They decorated it **so** beautifully.
It looks **good**.	She described it **well**.	This looks **really** good. She described it **really** well.
It's a **fast** elevator.	It moves **fast**.	It's **awfully** fast! It moves **awfully** fast!

Participial Adjectives

-*ing* Adjective	-*ed* Adjective
The apartment is **interesting**.	One couple is **interested** in the apartment.
It's an **interesting** one-bedroom apartment.	The **interested** couple called again.
My neighbor is **annoying**.	I'm **annoyed** by his loud music.
He's an **annoying** neighbor.	Another **annoyed** tenant complained.

Word Order: Adjectives before Nouns

	Opinion	Size	Age	Shape	Color	Origin	Material	Purpose	Noun (as Adj)	NOUN
a	peaceful	little						residential		area
some	interesting		young							tenants
your				round	blue	Chinese				vase
the		large	old				wooden		kitchen	table

GRAMMAR NOTES

1 Adjectives and adverbs describe or give more information about other words:

  a. Use **adjectives** to describe <u>nouns</u> (people, places, or things).

ADJECTIVE NOUN
- They are *safe* **streets**.

NOUN   ADJECTIVE
- The **streets** are *safe*.
(Safe *tells you more about the streets.)*

  b. Use **adverbs** to describe:

    • verbs

VERB   ADVERB
- The manager **talks** *quietly*.

    • adjectives

ADVERB   ADJECTIVE
- He's *extremely* **quiet**.

    • other adverbs

ADVERB   ADVERB
- He works *very* **quietly**.

2 Notice the **word order** of **adjectives** and **adverbs** and the words they describe:

  a. An **adjective** usually goes right <u>before the noun</u> it describes.

    It can also go <u>after a non-action verb</u> such as *be, look, seem, appear, smell,* or *taste.*

ADJECTIVE NOUN
- This is a *small* **house**.

VERB ADJECTIVE
- This house **looks** *small*.

  b. An **adverb** usually goes <u>after the verb</u> it describes.

VERB   ADVERB
- The apartment **rented** *quickly*.

  BE CAREFUL! Do NOT put an adverb between the verb and the object.

VERB   OBJECT   ADVERB
- She **decorated** the house *beautifully*.
NOT: She decorated ~~beautifully the house~~.

  c. An **adverb** usually goes right <u>before the adjective or adverb</u> it describes.

ADVERB ADJECTIVE
- It's an *extremely* **nice** house.

ADVERB ADVERB
- They found it *very* **quickly**.

(continued on next page)

3 Use **adverbs of manner** to describe or give more information about <u>action verbs</u>.

ACTION VERB   ADVERB
- They **decorated** the apartment *beautifully*!
- They **rented** it *quickly*.

ADJECTIVE
- We need a **quick** decision.

a. Form most adverbs of manner by **adding -*ly*** to the adjective:

adjective + -*ly* = adverb

ADVERB
- You should decide *quickly*.

MORE FORMAL		MORE INFORMAL
slowly	OR	slow
quickly	OR	quick
loudly	OR	loud
clearly	OR	clear

Some adverbs of manner also have a **form without -*ly*** (the same as the adjective). The form without -*ly* is more <u>informal</u>.

- Don't speak so **loudly**. OR Don't speak so **loud**.

ADJECTIVE
- It's a **lovely** apartment.

BE CAREFUL! Some **adjectives** also end in -*ly* —for example, *friendly*, *lonely*, *lovely*, and *silly*.

b. Some **common adverbs of manner** are NOT formed by adding -*ly* to adjectives:

The adverb form of ***good*** is ***well***.

ADJECTIVE   ADVERB
- He's a **good** driver. He drives **well**.

Early, *fast*, *hard*, *late*, and *wrong* have the <u>same adjective and adverb forms</u>.

ADJECTIVE   ADVERB
- She is a **hard** worker. She works **hard**.

BE CAREFUL! *Hardly* is not the adverb form of *hard*. *Hardly* means "almost not." *Lately* is not the adverb form of *late*. *Lately* means "recently."

- There's **hardly** enough room for a bed. (There's almost not enough room for a bed.)
- We haven't seen any nice houses **lately**. We're getting discouraged.

4 Use **degree adverbs** to make adjectives and other adverbs <u>stronger</u> or <u>weaker</u>.

absolutely	awfully	really	pretty	fairly	not at all
completely	terribly	so	quite		
		very			

←————————————————————→
100%   0%

Awfully and *terribly* can describe something **good** or something **bad**.

Not at all means "totally not."

Notice the word order for *not at all*:
- After a verb or verb + object
- After or before an adjective or another adverb

A: How fast can you get to work from here?
B: *Very* **fast**. The traffic is**n't** bad **at all**.

A: This apartment is *absolutely* **perfect**!
B: Really? It looks *very* **small** to me.
A: But it's in a *really* **good** neighborhood.
B: True. And you can get to work *quite* **easily**.

- The landlord was *awfully* **rude**.
- The apartment was *awfully* **nice**.

- I did**n't** like the apartment **at all**. (I totally didn't like it.)

- They did**n't** decorate (the place) **at all**.
- It was**n't** nice **at all**. OR It was**n't at all** nice.

5 | **Participial adjectives** are adjectives that end with **-ing** or **-ed**. They come from <u>verbs</u>.

VERB
- This story **amazes** me.

ADJECTIVE   ADJECTIVE
- It's an **amazing** story. I'm **amazed**.

Participial adjectives often describe **feelings**.

- Use the **-ing** form for someone or something that <u>causes</u> a feeling.

- Use the **-ed** form for the person who <u>has</u> the feeling.

- The fly is **disgusting**.
  (The fly causes the feeling.)

- I'm **disgusted**.
  (I have the feeling.)

6 | Sometimes we use **two or three adjectives before a noun**. If these adjectives belong to different categories, we usually follow this **order**:

opinion + size + age + shape + color + origin + material + purpose + noun (used as adjective) + NOUN

(OPINION)   (AGE)   (PURPOSE)
- It's in a **charming old residential** neighborhood.

(OPINION)   (COLOR)   (MATERIAL)
- I bought a **nice black leather** couch.

EXCEPTION: Size adjectives (such as *big* and *small*) often go first in a series of adjectives.

(SIZE)   (OPINION)   (NOUN AS ADJ)
- It's a **small affordable one-room** apartment. OR

(OPINION)   (SIZE)   (NOUN AS ADJ)
- It's an **affordable small one-room** apartment.

We do **NOT use commas** between adjectives that belong to <u>different categories</u>.

For adjectives that belong to the <u>same category</u>, the **order is not important**. Use **commas** to separate these adjectives.

(SIZE)   (SHAPE)   (ORIGIN)
- I got a **large round Mexican** mirror.
  NOT: I got a large round Mexican mirror.

- She's a **friendly, helpful, nice** woman. OR
- She's a **helpful, friendly, nice** woman. OR
- She's a **nice, helpful, friendly** woman.
  (All the adjectives are opinion adjectives, so the order can change.)

REFERENCE NOTES
For a list of **non-action verbs**, see Appendix 2 on page A-2.
For a list of **participial adjectives**, see Appendix 11 on page A-6.
For the **order of adjectives before a noun**, see Appendix 12 on page A-6.
For **spelling rules** for forming **-ly adverbs**, see Appendix 24 on page A-11.

STEP 3 FOCUSED PRACTICE

EXERCISE 1: Discover the Grammar

Read the notice from a university bulletin board. Underline the adjectives and circle the adverbs. Then draw an arrow from the adjective or adverb to the word it is describing.

APT. FOR RENT
140 Grant Street, Apartment 4B

Are you looking for a place to live? This charming apartment is in a new building and has two large comfortable bedrooms and a small sunny kitchen. The building is very quiet—absolutely perfect for two serious students. It's near the campus on a peaceful street. There's convenient transportation. The bus stop is an easy, pleasant walk, and the express bus goes directly into town. You can run or ride your bike safely in nearby parks. The rent is very affordable. Small pets are welcome. The apartment is available on June 1. Interested students should call Megan at 555-5050. We're sure you'll be satisfied. Don't wait! This apartment will rent fast. Nonsmokers, please.

EXERCISE 2: Adjective or Adverb

(Grammar Notes 1–5)

Circle the correct words to complete Maggie's email to her brother.

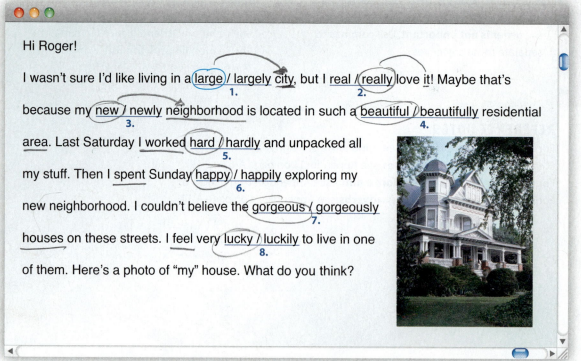

Hi Roger!

I wasn't sure I'd like living in a **large** / largely city, but I real / **really** love it! Maybe that's

1.   2.

because my **new** / newly neighborhood is located in such a **beautiful** / beautifully residential

3.   4.

area. Last Saturday I worked **hard** / hardly and unpacked all

5.

my stuff. Then I spent Sunday **happy** / happily exploring my

6.

new neighborhood. I couldn't believe the **gorgeous** / gorgeously

7.

houses on these streets. I feel very **lucky** / luckily to live in one

8.

of them. Here's a photo of "my" house. What do you think?

Hardly = not enough
Lately = recently

Adj. order = O + S + A + S + C + O + M + P + N

My apartment is on the second floor. It's really (great / greatly). I'm total / totally satisfied
9.   10.

with it. The other tenants are very nice / nicely. My next-door neighbor, Alice, seemed pretty
11.

shy / shyly at first, but I think we're going to become good / well friends very quick / quickly.
12.   13.   14.

She's an art student, and she likes to visit museums. We're going to the Modern Art Museum

together next Saturday. Life in the city is exciting / excitingly, but I get terrible / terribly
15.   16.

homesick. So I hope you visit me soon!

Love,
Maggie

*A dj + Noun
Verb + Adv.*

EXERCISE 3: Adverbs Before Adjectives and Other Adverbs   *(Grammar Notes 2, 4)*

Many different people went to see the apartment described in Exercise 1. Complete their comments about the apartment. Use the correct form of the words in parentheses. Go to Appendix 24 on page A-11 for help with spelling adverbs ending in -ly.

1. I am very interested. I think the apartment is _____ *extremely nice* _____.
   (extreme / nice)

2. I was expecting much bigger rooms. I was _____ *terribly disappointed* _____.
   (terrible / disappointed)

3. I thought it would be hard to get to, but the bus was _____ *surprisingly convenient* _____.
   (surprising / convenient)

4. I think it's a great place. I'm sure it will rent _____ *incredibly fast* _____.
   (incredible / fast)

5. The ad said it was quiet, but I heard the neighbors _____ *very clear* _____.
   (very / clear)

6. I heard them too. I thought their voices were _____ *awfully loud* _____.
   (awful / loud)

7. The ad described the apartment _____ *pretty accurate* _____.
   (pretty / accurate)

8. To be honest, this place is _____ *absolutely perfect* _____ for me!
   (absolute / perfect)

9. I'm going to feel _____ *really upset* _____ if I don't get it.
   (real / upset)

O + S + A + S + C + O + M + P + N

O + S + A + S + C + O + M + P + N

O + S + A + S + C + O + M + P + N

O + S + A + S + C + O + M + P + N

A living room in Wakefield House

A dj + Noun / verb + Adj.

EXERCISE 4: Word Order

(Grammar Notes 2–4)

Put the words in the correct order to complete the entry from Sylvie's journal.

I'm a _____*fairly cheerful person*_____ most of the time, but yesterday some
1. (cheerful / person / fairly)

_____ happened. The bus _____,
2. (things / upsetting / pretty)   **3. (late / arrived / really)**

so I missed an _____ at work. However, my boss
4. (important / meeting / awfully)

_____. She _____. Later, I
5. (well / quite / reacted)   **6. (at all / angry / didn't / seem)**

looked at a(n) _____. I thought it was exactly what I wanted, but
7. (apartment / charming / absolutely)

I needed to _____. When I called this morning, I found out it was
8. (it / think about / carefully / very)

already rented! Wow—_____! Next time I see a great place, I'll
9. (so / it / happened / quickly)

_____.
10. (it / immediately / take)

EXERCISE 5: Participial Adjectives

(Grammar Note 5)

Luis is talking to his friend Sylvie. Read their conversation. Complete it with the correct participial adjective form (-ing or -ed) of the verbs in parentheses.

SYLVIE: These apartment ads are really _____*annoying*_____. Just look at this one.
1. (annoy)

LUIS: Hmmm. It says, "cozy and _____ apartment." Why are you
2. (charm)

_____ at that?
3. (annoy)

SYLVIE: I saw the place—it's tiny, not cozy! And I wasn't _____ at all. In fact, I was
4. (charm)

pretty _____.
5. (disgust)

LUIS: Take it easy. It sounds like you had an _____ day. Let's relax and watch a
6. (exhaust)

movie tonight.

SYLVIE: You're right. I'm completely _____. I could use a _____
7. (exhaust)   **8. (relax)**

evening. What do you want to watch?

LUIS: There's a movie called *Lake House* on TV tonight. I hear it's _____.
9. (fascinate)

SYLVIE: *Lake House?* Great title! I'm _____ already. What's it about?
10. (fascinate)

LUIS: Well, the story's a little _____, but it happens in a beautiful glass house on a
11. (confuse)

peaceful lake.

SYLVIE: That sounds like a pretty _____ house. I wonder if *they're* looking for tenants.
12. (amaze)

EXERCISE 6: Word Order: Adjectives + Noun

(Grammar Note 6)

Sylvie has found a great place, and she's already moved in. Put the words in the correct order to complete the new entry in her journal. Remember to use commas when necessary.

I found a ____*nice, comfortable apartment*____ in this _____!
            1. (apartment / nice / comfortable)   **2. (old / house / charming)**

It's in a _____, and I can see a(n) _____
     3. (residential / neighborhood / peaceful)   **4. (tree / enormous / old)**

outside my _____. There's even a very lovely garden with a
     5. (bedroom / wide / window)

_____. The apartment is nicely furnished too. The kitchen has
     6. (stone / bench / Japanese)

a(n) _____. I do my homework there. And the people here are
     7. (beautiful / table / antique / large)

great. The manager is a _____. I've already met most of my
     8. (man / friendly / helpful)

neighbors. Across the hall from me is a _____. She took me to a(n)
     9. (Polish / young / woman)

_____ for dinner. I know I'll be happy here.
  10. (nice / neighborhood / restaurant / Italian)

EXERCISE 7: Editing

Read reviews of school dormitories. There are fourteen mistakes in the use of adjectives and adverbs. The first mistake is already corrected. Find and correct thirteen more.

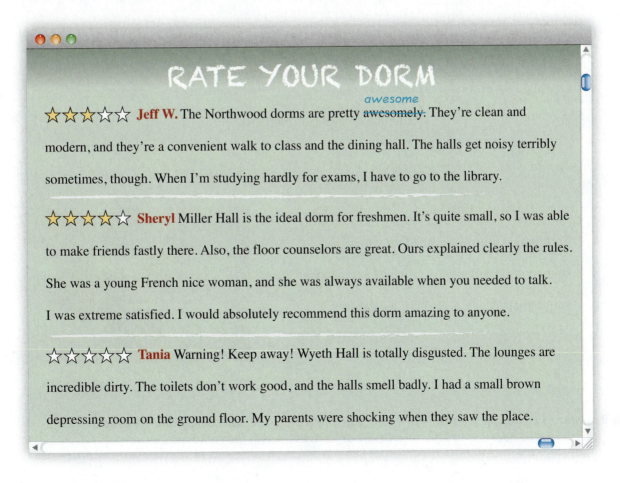

RATE YOUR DORM

★★★☆☆ **Jeff W.** The Northwood dorms are pretty ~~awesomely.~~ *awesome* They're clean and

modern, and they're a convenient walk to class and the dining hall. The halls get noisy terribly

sometimes, though. When I'm studying hardly for exams, I have to go to the library.

★★★★☆ **Sheryl** Miller Hall is the ideal dorm for freshmen. It's quite small, so I was able

to make friends fastly there. Also, the floor counselors are great. Ours explained clearly the rules.

She was a young French nice woman, and she was always available when you needed to talk.

I was extreme satisfied. I would absolutely recommend this dorm amazing to anyone.

★☆☆☆☆ **Tania** Warning! Keep away! Wyeth Hall is totally disgusted. The lounges are

incredible dirty. The toilets don't work good, and the halls smell badly. I had a small brown

depressing room on the ground floor. My parents were shocking when they saw the place.

EXERCISE 8: Listening

A | *A couple is discussing online apartment ads. Read the ads and guess the missing adjectives and adverbs.*

Janslist>bay area> housing > apts/housing for rent

$700 a month _____small_____ , charming 2 bedroom in Smithfield
1.

This is an _____ building very _____ all public transportation.
2.   **3.**

Keep your car in the garage and relax on the train!

Date: 12-10-2011 posted 10:00 PM PST
Call 555-3296 for an appointment today

FOSTER $750 Light and bright 2 BR on beautiful tree-lined street

This lovely apartment has been newly painted and is in _____ condition.
4.

_____ near shopping and schools.
5.

Date: 12-09-2011 posted 1:00 PM PST
Apply Online   Email for Appointment   See Photos

$650 Cute and Cozy 2 BR in Cumberland!

Our last 2-bedroom apartment has all _____ appliances.
6.

Enjoy the _____ residential area of Cumberland.
7.

Date: 12-14-2011 posted 8:53AM PST
Call 555-2343 ext. 27 OR email blanders@goodproperties.com Sorry, no pets. CLICK for photos.

LINCOLN Beautiful 2 bedroom only $850

Completely renovated building with _____
8.

kitchen and bath. All _____ appliances.
9.

Well-behaved pets welcome. Available _____ .
10.

Date: 12-09-2011 posted 7:00 AM PST
Call 555-4478 email: edgar.hodgins@Lincolntownhouse.com

B | *Listen to the couple's conversation. Did you guess the same adjectives that they used to describe the apartments? If not, write the adjectives used in the conversation.*

C | *Read the information in the chart. Then listen again to the conversation and check (✓) the couple's opinion of each apartment.*

Opinion	Apt 1	Apt 2	Apt 3	Apt 4
Sunny				
Sounds terrific!				
Not enough information	✓			
Awfully small				
Can't bring Loki				
Not near stores				

EXERCISE 9: Pronunciation

A | *Read and listen to the Pronunciation Note.*

> **Pronunciation Note**
>
> In phrases that include **adjective + noun**, the adjective and the noun are **both stressed**. When the **noun is new information**, the noun is often **stressed more strongly** than the adjective.
>
> EXAMPLES: **A:** Are you happy with your **new apartment**?
>
> **B:** Well, I've got a **noisy neighbor**.
>
> When we contrast information or add new information, we **stress** the **contrasting** or **new information more strongly**.
>
> EXAMPLES: **A:** This apartment is in a very **safe neighborhood**.
>
> **B:** No, it's not. It's in a very **dangerous area**.

B | *Listen to the short conversations. Put a small dot (•) or a large dot (•) over the nouns and adjectives to show stress.*

1. **A:** This is a **nice apartment**.

   B: And it's such a **sunny place** too!

2. **A:** Alice seems like a **friendly neighbor**.

   B: Yes, and she's a **helpful neighbor**, too.

3. **A:** It's got a **small kitchen**.

   B: No, it doesn't! It's the **perfect kitchen** for me.

(continued on next page)

4. A: Did the landlord give you **new appliances**?

   B: No. But these aren't **bad appliances**.

5. A: Do you have a **helpful landlord**?

   B: Yes, but he's a **nosy landlord**, too!

6. A: Well, I hope you like your **new home**.

   B: Thanks. I'm going to like it more than my **old home**.

C | *Listen again. Then practice the conversations with a partner.*

EXERCISE 10: What About You?

Work in small groups. Describe where you live. Answer the questions.

1. How did you find the place?
2. How did you first feel about it (pleased, disappointed, etc.)?
3. What does it look like?
4. How did you decorate it?
5. What is special about your place?

EXAMPLE: **A:** I found my apartment last summer. I was taking a walk in a beautiful neighborhood, and I saw . . .
   B: At first I was pretty happy about my dorm room, but then . . .
   C: My place is cozy, and it's got an old fireplace . . .

EXERCISE 11: Compare and Contrast

Work with a partner. There are many different types of housing. Describe the different types in the list. How are they similar? How are they different? Use your dictionaries to help you. Do these types of housing exist in other places you have lived?

- apartment
- boarding house
- dorm (dormitory)
- mansion
- mobile home
- private home
- rented room in someone's house
- studio apartment

EXAMPLE: **A:** A mobile home can be very convenient. You can move it from place to place.
   B: And it's easy to get away from noisy—or nosey—neighbors!

EXERCISE 12: Discussion

What is your ideal home? What does it look like? What kind of roommates, neighbors, and landlord does it have? Work in small groups. Take turns describing this perfect place. Talk about the people and their activities. Here are some words you can use.

Adjectives

affordable	convenient	honest	messy	peaceful
boring	cozy	interesting	modern	relaxed
cheerful	friendly	large	neat	reliable
considerate	helpful	loud	nosy	sunny

Adverbs of Manner

carefully	honestly	quickly
early	late	politely
easily	loudly	seriously
happily	noisily	well

Degree Adverbs

awfully	really
not . . . at all	so
pretty	totally
quite	very

EXAMPLE: **A:** My ideal home is small and modern. It's located . . .
B: My ideal neighbors are really interesting. They . . .
C: The perfect roommates always . . .

EXERCISE 13: Game: A Strange Story

Work in small groups. Student A keeps his or her book open. All the other students close their books. Student A asks each member of the group, in turn, for a type of adjective. Student A fills in the blanks with the words the group members give. At the end, Student A will read the story to the group. Expect a very strange story!

EXAMPLE: **A:** Enrique, I need a size adjective.
B: How about *enormous*?
A: OK. Lee, now I need an opinion adjective . . .

I was walking down the street one day when I saw a(n) _____ _____
                                                                                    1. (size adj)   **2. (opinion adj)**
_____ house. It was _____ _____. I took out my camera
3. (color adj)   **4. (degree adv)**   **5. (participial *-ing* adj)**
phone and _____ called my friend. He wasn't at home, so I took a picture.
              6. (*-ly* adv of manner)
    The house was _____ _____. It had three _____
                          7. (degree adv)   **8. (opinion adj)**   **9. (size adj)**
_____ windows and a _____ _____ door. There
10. (shape adj)   **11. (size adj)**   **12. (material adj)**
were two _____ _____ trees and a lot of _____
              13. (size adj)   **14. (age adj)**   **15. (opinion adj)**
_____ flowers. Under the tree was a(n) _____ _____
16. (color adj)   **17. (age adj)**   **18. (material adj)**
_____ bench. I was _____. I'd never seen anything like it before!
19. (origin adj)   **20. (participial *-ed* adj)**

Source: This game is based on the popular game *Mad Libs* invented in 1953 by Leonard Stern and Roger Price. *Mad Libs* books are published by Price Stern Sloan, an imprint of Penguin Group.

EXERCISE 14: Writing

A | *Write an ad like the one for Wakefield House on page 266. Describe your ideal home. Use adjectives and adverbs.*

EXAMPLE: Do you want to live in an exciting neighborhood with great stores that stay open late? Do you want a large modern apartment with a terrific view of all the action in the streets below? The apartments in the Atrium are . . .

B | *Check your work. Use the Editing Checklist.*

Editing Checklist

Did you use . . . ?

☐ adjectives to describe people, places, and things

☐ participial adjectives to describe feelings

☐ adverbs of manner to describe action verbs

☐ degree adverbs to describe adjectives and other adverbs

[handwritten at top: Adj. Order= O+S+A+S+C+O+M+P+N]

[handwritten: adj + noun / verb + adv.]

A | *Circle the correct words to complete the sentences.*

1. My neighbor is so annoyed /(annoying.) He plays loud music all night long.

2. The bus came late /(lately,) and I missed my class.

3. This apartment seems perfect / perfectly for you. Are you going to take it?

4. Ken worked very hardly /(hard) last semester. He deserved those A's. *[handwritten: hardly = not enough]*

5. My roommate is surprising /(surprisingly) shy. She doesn't even like to answer the phone.

B | *Unscramble the words to complete the sentences.*

1. Today I looked at a(n) ___interesting old house___ .
   (old / house / interesting)

2. I loved the ___cheerful big yellow kitchen___ .
   (yellow / big / kitchen / cheerful)

3. The house is on a ___peaceful residential street___ .
   (residential / peaceful / street)

4. Two ___nice young international students___ live next door.
   (international / nice / students / young)

5. But the landlord ___didn't seem friendly at all___ .
   (seem / friendly / didn't / at all)

6. There's a ___cute little Greek restaurant___ on the corner.
   (little / restaurant / cute / Greek)

7. It has a ___really beautiful garden___ in the back.
   (garden / beautiful / really)

8. We sat at a(n) ___wonderful old round wooden table___ .
   (round / table / wonderful / wooden / old)

9. I think I have to ___decide pretty quickly___ about this house.
   (quickly / pretty / decide)

10. I have a feeling that it's going to ___~~awfully rent fast~~___ *[handwritten correction: rent awfully fast]*
    (fast / awfully / rent)

C | *Find and correct five mistakes.*

The conditions in Parker Dorm are pretty ~~shocked~~ *[shocking]*. The rooms are ~~terrible~~ *[terribly]* small, and the furniture is incredibly ugly. The locks on the doors don't work ~~good~~ *[well]*, so your stuff is never ~~safely~~ *[safe]*.

The dorm counselors are great—they're all really nice, friendly people—but they can't make up for the ~~badly~~ *[bad]* conditions.

Adjectives: Comparisons with *As . . . as* and *Than*

FOOD

Before You Read

Look at the photo. Discuss the questions.

1. Would you like to order the pizza in the photo? Why or why not?
2. How often do you eat out?
3. What types of restaurant food do you enjoy?

Read

Read the newspaper restaurant review.

A New Place for Pizza
by Pete Tsa

AS FRESH AS IT GETS!

PIZZA PLACE, the chain of popular restaurants, has just opened a new one on Main Street, two blocks from the university. The last time that I ate there, the service was **not as good as** at the other Pizza Place restaurants in town. The young staff (mostly students) probably needs time to become **more professional**. But the pizza was incredible! It seemed **bigger** and **better than** at the other six locations in town. As with all food, **the fresher** the ingredients,[1] **the better** the pizza. The ingredients at the new Pizza Place are **as fresh as** you can get (absolutely no mushrooms from a can here!), and the choices are much **more varied than** at their other locations. We ordered two different types. The one with mashed potatoes and garlic was a lot **more interesting than** the traditional pizza with cheese and tomato sauce, but both were delicious.

Each Pizza Place is different. The one on Main Street is a little **larger** (and **louder**) **than** the others. It's also a lot **more crowded** because students love it. At lunchtime the lines outside this new eatery are getting **longer and longer**. Go early for a **quieter**, **more relaxed** meal.

---

[1] *ingredients:* things that go into a recipe (example: tomatoes, cheese, mushrooms, salt . . .)

A | Vocabulary: *Circle the letter of the word or phrase that best completes each sentence.*

1. **Delicious** food _____.

   a. is healthy

   b. tastes very good

   c. costs a lot

2. **Fresh** food _____.

   a. comes in a can

   b. is not old

   c. is always hot

3. If a meal is **relaxed**, you don't feel _____.

   a. in a hurry

   b. too full

   c. comfortable

4. A **varied** menu has _____.

   a. pizza and hamburgers

   b. very good food

   c. a lot of different types of food

5. In a **crowded** restaurant people or things are _____.

   a. close together

   b. not interesting

   c. far apart

6. _____ is NOT a **traditional** pizza ingredient.

   a. Cheese

   b. Tomato sauce

   c. Fruit

B | Comprehension: *Check (✓)* **all** *the words that describe each item.*

1. **the restaurant** ☐ crowded ☐ new ☐ quiet ☐ popular

2. **the staff** ☐ professional ☐ young ☐ relaxed ☐ loud

3. **the food** ☐ delicious ☐ fresh ☐ expensive ☐ good

ADJECTIVES: COMPARISONS WITH *AS . . . AS* AND *THAN*

Comparisons with *As . . . as*				
	(Not) As	**Adjective**	**As**	
The new restaurant is	(not) as	**large** **busy** **good** **interesting** **expensive**	as	the other ones.

Comparisons with *Than*		
	Comparative Adjective Form	*Than*
The new restaurant is	**larger** **busier** **better** **more interesting** **less expensive**	than	the other ones.

GRAMMAR NOTES

1

Use *as* + **adjective** + *as* to show how people, places, or things are <u>the same or equal</u>.

- The new menu is **as good as** the old.

Use *just* to make the comparison stronger.

- The new menu is *just* **as good as** the old.
  (*The new menu and the old menu are equally good.*)

Use *not as* + **adjective** + *as* to show how they are <u>NOT the same or equal</u>.

- The new menu is**n't as varied as** the old.
  (*The old menu was more varied.*)

REMEMBER: It is not necessary to mention both parts of the comparison when the meaning is clear.

A: I liked the old menu. It had more choices.
B: Too bad the new one is**n't as varied**.
  (*It isn't as varied as the old menu.*)

2 Use **comparative adjectives** + **than** to show how people, places, or things are <u>different</u>.

- The new room is **bigger than** the old room.
- The new waiters are **more professional than** the old waiters.

Use **even** to make the comparison stronger.

- The old waiters were very professional, but the new waiters are **even more professional than** the old waiters.

USAGE NOTE: We usually do NOT use **less . . . than** with <u>one syllable adjectives</u>. Instead we use:
- **not as . . . as**
  OR
- another adjective with the <u>opposite meaning</u>.

NOT: Our server is ~~less fast than~~ theirs.

- Our server is**n't as fast as** theirs.
  OR
- Our server is **slower than** theirs.

REMEMBER: It is not necessary to mention both parts of the comparison when the meaning is clear.

- The new tables are **smaller**.
  (They are smaller than the old tables.)

3 There are several ways of **forming comparative adjectives**.

a. For **short adjectives** (one syllable and two syllables ending in -y), use **adjective + -er**.

There are often **spelling changes** when you add **-er**.

Some short adjectives have **irregular** comparative forms.

ADJECTIVE	COMPARATIVE
loud	loud**er**
friendly	friendl**ier**
late	lat**er**
big	big**ger**
early	earl**ier**
good	**better**
bad	**worse**
far	**farther**

b. For **long adjectives** (two or more syllables), use **more / less + adjective**.

EXCEPTION: The **short adjective fun** forms the comparative in the same way as a long adjective.

expensive	**more** expensive
	less expensive
fun	**more** fun NOT: ~~funner~~
	less fun

c. For **some adjectives**, such as *lively, lovely, friendly,* and *quiet,* you can use: **-er** or **more**

- The Inn is **livelier** than Joe's.
  OR
- The Inn is **more lively** than Joe's.

(continued on next page)

| **4** | Repeat the **comparative adjective** to show <u>increase or decrease</u>:

| comparative adjective | + *and* + | comparative adjective |

With long adjectives, repeat only ***more*** or ***less***. | • The lines are getting **longer and longer**.
(Their length is increasing.)

• It's getting **more and more popular**.
(Its popularity is increasing.)
NOT: It's getting more ~~popular~~ and more popular. |

| **5** | Use **two comparative adjectives** to show <u>cause and effect</u>:

the + comparative + *the* + comparative
    adjective   adjective

When both comparative adjectives describe the same person, place, or thing, we often <u>leave out the noun</u>. | • **The more crowded** the restaurant, **the slower** the service.
(The service is slower because the restaurant is more crowded.)

A: The service is really fast here.
B: **The faster, the better.**
(The faster the service, the better the service.) |

REFERENCE NOTES

For a list of **adjectives** that use **both forms of the comparative**, see Appendix 9 on page A-5.
For a list of **irregular comparative adjectives**, see Appendix 10 on page A-6.
For **spelling rules** for the **comparative form of adjectives**, see Appendix 23 on page A-11.

STEP 3 FOCUSED PRACTICE

EXERCISE 1: Discover the Grammar

*Read the information about two brands of frozen pizza on the next page. Then decide if each statement is **True (T)** or **False (F)**.*

	Maria's Pizza	John's Pizza
Size	12 inches	12 inches
Weight	27 ounces	24 ounces
Price	$5.99	$6.99
Calories*	364	292
Salt content*	731 milligrams	600 milligrams
Fat content*	11 grams	11 grams
Baking time	20 minutes	16 minutes
Taste	★ ★ ★	★ ★ ★ ★

* for a five-ounce serving

<u>F</u> **1.** Maria's pizza is bigger than John's.

_____ **2.** John's pizza is just as big as Maria's.

_____ **3.** John's isn't as heavy as Maria's.

_____ **4.** Maria's is just as expensive as John's.

_____ **5.** John's is more expensive than Maria's.

_____ **6.** Maria's is higher in calories than John's.

_____ **7.** Maria's is saltier than John's.

_____ **8.** John's pizza is just as high in fat as Maria's pizza.

_____ **9.** The baking time for Maria's isn't as long as the baking time for John's.

_____ **10.** John's tastes better than Maria's.

EXERCISE 2: Comparisons with *As . . . as*

(Grammar Note 1)

Look at the consumer magazine chart comparing three brands of pizza cheese. Complete the sentences. Use **as . . . as** *or* **not as . . . as** *and the correct form of the words in parentheses.*

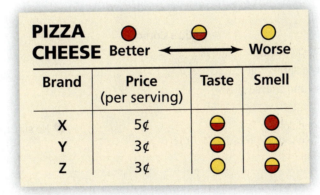

1. Brand Z _____ *is as expensive as* _____ brand Y.
   (be / expensive)

2. Brand Y _____ brand X.
   (be / expensive)

3. Brand X _____ brand Y.
   (taste / good)

4. Brand Z _____ brand Y.
   (taste / good)

5. Brand Y _____ brand X.
   (smell / delicious)

6. Brand Y _____ brand Z.
   (smell / delicious)

Adjectives: Comparisons with *As . . . as* and *Than* **287**

EXERCISE 3: Comparisons with *Than*

(Grammar Note 2–3)

*Look at the menu. Then complete the sentences comparing items on the menu. Use the appropriate comparative form of the adjectives in parentheses and **than**.*

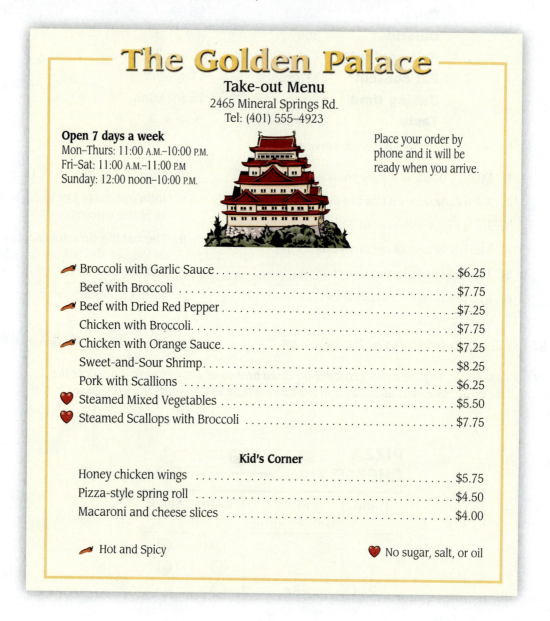

The Golden Palace

Take-out Menu

2465 Mineral Springs Rd.
Tel: (401) 555-4923

Open 7 days a week
Mon–Thurs: 11:00 A.M.–10:00 P.M.
Fri–Sat: 11:00 A.M.–11:00 P.M
Sunday: 12:00 noon–10:00 P.M.

Place your order by
phone and it will be
ready when you arrive.

Broccoli with Garlic Sauce $6.25
Beef with Broccoli $7.75
Beef with Dried Red Pepper $7.25
Chicken with Broccoli. $7.75
Chicken with Orange Sauce. $7.25
Sweet-and-Sour Shrimp. $8.25
Pork with Scallions $6.25
Steamed Mixed Vegetables $5.50
Steamed Scallops with Broccoli $7.75

Kid's Corner

Honey chicken wings $5.75
Pizza-style spring roll $4.50
Macaroni and cheese slices $4.00

Hot and Spicy   No sugar, salt, or oil

---

1. The sweet-and-sour shrimp is _____*more expensive than*_____ the steamed scallops.
   (expensive)

2. The beef with red pepper is _____ the beef with broccoli.
   (hot)

3. The pork with scallions is _____ the sweet-and-sour shrimp.
   (expensive)

4. The chicken with orange sauce is _____ the steamed scallops.
   (spicy)

5. The steamed vegetables are _____ the pork with scallions.
   (salty)

6. The steamed vegetables are _____ the beef with red pepper.
   (healthy)

7. The broccoli with garlic is _____ the chicken with broccoli.
   (cheap)

8. The shrimp dish is _____ the scallop dish.
   (sweet)

9. The restaurant's hours on Sunday are _____ on Saturday.
   (short)

10. The children's menu is _____ the adult's menu.
    (varied)

11. The children's menu is _____ too.
    (expensive)

12. The chicken wings are _____ the macaroni and cheese slices.
    (sweet)

EXERCISE 4: Increase or Decrease; Cause and Effect

(Grammar Notes 4–5)

Complete the conversations. Use the comparative form of the adjectives in parentheses to show an increase or decrease or a cause and effect.

1. **A:** Wow! The lines here are getting _____*longer and longer*_____.
   (long)

   B: I know. And _____*the longer*_____ the wait, _____*the hungrier*_____ I get.
   (long)   (hungry)

2. **A:** It's worth the wait. The food here is getting _____.
   (good)

   B: But _____ the food, _____ the bill!
   (good)   (high)

3. **A:** The lunch crowd is leaving. It's getting _____.
   (crowded)

   B: Great. These books were starting to feel _____.
   (heavy)

4. **A:** The menu is getting _____.
   (interesting)

   B: I know, but that means it's also _____ to choose something.
   (difficult)

5. **A:** There's Professor Lee. You know, his course is getting _____.
   (popular)

   B: It's amazing. _____ it is, _____ it gets.
   (hard)   (popular)

   He's a great teacher.

6. **A:** Is it the hot sauce, or has your cough been getting _____?
   (bad)

   B: It's the hot sauce, but I love it. For my taste, _____,
   (spicy)

   _____.
   (good)

7. **A:** The service used to be slow here, but it's getting _____.
   (fast)

   B: Right. _____ the service, _____ the lines!
   (fast)   (short)

EXERCISE 5: Editing

Read the student's essay. There are ten mistakes in the use of **as ... as** *and comparatives with* **than**. *The first mistake is already corrected. Find and correct nine more.*

When I was a teenager in the Philippines, I was an expert on snacks and fast foods. I was

growing fast, so the more I ate, the ~~hungry~~ *hungrier* I felt. The street vendors in our town had the

better snacks than anyone else. In the morning, I used to buy rice muffins on the way to

school. They are more sweeter that American muffins. After school, I ate fish balls on a stick

or *adidas* (chicken feet). Snacks on a stick are small than traditional American hot dogs and

burgers, but they are much varied, and the food is much fresher. My friend thought

banana-cue (banana on a stick) was really great. However, they weren't as sweet from

kamote-cue (fried sweet potatoes and brown sugar), my favorite snack.

When I came to the United States, I didn't like American fast food at first. To me, it was

interesting than my native food and less tastier too. Now I'm getting used to it, and it seems

deliciouser and deliciouser. Does anyone want to go out for a pizza?

STEP 4 COMMUNICATION PRACTICE

EXERCISE 6: Listening

A | *Read the statements. Then listen to the conversation. Listen again and circle the correct information.*

1. The couple is <u>in a restaurant</u> / <u>at a supermarket</u>.

2. They are going to have <u>fresh / frozen</u> pizza for dinner.

3. They are comparing <u>two / three</u> brands of pizza.

4. They first discuss the <u>size / price</u> of the pizza.

5. The <u>woman / man</u> reads the nutrition information.

6. The expiration date tells them the latest date they should <u>eat / buy</u> the pizza.

7. In the end, the couple decides to buy <u>Angela's / Di Roma's</u> pizza.

B | *Listen again to the conversation and check (✓) the pizza that is better in each category.*

	Di Roma's	Angela's
1. cheap	✓	☐
2. big	☐	☐
3. healthy	☐	☐
4. tasty	☐	☐
5. fresh	☐	☐

EXERCISE 7: Pronunciation

A | *Read and listen to the Pronunciation Note.*

> **Pronunciation Note**
>
> In **conversation** we often pronounce *as* /əz/ and *than* /ðən/.
>
> **EXAMPLES:** It's **as** good **as** John's pizza.
> It's better **than** Maria's.

B | *Listen to the short conversations. Notice the pronunciation of* **as** *and* **than.**

1. **A:** The new restaurant is just **as** crowded **as** the old one.

   B: It's even more crowded **than** the Pizza Place.

2. **A:** The menu was more varied **than** at Joe's.

   B: And the prices were just **as** good.

3. **A:** The fish was just **as** expensive **as** the scallops.

   B: It was even more expensive **than** the shrimp.

4. **A:** The restaurant didn't feel **as** relaxed **as** it used to.

   B: But the service was better **than** it was.

5. **A:** It's just **as** noisy **as** Joe's at lunchtime.

   B: It's even noisier **than** Joe's at dinnertime.

C | *Listen again. Then practice the conversations with a partner.*

EXERCISE 8: Compare and Contrast

Look at some of these favorite international pizza toppings. Discuss them with a partner. Make comparisons using some of the adjectives from the box.

| delicious | filling | healthy | interesting | spicy | tasty | traditional | unusual |

1. Australia

2. Mexico

3. Hong Kong

4. Greece

5. Poland

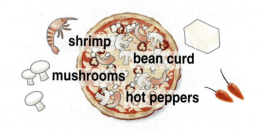

6. Indonesia

EXAMPLE: **A:** The pizza from Hong Kong looks less filling than the one from Mexico.
B: Yes, but it looks just as spicy.

EXERCISE 9: Role Play: Your Restaurant

A | *Work in small groups. Imagine that you have a small restaurant. Give your restaurant a name and decide what to put on the menu. Discuss dishes and prices for each category. Use comparisons in your discussion.*

EXAMPLE: **A:** We need a soup. How about chicken noodle?
B: Too boring! Gazpacho is more interesting.

Soups and Appetizers

_____ . . . . $ _____

_____ . . . . $ _____

Entrées

_____ . . . . $ _____

_____ . . . . $ _____

Salads and Side Dishes

_____ . . . . $ _____

_____ . . . . $ _____

Desserts

_____ . . . . $ _____

_____ . . . . $ _____

Beverages

_____ . . . . $ _____

_____ . . . . $ _____

B | *With your group, role-play ordering from your menu. One person is the server; the others are customers.*

EXAMPLE: **A:** Is the gazpacho as spicy as the hot-and-sour soup?
B: No, the hot-and-sour soup is much spicier.
C: Great! I love spicy food. The spicier the better!

EXERCISE 10: Writing

A | *Write a paragraph comparing your country's food with the food of another country.*

> **EXAMPLE:** Food in Taiwan is fresher than food in the United States. Taiwan is a small island, and there are a lot of farms . . .

B | *Check your work. Use the Editing Checklist.*

Editing Checklist

Did you . . . ?

☐ use comparisons with **as . . . as** to show how food is or is not similar

☐ use comparisons with **than** to show how food is different

☐ form comparative adjectives (long and short) correctly

☐ use **just** or **even** to make the comparisons stronger

Check your answers on page UR-5.

Do you need to review anything?

A | *Circle the correct words to complete the sentences.*

1. Rosa's spaghetti is just as good <u>as / than</u> Maria's.

2. My mother's tomato sauce is <u>good / better</u> than Rizzo's bottled sauce.

3. These chairs are <u>more / as</u> comfortable than the old ones.

4. I don't like the new menu. It's <u>more / less</u> interesting than the old one.

5. The lines in my supermarket are getting <u>long / longer</u> and longer.

6. The longer the line, <u>the more impatient / more impatient</u> I get.

B | *Complete the sentences with the comparative form of the words in parentheses.*
*Use **than** where necessary.*

1. Tony's pizza is _____ Sal's, so I can't buy it often.
   (expensive)

2. It's also _____, so it's worth the price.
   (big)

3. Tony's restaurant is _____ Sal's. They have more tables.
   (large)

4. But Sal's hours are _____. They're open until midnight.
   (convenient)

5. Tony's is _____ from school. It's 10 blocks away.
   (far)

C | *Find and correct nine mistakes.*

    Last night, I had dinner at the new Pasta Place on the corner of Main Street and Grove. This new Pasta Place is just as good than the others, and it has just as many sauces to choose from. No one makes a more good traditional tomato sauce them. But there are much interestinger choices. Their mushroom cream sauce, for example, is as better as I've ever had. Try the mushroom and tomato sauce for a healthier than meal. It's just as delicious. The new branch is already popular. The later it is, longer the lines. My recommendation: Go early for a more short wait. And go soon. This place will only get more popular and more popular!

Adjectives: Superlatives
CITIES

Before You Read

Look at the photo. Discuss the questions.

1. Do you recognize this city? Where do you think it is?
2. What are some important features for a city to have?

Read

Read the travel brochure.

A Superlative[1] City

TORONTO. It's the capital of the province of Ontario. It's also . . .

* **the largest** city in Canada
* **the most important** economic and financial center of the country
* one of **the most multicultural** places on earth (Over 100 languages are spoken in the city!)
* one of **the easiest** places to get around (It has **the** second **largest** public transportation system in North America.)
* **the safest** city on the continent, and one of **the most peaceful** of all large, international cities on earth

All of these features, and many more, make Toronto one of **the most dynamic** cities in the world. Come visit and find out for yourself!

[1] **superlative**: excellent

After You Read

A | Vocabulary: *Circle the letter of the word or phrase that best completes each sentence.*

1. A **financial** center has a lot of _____.

   a. banks

   b. parks

   c. hospitals

2. A **multicultural** city has people from many different _____.

   a. schools

   b. theaters

   c. countries

3. An important **feature** of Toronto is its _____.

   a. city

   b. name

   c. safety

4. The transportation system is **public**. _____ can use it.

   a. Only important people

   b. Everyone

   c. Nobody

5. A **dynamic** city is NOT _____.

   a. interesting

   b. exciting

   c. boring

B | Comprehension: *Check (✓)* **True** *or* **False**. *Correct the false statements.*

	True	False
1. Some Canadian cities are larger than Toronto.	☐	☐
2. Some Canadian cities are more important financially than Toronto.	☐	☐
3. Many cities in the world aren't as multicultural as Toronto.	☐	☐
4. It's easy to get around Toronto.	☐	☐
5. Some cities in North America are safer than Toronto.	☐	☐

ADJECTIVES: SUPERLATIVES

Superlatives			
	Superlative Adjective Form		
This is	the largest the busiest the best the most interesting the least expensive	city	*in* the world. *of* all. I've *ever* visited.

GRAMMAR NOTES

1	Use **superlative adjectives** to compare one person, place, or thing with other people, places, or things in a group.	• Toronto is **the largest** city in Canada. • It's **the most multicultural** city in the country.

2	There are several ways of **forming superlative adjectives**.		
		ADJECTIVE	**SUPERLATIVE**
	a. For **short adjectives** (one syllable and two syllables ending in *-y*), use: *the* + **adjective** + *-est*	loud pretty	**the** loud**est** **the** prett**iest**
	There are often **spelling changes** when you add *-est*.	late big early	**the** lat**est** **the** big**gest** **the** earl**iest**
	Some adjectives have **irregular** superlative forms.	good bad far	**the best** **the worst** **the farthest**
	b. For **long adjectives** (two or more syllables), use *the most / the least* + **adjective**.	expensive	**the most** expensive **the least** expensive
	EXCEPTION: The **short adjective** *fun* forms the superlative the same way as a long adjective.	fun	**the most** fun NOT: the ~~funnest~~ **the least** fun
	c. For **some adjectives**, such as *lively, lovely, friendly,* and *quiet*, you can use: *the . . . -est* OR *the most / the least*	• Rio is **the liveliest** city in the world. OR • Rio is **the most lively** city in the world.	

3 We often use the superlative with other **words and expressions**:

a. phrases with *in* and *of*

- This is **the least expensive** hotel *in town*.
- It's **the greatest** city *in the world*.
- This was **the best** day *of our visit*.

b. *one of* or *some of*
Use a <u>plural count noun</u> with *one of*.

- Toronto is *one of* **the most dynamic** *cities* in the world.
  Not: Toronto is one of the most dynamic ~~city~~ in the world.

With *some of* you can use:
- a <u>plural count noun</u>
- a <u>non-count noun</u>

- *Some of* **the best** *cities* have large parks.
- Toronto has *some of* **the best** *food* in Canada.

c. *second (third, fourth . . .)*

- It has **the** *second* largest transportation system.

d. *ever* + present perfect

- This is **the biggest** building I *'ve ever seen*.

REFERENCE NOTES

For a list of **adjectives** that use **both forms of the superlative**, see Appendix 9 on page A-5.
For a list of **irregular superlative adjectives**, see Appendix 10 on page A-6.
For **spelling rules** for the **superlative form of adjectives**, see Appendix 23 on page A-11.

STEP 3 FOCUSED PRACTICE

EXERCISE 1: Discover the Grammar

Read more information about Toronto. Underline all the superlative adjectives.

What to Do and See in Toronto

🍁 **Go to the CN Tower**. It's one of <u>the tallest</u> buildings in the world. From there you can get the best view of the city and countryside.

🍁 **Drive along Yonge Street**. At 1,200 miles (1,800 km), it's the longest street in the world. For one weekend in July it's one of the liveliest too. Come and join 1 million others for the exciting Yonge Street Festival.

🍁 **Visit PATH**, the world's largest underground shopping complex.

🍁 **Explore the Old Town of York**. It has the most historic buildings in the whole city.

🍁 **Take the Yuk Yuk's Comedy Tour** of the Entertainment District—you'll have a good time on the funniest bus ride in town.

🍁 **Visit the Toronto Zoo**. There's always something new and fascinating going on. Local people call it the best family outing in Toronto.

EXERCISE 2: Superlative Adjectives

(Grammar Notes 1–2)

Look at the chart. Complete the sentences. Use the superlative form of the correct adjectives in parentheses.

CITY STATISTICS

		BEIJING	SEOUL	MEXICO CITY	TORONTO
	Population	8,614,000	17,500,000	17,400,000	4,367,000
	Area	748 sq km 289 sq mi	1,049 sq km 405 sq mi	2,072 sq km 800 sq mi	1,655 sq km 639 sq mi
	Average January Temperature	−4°C 28°F	−2.7°C 27°F	13.3°C 55.9°F	−6.4°C 20.5°F
	Average July Temperature	24°C 75°F	24.7°C 76.5°F	16.7°C 62.1°F	20.7°C 69.3°F
	Average Rainfall per Year	576.9 mm 22.71 in	1,242 mm 49 in	634.3 mm 25 in	877.7 mm 32.2 in
	Cost of a Cup of Coffee ($US)	$2.92	$3.00	$1.15	$3.26
	Cost of a Bus Ticket ($US)	$1.17	$0.44	$0.35	$1.86

1. Seoul has _____the largest_____ population of all four cities. But Mexico City
   (large / small)
   is _____ city in area.
   (big / small)

2. Beijing is _____ city in area.
   (big / small)

3. Toronto is _____ city in population, but not in area.
   (big / small)

4. In winter, _____ city is Toronto.
   (warm / cold)

5. Seoul has _____ July temperatures.
   (hot / cool)

6. Of all the cities in the chart, Mexico City is _____ in July,
   (hot / cool)
   and it is _____ in January. Mexico City definitely has
   (warm / cold)
   _____ climate of all.
   (comfortable / uncomfortable)

7. _____ city is Seoul. _____
   (dry / rainy)   (dry / rainy)
   city is Beijing.

8. You'll find _____ cup of coffee in Mexico City, and you'll find
   (cheap / expensive)
   _____ in Toronto.
   (cheap / expensive)

9. The city with _____ public buses is Mexico City. Toronto has
   (cheap / expensive)
   _____.
   (cheap / expensive)

EXERCISE 3: Superlative Adjectives

(Grammar Notes 1–3)

Read about the CN Tower. Complete the information. Use the superlative form of the correct adjective from the box.

| clear | famous | fast | heavy | long | popular | ~~tall~~ |

The CN Tower / La Tour CN

1. At 1,815 feet, 5 inches (553.33 m), the CN Tower is one of _____ the tallest _____

   structures in the world.

2. Everyone recognizes the CN Tower. It is _____ building in Canada.

3. At 130,000 tons (117,910 metric tonnes), the impressive CN Tower is one of the

   _____ buildings in the world.

4. With 2 million visitors every year, it is one of _____ tourist

   attractions in the country.

5. Because of its very high antenna, the tower provides the people of Toronto with some of

   _____ radio and TV reception in North America.

6. Moving at 15 miles (22 km) per hour, the six elevators are among _____

   in the world. The ride to the Look Out Level takes just 58 seconds.

7. If you don't want to take the elevator, you can try the stairs! The CN Tower has

   _____ metal staircase in the world.

EXERCISE 4: *The Most* and *The Least* + *Ever*

(Grammar Note 3)

Write superlative sentences about your own experiences. Use the words in parentheses with **the most** or **the least** + **ever** and the present perfect. Write two sentences for each item. Go to Appendix 1, page A-1 for help with the irregular past participles.

EXAMPLE: Toronto is the most multicultural city I've ever visited.
            Meadville is the least multicultural city I've ever visited.

1. (multicultural / city / visit)

   _____

   _____

(continued on next page)

2. (comfortable / place / stay)

_____

_____

3. (friendly / people / meet)

_____

_____

4. (expensive / trip / take)

_____

_____

5. (attractive / place / see)

_____

_____

6. (exciting / team / watch)

_____

_____

EXERCISE 5: Editing

Read the postcard. There are eight mistakes in the use of superlative adjectives. The first mistake is already corrected. Find and correct seven more.

most beautiful
Greetings from Toronto—the ~~beautifulest~~ city I've ever visited. Yesterday we went to the CN Tower—the more recognizable structure in all of Canada. From there you get the best view of the city—the different neighborhoods, the harbor, the fast traffic—it made my head spin! This is one of most dynamic places I've ever visited! The restaurant was the most expensivest I've ever seen, so we just enjoyed the view and then went to Kensington Market to eat. This place has the baddest crowds but the cheapest and the goodest food we've had so far. We're staying in East Toronto. It's not the closer place to downtown, but it has some of most historic buildings. In fact, our bed-and-breakfast is called _1871 Historic House_. John Lennon slept here!

Love, Marissa

EXERCISE 6: Listening

A | *May and Dan are planning a vacation. Read the sentences. Listen to May and Dan's conversation. Then listen again and complete the sentences.*

1. May and Dan are going to go to _____Toronto_____ next summer.

2. They are trying to decide among _____ hotels.

3. The Westin Harbour Castle has a _____ with views of both the lake and the _____.

4. The Hôtel Le Germain is close to the entertainment _____.

5. The rooms at Hôtel Le Germain start at _____.

6. The Delta Chelsea has _____ rooms.

7. Dan says, "This is going to be the _____ vacation we've ever had."

B | *Listen again to the conversation and check (✓) the correct hotel for each feature.*

FEATURES	Westin Harbour Castle	Hôtel Le Germain	Delta Chelsea
the best view	✔		
the most convenient			
the least convenient			
the most comfortable			
the most expensive			
the least expensive			
the biggest			
the smallest			

EXERCISE 7: Pronunciation

A | *Read and listen to the Pronunciation Note.*

> **Pronunciation Note**
>
> In **words that end in -st**, we often **drop the final -t sound** before a word that begins with a **consonant** sound. For example, we drop the *t* in the word ***most*** and pronounce it "***mos'***" when the following word begins with a consonant sound.
>
> **EXAMPLES:** It's the **most beautiful** city. → "It's the **mos' beautiful** city."
> It's the **safest place**. → "It's the **safes' place**."

B | *Listen to the short conversations. Draw a slash (/) through the final -t when it is not pronounced in the superlative adjectives.*

1. **A:** The view from here is great.

    B: But the **best view** is from the CN Tower.

2. **A:** This restaurant is expensive.

    B: Yes, it's the **most expensive** restaurant in town.

3. **A:** This is an interesting part of town.

    B: It is. But it's not the **most interesting** part.

4. **A:** Toronto's a very safe city.

    B: Yes, it's the **safest city** in Canada.

5. **A:** This hotel is pretty expensive.

    B: Yes, but it's the **least expensive** one in this part of town.

6. **A:** I love Toronto.

    B: Me too. I think it's one of the **nicest places** in the world.

C | *Listen again and repeat each response. Then practice the conversations with a partner.*

EXERCISE 8: What About You?

Work with a partner. Talk about your answers to Exercise 4 on page 301. Keep the conversation going by asking more questions like these:

- Which . . . did you like best?
- Why do you say that?
- Sounds great! What else did you like?
- Who did you meet?

EXAMPLE: **A:** What's the most interesting city you've ever visited?
B: Toronto. People from all over the world live there. It's very multicultural.
A: Are there interesting neighborhoods?
B: Oh, yes. Greektown is one of the most dynamic places I've ever seen.

EXERCISE 9: Discussion

Work in small groups. Discuss cities in your countries. You can use some of the adjectives from the box.

beautiful	crowded	exciting	interesting	multicultural
clean	dynamic	friendly	modern	old

EXAMPLE:
A: What's the most interesting city in Argentina?
B: I think Buenos Aires is the most interesting city in Argentina. There's so much to do—theater, sports, movies. It's also the most multicultural city in the country. People from all over the world live there.
C: It sounds very exciting. What's the most exciting city in your country, Chen?

EXERCISE 10: Writing

A | Write a fact sheet for your hometown or city. Use Exercise 1 on page 299 as a model. Include superlatives.

EXAMPLE: **What to Do and See in Meadville**
- Go to Joe's for the best pizza in town.
- Ride the number 53 bus for one of the cheapest and best ways to see the major sights.

B | Check your work. Use the Editing Checklist.

Editing Checklist

Did you . . . ?
☐ use superlative adjectives
☐ form them correctly
☐ use words and expressions such as *in the city*

A | Complete each sentence with the superlative form of the correct word from the box.

| big | cheap | dry | expensive | rainy | short |

1. The _____ river in the world is the Roe River in the United States. It's only

    200 feet long.

2. The _____ lake is Lake Superior in North America. It's 32,000 square miles.

3. Calama, Chile, is one of the _____ towns on earth. It gets only .004 inches

    of rain a year.

4. Cherrapunji, India, is one of the _____. It gets around 400 inches.

5. Tokyo, Japan, is one of the _____ cities. A cup of coffee costs $4.00.

6. Johannesburg, South Africa, is one of the _____. A cup of coffee is $1.35.

B | Complete the conversation with the superlative form of the adjectives in parentheses.

A: Welcome back! You just missed _____ week of the year so far.
    1. (cold)

B: But Florida was great! The Magic Kingdom is _____ place.
    2. (fantastic)

A: It's _____ amusement park. It's also _____.
    3. (popular)   **4. (crowded)**

B: True. The long lines were _____ part of the trip.
    5. (fun)

A: What was _____ part?
    6. (good)

B: Monsters, Inc. It's not _____ show in the world, but it's quite good.
    7. (funny)

C | Find and correct seven mistakes.

Small towns aren't most dynamic places to visit, and that's just why we love to vacation on

Tangier Island. This tiny island is probably the less popular vacation spot in the United States.

Almost no one comes here. But it's also one of the most safest places to visit. And you'll find some

of the goodest seafood and the beautiful beaches here. It's one of the easiest place to get around

(there are no cars on the island). If you get bored, just hop on the ferry. You're only a few hours

from Washington, D.C., and a few more hours from New York and the excitingest nightlife ever.

UNIT 22 Adverbs: *As . . . as*, Comparatives, Superlatives

SPORTS

STEP 1 GRAMMAR IN CONTEXT

Before You Read

Look at the photo. Discuss the questions.

1. What game are they playing?
2. Which sports do you like to watch?
3. Do you play any sports? Which ones?
4. Why do you like them?

Australia vs France

Read

Read the transcript of a TV sports program.

The Halftime¹ Report

CINDY: What a game! Spero, have you ever seen two teams play **more aggressively**?

SPERO: No, I haven't, Cindy. Folks, we're in Bangkok, Thailand, watching the Australian and French teams battle for the Women's World Basketball Championship. It's halftime, and just listen to that crowd! I think the Australians cheer **the loudest** of any fans in the game!

CINDY: Well, the court really belonged to France for the first few minutes of the game, Spero. But the Australian team recovered quickly. They've scored almost **as frequently as** the French in the first half. The score is now 30-28, France, and no one can predict a winner at this point.

SPERO: I heard that Elizabeth Cambage, Australia's star player, injured her arm yesterday, but you can't tell from the way she's playing today. So far, she's scored **the most** of any player on her team.

CINDY: And with an injury too! Spero, I have to say that's pretty amazing. But Maud Medenou of France isn't that far behind. Did you notice that she's been playing **more and more intensely** in this tournament? You can see that she really wants the ball, and she's getting it **more consistently** in every game.

SPERO: You're right, Cindy. And **the harder** she plays, **the more** she scores.

CINDY: The Australians have really been playing a great defense tonight. They've been blocking Medenou **more effectively than** any other team this season. But can they stop her?

SPERO: We'll find out soon! The second half is ready to begin. See you again after the game.

---

¹ *halftime:* a period of rest between two parts of a game such as football or basketball

After You Read

A | Vocabulary: *Match the sentences on the left with the sentences on the right.*

___d___ **1.** Medenou is playing very **aggressively**.

___e___ **2.** Farley is playing **consistently**.

___b___ **3.** France blocked Cambage **effectively**.

___c___ **4.** Thizy gets hurt the most **frequently**.

___a___ **5.** Cambage is playing pretty **intensely**.

a. She's got a lot more energy and focus.

b. Cambage wasn't able to score.

c. She's had a lot of injuries.

d. She just pushed Jarry off the court.

e. She's played well in the last five games.

B | Comprehension: *Check (✓) the boxes to complete the sentences.*

1. The teams are competing in _____.
- ☑ Thailand
- ☐ Australia
- ☐ France

2. In the beginning of the game, _____ was losing.
- ☐ France
- ☑ Australia
- ☐ Thailand

3. At halftime, Australia had _____ France.
- ☑ a lower score than
- ☐ a higher score than
- ☐ the same score as

4. Cambage _____ today.
- ☐ can't play
- ☐ injured her arm
- ☑ has scored a lot

5. Medenou is _____ Cambage.
- ☑ almost as good as
- ☐ better than
- ☐ just as good as

6. At halftime, _____ knows which team is going to win.
- ☐ Cindy
- ☐ Spero
- ☑ nobody

ADVERBS: *AS . . . AS*, COMPARATIVES, SUPERLATIVES

As . . . as					
		As	**Adverb**	**As**	
France	played didn't play	**as**	**hard** **well** **aggressively** **consistently**	**as**	Australia.

Comparatives				
		Comparative Adverb Form	**Than**	
France	played	**harder** **better** **more aggressively** **less consistently**	**than**	Australia.

Superlatives			
		Superlative Adverb Form	
The star player	played	**the hardest** **the best** **the most aggressively** **the least consistently**	**of** anyone in the game.

GRAMMAR NOTES

1 Use *as* + **adverb** + *as* to compare actions and show how they are <u>the same or equal</u>.

- Girard plays **as well as** Farley.

Use *just* to make the comparison stronger.

- Girard plays *just* **as well as** Farley.
  (Girard and Farley play equally well.)

Use *not as* + **adverb** + *as* to show how the actions are <u>NOT the same or equal</u>.

- Girard did**n't** play **as aggressively as** Kunek.
  (Girard and Kunek didn't play the same. Kunek played more aggressively.)

(continued on next page)

2 Use **comparative adverbs** + *than* to show how the actions of two people or things are <u>different</u>.

Use *even* to make the comparison stronger.

USAGE NOTE: We usually do NOT use *less . . . than* with <u>one syllable adverbs</u>. Instead we use:
- *not as . . . as*

  OR
- another adverb with the <u>opposite meaning</u>

REMEMBER: When the meaning is clear, it's not necessary to mention both parts of a comparison with *as . . . as* or comparative adverbs.

- France played **better than** Australia.
- Cambage played **more skillfully than** Datchy.

- She played *even* **more skillfully than** Datchy.

NOT: Riley runs ~~less fast than~~ Cash.

- Riley does**n't** run **as fast as** Cash.

  OR
- Riley runs **slower than** Cash.

- He played hard. She played just **as hard**.
  (*. . . as hard as he played*)
- Beard shot **more consistently**.
  (*. . . more consistently than King shot*)

3 Use **superlative adverbs** to compare <u>one</u> action with the actions of other people or things in a <u>group</u>.

We often use the superlative with **expressions** beginning with *of*.

- All the players worked hard, but Robins worked **the hardest**.

- She scored **the most frequently** *of any player* on the team.

4 There are several ways of **forming comparative and superlative adverbs**.

a. For most **short adverbs** (one syllable), use:
adverb + -er OR **the + adverb + -est**

Some short adverbs have **irregular** comparative and superlative forms.

b. For **long adverbs** (two or more syllables), use:
more / less + **adverb** OR *the most / the least* + **adverb**

c. **Some adverbs of manner** have <u>two comparative</u> and <u>two superlative</u> forms.

The *-er / -est* forms are more common in <u>spoken English and informal writing</u>.

REMEMBER: Do NOT put an adverb of manner <u>between the verb and the object</u>.

ADVERB	COMPARATIVE	SUPERLATIVE
fast	fast**er**	**the** fast**est**
hard	hard**er**	**the** hard**est**
well	**better**	**the best**
badly	**worse**	**the worst**
far	**farther**	**the farthest**
much/a lot	**more**	**the most**
a little	**less**	**the least**
skillfully	**more / less** skillfully	**the most / the least** skillfully
quickly	**more** quickly **quicker**	**the most** quickly **the quickest**

MORE COMMON: Davis ran **quicker**.
LESS COMMON: Davis ran **more quickly**.

- She **handled** *the ball* **better** than Farley.
  NOT: She handled ~~better the ball~~ than Farley.

5	Repeat the **comparative adverb** to show <u>increase or decrease</u>:	
	comparative + *and* + **comparative** adverb adverb With long adverbs, repeat only *more* or *less*.	• Kukoc is playing **better and better** as the season continues. *(His performance keeps getting better.)* • He's playing **more and more aggressively**. NOT: He's playing more ~~aggressively~~ and more aggressively.

6	Use **two comparative adverbs** to show <u>cause and effect</u>: *the* + **comparative** + *the* + **comparative** adverb adverb	• **The harder** he played, **the better** he got. *(When he played harder, he got better.)*

REFERENCE NOTES

For a list of **irregular comparative and superlative adverbs** see Appendix 10 on page A-6.
For more information about **adverbs**, see Unit 19 on page 268.

STEP 3 FOCUSED PRACTICE

EXERCISE 1: Discover the Grammar

Read the story from the sports section of the newspaper. Underline all the comparisons with
(not) as + *adverb* + **as,** *and all the comparative and superlative adverb forms.*

Comets Beat Lions!

In the first basketball game of the season, the Comets beat the Lions, 90 to 83. The Lions played a truly fantastic game, but their defense is still weak. The Comets defended the ball much more aggressively than the Lions did.

Of course, Ace Hernandez certainly helped win the game for the Comets. The Comets' star player was back on the court today to the delight of his many fans. He was hurt badly at the end of the last season, but he has recovered quickly. Although he didn't play as well as people expected, he still handled the ball like

the old Ace. He certainly handled it the most skillfully of anyone on the team. He controlled the ball the best, shot the ball the most accurately, and scored the most consistently of any of the players on either team. He played hard and helped the Comets look good. In fact, the harder he played, the better the Comets performed. Watch Ace this season.

And watch the Lions. They have a new coach, and they're training more seriously this year. I think we'll see them play better and better as the season progresses.

EXERCISE 2: Comparisons with *As . . . as*

(Grammar Note 1)

Read the chart comparing several brands of basketball shoes. Complete the sentences. Use
(not) as + *adverb* + **as** *and the words in parentheses.*

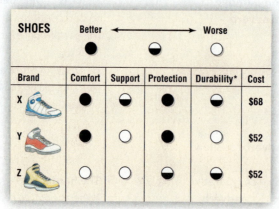

*how long the product lasts

1. Brand X _____ *fits as comfortably as* _____ brand Y.
   (fit / comfortable)

2. Brand Z _____ doesn't fit as comfortably as _____ brand X or Y.
   (fit / comfortable)

3. Brand Y _____ support the ankles as well as _____ brand Z.
   (support / the ankles / good)

4. Brands Y and Z _____ don't support the ankles as well as _____ brand X.
   (support / the ankles / good)

5. Brand Z _____ doesn't protect the feet as effectively as _____ brand X or Y.
   (protect / the feet / effective)

6. Brand X _____ protect the feet as effectively as _____ brand Y.
   (protect / the feet / effective)

7. Brand X _____ lasts as long as _____ brand Z.
   (last / long)

8. Brand Y _____ doesn't last as long as _____ brand X or Z.
   (last / long)

9. Brands Y and Z _____ cost less than / don't cost as much as _____ brand X.
   (cost / much)

EXERCISE 3: *As . . . as,* Comparative and Superlative Adverbs

(Grammar Notes 1–6)

*Complete the conversation between sports commentator Carla Lobo and player Elena
Bard. Change the adjectives in parentheses to adverbs. Use them with* **as . . . as** *or with the
comparative or superlative forms. Add* **the** *or* **than,** *and choose between* **more** *or* **less** *where
necessary.*

LOBO: Why do people still take female basketball players _____ *less seriously than* _____
                                                                    1. (serious)

male players? Do women really play _____ men?
                                                   2. (aggressive)

BARD: Absolutely not! We play just _____. And when we fall, we hit
                                               3. (aggressive)

the floor just _____ the guys do.
                        4. (hard)

LOBO: You could sure see that in tonight's game. Jackson played _____
                                                                        5. (effective)

of any player I've seen, male or female. She never let Cash anywhere near the basket.

BARD: Yes. And she performs like that much _____ a lot of the
6. (consistent)

men. Jackson always gets the job done.

LOBO: Some people say women play _____ men.
7. (cooperative)

BARD: I agree. I think we have better teamwork—we play _____
8. (good)

on a team. We're also more patient. I have noticed that most women players are able to wait

_____ for a good chance to shoot.
9. (long)

LOBO: Tickets for women's basketball games cost _____ tickets for
10. (little)

men's games. Does that bother you?

BARD: Sure, but _____ women players attract fans,
11. (fast)

_____ the women's leagues will make money.
12. (fast)

EXERCISE 4: Comparative and Superlative Adverbs

(Grammar Notes 2–4)

*Look at the chart. Then complete the sentences. Use the comparative or superlative adverb
form of the words from the box. You will use some words more than once.*

bad	far	fast	good	high	slow

	Broad Jump (distance)	Pole Vaulting (height)	5-mile Run (speed)
Nolan	14.3 feet	7 feet, 3 inches	24 minutes
Smith	14.1 feet	7 feet, 2 inches	28 minutes
Diaz	15.2 feet	7 feet, 8 inches	30 minutes
Wang	15.4 feet	8 feet, 2 inches	22 minutes

1. Nolan jumped _____*farther than*_____ Smith.

2. Wang vaulted _____*the highest*_____ of all.

3. Diaz ran _____.

4. Smith ran _____ Wang.

5. Wang jumped _____.

6. Nolan ran _____ Smith.

7. Wang vaulted _____ Smith.

8. All in all, Wang did _____.

9. All in all, Smith did _____.

EXERCISE 5: Editing

Read the article from a student newspaper. There are nine mistakes in the use of adverbs.
The first mistake is already corrected. Find and correct eight more.

The Last Game is the Lions' Best

Last night was the last game of the

season, and the Lions played the ~~goodest~~ *best*

they've played for months. Both the Cubs

and Lions play a great offensive game, but

this time the Lions really played defense

much more effectively as the Cubs.

Hernandez, the Cubs' star player, has

been shooting more aggressively and more

aggressively all season. But in last night's

game, the more aggressive he played, the

most closely the Lions guarded him. Then,

in the last two minutes, "Tiny Tim"

O'Connell made the winning shot for the

Lions. "He's less than six feet tall, but he

runs more fastly than anyone else on the

court," the Cubs' coach said. "O'Connell

doesn't shoot as often other players, but

he's a lot more accurately than the bigger

guys." The Cubs played a great game last

night too, but they just didn't play as good

as the Lions. Can the Lions play like this

consistently? If so, they may be this

season's new champions.

STEP 4 COMMUNICATION PRACTICE

EXERCISE 6: Listening

A | *Read the names of the horses in the horse race. Then listen to the sportscasters*
*describing the race. Listen again and rank the horses from first place (**1**) to last place (**5**).*

_____ Exuberant King

_1_ Get Packin'

_____ Inspired Winner

_____ Señor Speedy

_____ Wild Whirl

A fast start to an exciting race

B | *Read the statements about the race. Then listen again to the sportscasters and circle the correct information.*

1. The race was in Sydney / (Dubai).

2. Inspired Winner / Wild Whirl has been winning the most consistently.

3. In the first turn, Inspired Winner and Wild Whirl ran faster / slower than Get Packin'.

4. In the first turn, Señor Speedy and Exuberant King ran the slowest / fastest of all the horses.

5. In the second turn, Señor Speedy and Exuberant King ran slower / faster than in the first turn.

6 In the second turn, Inspired Winner ran better and better / slower and slower.

7. Get Packin' competed the most / least aggressively of all the horses in the race.

EXERCISE 7: Pronunciation

A | *Read and listen to the Pronunciation Note.*

> **Pronunciation Note**
>
> We often **link final consonants to beginning vowels** in *as* + **adverb** + *as* phrases:
>
> **Link "s"** in *as* to a beginning vowel in the adverb.
>
> **EXAMPLE:** as easily
>
> For **adverbs** that **end in the letter y**, use the **sound "y"** as in the word *yes* to **link the adverb to as.**
>
> **EXAMPLE:** as easily as

B | *Listen to the short conversations. Notice the pronunciation of* **as** + *adverb* + **as.**

1. **A:** Who scores more easily, Cash or Riley?
   B: Cash can't score **as easily as** Riley.

2. **A:** Our team should play more aggressively.
   B: Nah. We play just **as aggressively as** the other team.

3. **A:** So why do we keep losing this season?
   B: I don't know. Maybe we're not training **as effectively as** we did last year.

4. **A:** Johnson's energy is incredible.
   B: I know. Nobody plays **as intensely as** she does.

5. **A:** I wonder what's wrong with her tonight.
   B: Something is. She's not shooting **as accurately as** usual.

C | *Listen again to the conversations and repeat the responses. Then practice the conversations with a partner.*

EXERCISE 8: Compare and Contrast

Work as a class. Name several famous athletes for one sport. Compare their abilities. Use some of the verbs and adverbs in this list.

Verbs	Adverbs
catch	carefully
hit	defensively
kick	easily
race	fast
run	intensely
play	powerfully
throw	straight
train	successfully

Usain "Lightning" Bolt celebrates a world record in Beijing.

EXAMPLE: Usain Bolt is a runner from Jamaica. He runs faster than anyone else on earth.

EXERCISE 9: Questionnaire: Work and Play

A | *How well do you balance work or study and leisure time? Complete the questionnaire.*

1. How many hours do you work every week? _____

2. How many hours do you study every week? _____

3. How many books have you read for pleasure this month? _____

4. How many hours a week do you watch TV every week? _____

5. How many hours do you spend with your family and friends every week? _____

6. When did you last watch a sports event? _____

7. How many hours a week do you play sports? _____

8. How many days a week do you exercise? _____

9. How many vacation trips have you taken in the last year? _____

B | *Now add your own questions.*

10. _____

11. _____

12. _____

C | *Work in small groups. Compare your answers to questions 1–9 with those of your classmates. Ask the group your own questions (10–12) and compare the answers.*

Find out:

1. Who works the hardest?

2. Who studies the most?

3. Who reads the most?

4. Who has watched a sports event the most recently?

5. Who plays sports the most regularly?

6. Who has traveled the most frequently?

7. Who balances work and play the most effectively?

   EXAMPLE: Sharif works the hardest. He works 45 hours every week.

EXERCISE 10: Writing

A | *Write a paragraph comparing two sports figures. Choose two people that you know or two famous athletes. You can use the vocabulary from Exercise 8.*

   EXAMPLE: My friends Paul and Nick are both good soccer players, but they have different styles. Nick plays more aggressively than Paul, but Paul runs faster and passes more frequently. Nick scores more often, but Paul plays more cooperatively . . .

B | *Check your work. Use the Editing Checklist.*

Editing Checklist
Did you . . . ?   ☐ use *as . . . as* to show how two actions are the same or equal   ☐ use comparative adverbs with ***than*** to show how actions are different   ☐ use superlative adverbs to compare one person's actions to actions of a group   ☐ form comparative and superlative adverbs correctly

A | Circle the correct words to complete the sentences.

1. Chen plays just as <u>good / well</u> as Sanchez.

2. Maya is a slow runner. She <u>runs / doesn't run</u> as fast as her teammates.

3. Dan always shoots the ball <u>more accurately / the most accurately</u> than Will.

4. Inez plays the most aggressively <u>of / than</u> all the other players.

5. Our team didn't play <u>the worst / as well as</u> I expected. I was disappointed.

6. The faster Tranh runs, <u>the more tired he gets / he gets more tired</u>.

7. We need to practice <u>harder / hardly</u> if we want to win.

8. You're playing <u>well / better</u> and better!

B | Complete the sentences with the correct form of the words in parentheses.

1. You play just as _____ as Tomás.
   (good)

2. Olga runs _____ than any of her teammates.
   (fast)

3. Diego shoots the ball _____ of all the players.
   (accurate)

4. He practices _____ of all.
   (hard)

5. Their team played _____ of all the teams.
   (bad)

C | Find and correct seven mistakes.

Last night's game was a very exciting one. The Globes played the best they've played all season. But they still didn't play as good as the Stars. The Stars hit the ball more frequent and ran more fast than the Globes, and their pitcher, Kevin Rodriguez, threw the ball more accurately. Their catcher, Scott Harris, handled better the ball than the Globes' catcher. The Globes are good, but they are less good than the Stars. All in all, the Stars just keep playing good and better. And the better they play, the hardest it is for their fans to get tickets! These games sell out quicker than hotcakes, so go early if you want to get a chance to see the Stars.

PART VI

From Grammar to Writing

USING DESCRIPTIVE ADJECTIVES

Descriptive adjectives can help your reader better picture what you are writing about.

EXAMPLE: I live in an apartment. ➔
I live in a **small comfortable one-bedroom** apartment.

1 | *Read the description of an apartment and the writer's feelings about it. Circle all the adjectives that the writer uses.*

> I live in a (small) comfortable one-bedroom apartment with a convenient location close to school. The living room is my favorite room. It's sunny, warm, and peaceful. Its best feature is the old brick fireplace, which I use frequently on cold winter nights. In the corner there's a large soft green couch. I like to sit there and read. Next to it is a small wood table with a charming modern lamp that I bought in town. It's a cozy living room, and I enjoy spending time here. It's an ideal room for a student.

2 | *Complete the word map with the circled words from Exercise 1.*

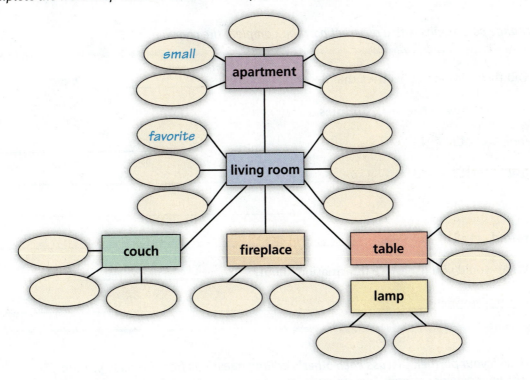

1. Work in small groups. Put the adjectives from the box into the correct categories. Brainstorm other adjectives for each category. You can use a dictionary for help.

~~attractive~~	cozy	gorgeous	huge	lovely	~~soft~~
coarse	cute	~~hard~~	~~large~~	rough	tiny
comfortable	enormous	hideous	~~little~~	~~run-down~~	ugly

a. things that are big: *large,* _____

b. things that are small: *little,* _____

c. things that look good: *attractive,* _____

d. things that look bad: *run-down,* _____

e. things that feel good: *soft,* _____

f. things that feel bad: *hard,* _____

2. Think about a room you know. On a separate piece of paper, draw a word map like the one in Exercise 2. Use some of the adjectives in the box above.

3. Discuss your map with a partner. Do you want to add or change any adjectives?

   EXAMPLE: **A:** How small is the dining room?
   B: Oh, it's tiny.

4 | Write a paragraph about the room from Exercise 3. Use your word map.

5 | Exchange paragraphs with a different partner. Complete the chart.

Did the writer use adjectives that describe how things _____?

	Yes	No	Examples
look	☐	☐	_____
feel	☐	☐	_____
smell	☐	☐	_____
sound	☐	☐	_____

What would you like more information about? _____

_____

6 | Work with your partner. Discuss each other's editing questions from Exercise 5. Then rewrite your own paragraph. Answer any questions your partner asked.

GERUNDS AND INFINITIVES

STEP 1 GRAMMAR IN CONTEXT

Before You Read

Look at the cartoon. Discuss the questions.

1. Why are the people standing on the ledge of the building?
2. How do you think they feel about it?
3. How do *you* feel about it?

Read

Read the article about smoking regulations.

NO SMOKING
AROUND THE WORLD FROM A–Z

In the past few decades,[1] life has become more and more difficult for people who **enjoy lighting up**.[2] At the same time, it has become more comfortable for people who don't smoke. And for those who want to **quit smoking**, it has become easier as countries around the world introduce laws that **limit** or **ban smoking** in public, and sometimes even private spaces. Here are some examples, from **A** to **Z**:

⊘ In **A**ustria, the law **prohibits smoking** in many public places, including trains and train stations. It's also banned in offices unless all employees are in favor **of permitting** it. Large restaurants must provide areas for non-smokers, but smaller ones can choose **between permitting smoking** or **being** smoke-free.

⊘ In many provinces of **C**anada, it's against the law to smoke in a car if there is a child or young adult present.

⊘ In some cities in **J**apan, it's illegal to smoke on the streets.

⊘ In **M**exico, **smoking** is not permitted at all in restaurants. The government has also **banned advertising** tobacco products on TV or radio.

⊘ The **U**nited Arab Emirates has recently **started banning** cigarettes in shopping malls and other public places including cafés and nightclubs.

⊘ In **Z**ambia, the law **bans smoking** in all public places. **Not obeying** the law can result in fines and even jail time.

---

[1] *decade:* a ten-year period
[2] *lighting up:* lighting a cigarette

NO SMOKING

Smoking is bad for your health. By now, almost everyone agrees. But, although many people approve of the new laws, not everyone is in favor **of prohibiting** public smoking. "It's one thing to try to discourage the habit **by putting** a high tax on cigarettes," says one smoker, "but some of the new laws go too far." Smokers argue that the laws limit personal freedom. They say everyone today knows the dangers **of lighting up**. So, if someone won't **quit smoking** and wants to smoke outdoors in a park or on the beach, it is that person's choice. Those smokers are only hurting themselves. There are many things that people do that are not good for them, such as **eating** junk food[3] and **not exercising**. But there are no laws that regulate[4] those behaviors.

[3] **junk food:** food that is bad for you (usually with a lot of sugar and fat)
[4] **regulate:** to control with rules or laws

After You Read

A | Vocabulary: *Which words can you use to talk about something that is **OK** to do? Something that is **NOT OK** to do? Complete the word maps with the words from the box.*

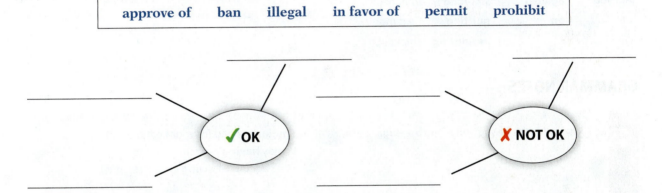

| approve of | ban | illegal | in favor of | permit | prohibit |

✓ OK   ✗ NOT OK

B | Comprehension: *Complete each sentence with the name of the country.*

1. Smoking outside is illegal in some parts of _____.

2. In _____, workers can decide on permitting smoking in the workplace or not.

3. In parts of _____, smoking is sometimes banned on people's own property.

4. Breaking non-smoking laws is a very serious crime in _____.

5. In _____, people can choose between dining in a smoke-free restaurant or in a smaller cigarette-friendly place.

6. You won't see any cigarette ads on TV in _____.

7. _____ has recently started having laws against smoking.

GERUNDS: SUBJECT AND OBJECT

Gerund as Subject		
Gerund (Subject)	**Verb**	
Smoking	causes	health problems.
Not smoking	is	healthier.

Gerund as Object		
Subject	**Verb**	**Gerund (Object)**
You	should quit	**smoking.**
We	suggest	**not smoking.**

Gerund as Object of a Preposition			
	Preposition	**Gerund**	
Are you	**against**	**smoking**	in public?
I plan	**on**	**quitting**	next month.
I'm in favor	**of**	**permitting**	smoking.

GRAMMAR NOTES

1 A **gerund** is the **base form of verb** + *-ing*.

- **Smoking** is bad for your health.
- I enjoy **having** a cigarette in the park.
- She's against **allowing** cigarettes at work.

BASE FORM	GERUND
smoke	smok**ing**
permit	permit**ting**
die	d**ying**

BE CAREFUL! There are often **spelling changes** when you add *-ing*.

Form the **negative** by placing *not* before the gerund.

- **Not exercising** is bad for you.
- The doctor suggested **not drinking** coffee.
- She's happy about **not working** today.

2 A gerund is a verb that we use **like a noun**.

a. A gerund can be the **subject** of a sentence. It is always <u>singular</u>. Use the third-person-singular form of the verb after gerunds.

- **Eating** junk food *makes* me sick.
- **Advertising** cigarettes on TV *is* illegal.

GERUND
- **Drinking** a lot of coffee is unhealthy.

PROGRESSIVE FORM
- He **is drinking** coffee right now.

BE CAREFUL! Do NOT confuse a <u>gerund</u> with the <u>progressive form</u> of the verb.

b. A gerund can be the **object** of certain verbs. Use a gerund **after these verbs**:

admit	consider	keep	resist
advise	deny	like	risk
appreciate	dislike	mind	start
avoid	enjoy	miss	stop
can't stand	finish	quit	suggest

- Jiang *avoids* **hanging out** with smokers.
- Have you ever *considered* **quitting**?
- I *dislike* **sitting** near smokers in cafés.
- We *finished* **studying** and went out.
- Did you *miss* **smoking** after you quit?
- Dr. Ho *suggested* **not staying up** late.

c. We often use *go* + **gerund** to describe <u>activities</u> such as *shopping, fishing, skiing, swimming,* and *camping*.

- Let's *go* **swimming** in the lake.
- I *went* **shopping** for running shoes at the mall.

3 A gerund can also be the **object of a preposition**.

Use a gerund **after prepositions** such as:

about	before	for	on
against	between	in	to
at	by	of	with / without

- It's all *about* **getting** fit.
- I'm *against* **smoking** in public.
- You'll improve your health *by* **quitting**.
- I'm *for* **banning** tobacco ads.

There are many **expressions with prepositions**. You can use a gerund after expressions with:

- **verb + preposition**
  advise *against*   believe *in*   count *on*

- I *believe in* **taking** care of my health.

- **adjective + preposition**
  afraid *of*   bored *with*   excited *about*

- I'm *excited about* **joining** the health club.

BE CAREFUL! Use a **gerund**, not an infinitive (*to* + **base form of verb**), after **expressions with the preposition *to***:
look forward *to*   be opposed *to*   object *to*

- I *look forward to* **seeing** you.
  NOT: I look forward ~~to see~~ you.

REFERENCE NOTES
For **spelling rules for verb + *-ing*,** see Appendix 21 on page A-10.
For a more complete list of **verbs** that can be **followed by gerunds**, see Appendix 13 on page A-7.
For a list of **adjectives followed by prepositions**, see Appendix 17 on page A-7.
For a list of **verbs followed by prepositions**, see Appendix 18 on page A-8.

STEP 3 FOCUSED PRACTICE

EXERCISE 1: Discover the Grammar

Read the online bulletin board about smoking. Underline all the gerunds.

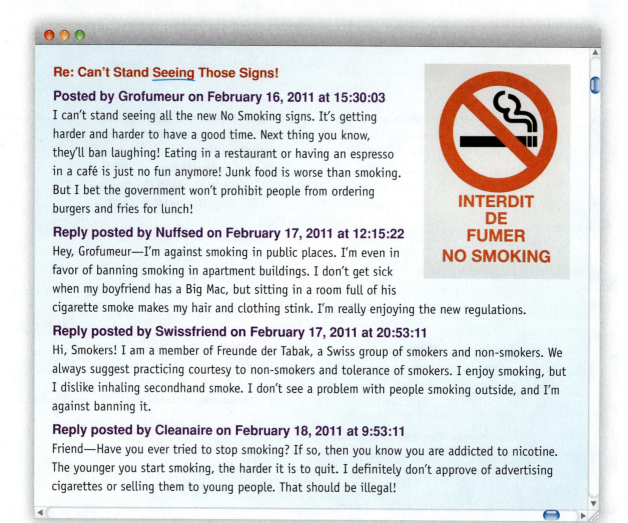

Re: Can't Stand Seeing Those Signs!

Posted by Grofumeur on February 16, 2011 at 15:30:03
I can't stand seeing all the new No Smoking signs. It's getting harder and harder to have a good time. Next thing you know, they'll ban laughing! Eating in a restaurant or having an espresso in a café is just no fun anymore! Junk food is worse than smoking. But I bet the government won't prohibit people from ordering burgers and fries for lunch!

Reply posted by Nuffsed on February 17, 2011 at 12:15:22
Hey, Grofumeur—I'm against smoking in public places. I'm even in favor of banning smoking in apartment buildings. I don't get sick when my boyfriend has a Big Mac, but sitting in a room full of his cigarette smoke makes my hair and clothing stink. I'm really enjoying the new regulations.

Reply posted by Swissfriend on February 17, 2011 at 20:53:11
Hi, Smokers! I am a member of Freunde der Tabak, a Swiss group of smokers and non-smokers. We always suggest practicing courtesy to non-smokers and tolerance of smokers. I enjoy smoking, but I dislike inhaling secondhand smoke. I don't see a problem with people smoking outside, and I'm against banning it.

Reply posted by Cleanaire on February 18, 2011 at 9:53:11
Friend—Have you ever tried to stop smoking? If so, then you know you are addicted to nicotine. The younger you start smoking, the harder it is to quit. I definitely don't approve of advertising cigarettes or selling them to young people. That should be illegal!

EXERCISE 2: Gerunds: Affirmative and Negative

(Grammar Notes 1–2)

Complete the article with gerunds. Use the verbs from the box. You will use one verb more than once. Choose between affirmative and negative.

eat	exercise	go	increase	join	pay	smoke	start	stay

_____*Not paying*_____ attention to their health is a mistake a lot of college students make.
1.

_____ healthy will help you do well in school and help you enjoy your college
2.

experience. Here are some tips:

- Smokers have more colds and less energy. Quit _____ now or don't start.

    3.

- _____ regularly reduces stress and brings more oxygen to your brain. If you

    4.

  don't exercise, I suggest _____ every day with a walk or run around campus.

    5.

- _____ breakfast is a common mistake. It's the most important meal of the day.

    6.

- Avoid _____ junk food. Your brain will thank you!

    7.

- Health experts advise _____ the fruits and vegetables in your diet. You need at

    8.

  least four and a half cups a day, but more is better.

- _____ to the doctor when you're sick is another common mistake. Know where

    9.

  your school Health Service is, and use it when you need it.

- Better yet—consider _____ Healthy Campus—a program for staying healthy.

    10.

EXERCISE 3: Gerund as Object

(Grammar Note 2)

Write a summary sentence for each conversation. Use the correct form of the verbs from the box and the gerund form of the verbs in parentheses.

admit	avoid	consider	deny	enjoy	go	mind	~~quit~~

1. **RALPH:** Would you like a cigarette?

   MARTA: Oh, no, thanks. Since restaurants have banned cigarettes, I don't smoke anymore.

   SUMMARY: Marta _____*quit smoking*_____.
                              (smoke)

2. **BRIAN:** Where are the cookies I bought? You ate them, didn't you?

   ELLEN: No, I didn't.

   SUMMARY: Ellen _____ the cookies.
                                      (eat)

3. **ANN:** Do you want to go running with me before work?

   TOM: Running? Are you kidding? I hate it!

   SUMMARY: Tom doesn't _____.
                                          (run)

4. **CHEN:** What are you doing after work?

   AN-LING: I'm going to that new swimming pool. Would you like to go with me?

   SUMMARY: An-ling is going to _____.
                                              (swim)

(continued on next page)

5.

      IRENE: You're lazy. You really need to exercise more.

      MIKE: You're right. I *am* lazy.

  SUMMARY: Mike _____ lazy.
                                       (be)

6.

     MONICA: Would you like a piece of chocolate cake?

       PAULO: No, thanks. I try to stay away from sweets.

  SUMMARY: Paulo _____ sweets.
                                         (eat)

7.

      CRAIG: I know exercise is important, but I hate it. What about you?

      VILMA: Well, I don't *love* it, but it's OK.

  SUMMARY: Vilma doesn't _____.
                                        (exercise)

8.

      ALICE: We've been working too hard. Maybe we need a vacation.

        ERIK: A vacation? Hmmm. That's an interesting idea. Do you think we can afford it?

  SUMMARY: Erik and Alice _____ a vacation.
                                       (take)

EXERCISE 4: Gerund as Object of a Preposition   *(Grammar Note 3)*

Combine the pairs of sentences to make statements about the Healthy Campus Program. Use the prepositions in parentheses plus a gerund.

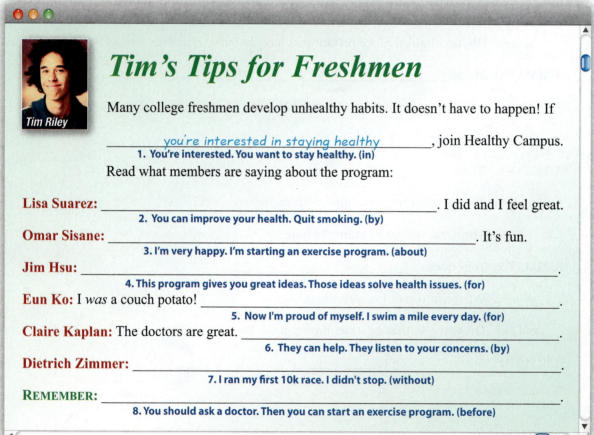

Tim's Tips for Freshmen

Tim Riley

Many college freshmen develop unhealthy habits. It doesn't have to happen! If

_____ *you're interested in staying healthy* _____, join Healthy Campus.
     1. You're interested. You want to stay healthy. (in)

Read what members are saying about the program:

Lisa Suarez: _____. I did and I feel great.
     2. You can improve your health. Quit smoking. (by)

Omar Sisane: _____. It's fun.
     3. I'm very happy. I'm starting an exercise program. (about)

Jim Hsu: _____.
     4. This program gives you great ideas. Those ideas solve health issues. (for)

Eun Ko: I *was* a couch potato! _____.
          5. Now I'm proud of myself. I swim a mile every day. (for)

Claire Kaplan: The doctors are great. _____.
          6. They can help. They listen to your concerns. (by)

Dietrich Zimmer: _____.
          7. I ran my first 10k race. I didn't stop. (without)

REMEMBER: _____.
     8. You should ask a doctor. Then you can start an exercise program. (before)

EXERCISE 5: Editing

Read part of an ex-smoker's journal. There are sixteen mistakes in the use of gerunds as subject and object. The first mistake is already corrected. Find and correct fifteen more. Remember to check for spelling mistakes.

DAY 1 I quit ~~to smoke~~ *smoking*! This was the first day of the rest of my life as a non-smoker. Get through the day wasn't too difficult. I quit drinking coffee today too, and I think that helped. I used to enjoy had a cigarette with a cup of coffee in the morning. But now I'm looking forward to get healthier.

DAY 3 Today was harder. I called Dinah and admitted wanted to smoke. She advised takeing deep breaths and staying busy. That worked. I have to resist eat too much. Gaining 5 pounds aren't a big deal, but I don't want to gain more than that.

DAY 5 I got through the workweek smoke free. My boss definitely approves of the new me. She keeps tells me, "You can do it." I really appreciate to have her support. I miss smoking, but I don't miss to standing outside in the cold just to smoke. I also don't mind don't burning holes in my clothes!

DAY 7 Dinah suggested to go out to dinner, but I can't risk be around smokers. Instead, we went shoping, and I bought a shirt with the money I saved during my first week as a non-smoker. Also, I'm happy about have clothes that smell fresh! Not smoking has advantages.

STEP 4 COMMUNICATION PRACTICE

EXERCISE 6: Listening

A | *A doctor is giving advice to a patient. Some things are **OK to Do** for this patient, but other things are **Not OK to Do**. Read the list. Then listen to the conversation between doctor and patient. Listen again and check (✓) the correct column.*

	OK to Do	Not OK to Do
1. smoking	☐	☑
2. drinking a little coffee	☐	☐
3. losing more weight	☐	☐

(continued on next page)

	OK to Do	Not OK to Do
4. eating more complex carbohydrates	☐	☐
5. running every day	☐	☐
6. riding a bike every day	☐	☐
7. working eight hours a day	☐	☐

B | *Read the statements. Then listen again to the conversation and circle the correct information.*

1. The patient is going to try to stop drinking coffee / (smoking).

2. The doctor says the patient should gain / stay the same weight.

3. The patient thanks the doctor for giving him a list of foods that are high in

   complex carbohydrates / protein.

4. The patient says he enjoys running / cycling.

5. The patient is not going to quit running / working every day.

EXERCISE 7: Pronunciation

A | *Read and listen to the Pronunciation Note.*

> **Pronunciation Note**
>
> Gerunds end in **-ing**. When a word beginning with a vowel sound follows a gerund, we usually **link the -ing with the vowel sound**.
>
> **EXAMPLES: Swimming is** fun.
>
> They shouldn't allow **smoking on** the street.

B | *Listen to the sentences. Draw linking lines (‿) between the gerunds and the words beginning with a vowel.*

1. **Smoking** is bad for your health.

2. **Smoking** causes health problems.

3. **Quitting** is very difficult.

4. He's opposed to **smoking** near other people.

5. He's even opposed to **smoking** outside.

6. She doesn't like **seeing** those signs.

7. She used to enjoy **lighting** up after dinner.

8. She plans on **quitting** in April.

C | *Listen again and repeat the sentences.*

EXERCISE 8: Survey

A | *Take a class survey. How many students agree with the statements? Write the numbers in the appropriate column.*

	Agree	Disagree	No Opinion or Don't Know
Smoking a few cigarettes a day is safe.			
Quitting is very difficult.			
Increasing the price of cigarettes encourages quitting.			
Banning all cigarette ads is a good idea.			
TV programs shouldn't allow scenes with smoking.			
Health insurance should be higher for smokers.			
They should allow smoking on the street.			
Selling cigarettes to teenagers should be illegal.			

B | *Discuss your survey results.*

> **EXAMPLE:** **A:** Only three students agree that smoking a few cigarettes a day is safe. Ten students disagree. Three students have no opinion or don't know.
> **B:** It seems that most students think that smoking is bad for people's health.
> **C:** Great! . . . Now how do they feel about quitting smoking?

EXERCISE 9: For or Against

Many people agree with laws that prohibit smoking. What is your opinion? Work in small groups. Think of arguments for and against allowing smoking in these places:

- in restaurants
- outside of schools
- at outdoor bus stops
- in parks
- in a car with children under 18
- in elevators
- in outdoor sports arenas
- in indoor shopping malls

> **EXAMPLE:** **A:** I'm in favor of banning smoking in restaurants.
> **B:** I agree. Sitting in a room full of smoke is unhealthy.
> **C:** But some restaurants have outdoor seating. I'm not against allowing smoking at tables outside.

EXERCISE 10: Writing

A | *Smoking is just one of many topics that people disagree about. Write a two-paragraph opinion essay for or against one of these topics:*

- allowing dogs in restaurants and stores
- texting or talking on cell phones while driving
- riding a motorcycle without wearing a helmet on your head
- forcing drivers over age 75 to pass a road test
- listing calories and fat content on restaurant menus
- eating junk food

EXAMPLE: In the United States, bringing your dog into a restaurant is illegal in most places. Some people don't like dogs. They don't want to eat dinner with one nearby. Other people are afraid of getting sick because a server touched a dog and didn't wash his or her hands . . .

B | *Check your work. Use the Editing Checklist.*

Editing Checklist
Did you use gerunds . . . ? ☐ as subjects ☐ as objects after certain verbs ☐ after prepositions ☐ with third-person-singular verbs

Check your answers on page UR-6.

Do you need to review anything?

A | Complete each sentence with the gerund form of the correct verbs from the box. Choose between affirmative and negative.

| eat | feel | improve | join | like | smoke | swim |

1. I admit _____ exercise. I've never enjoyed it.

2. I'm going to quit _____ on my birthday. This is my last pack.

3. You can count on _____ better as soon as you quit. You'll sleep better too.

4. Are you interested in _____ a gym?

5. Rafe goes _____ almost every day.

6. Sally doesn't mind _____ sweets anymore. She doesn't miss them.

7. I'd like some ideas for _____ my health. I catch too many colds.

B | Complete the sentences with the correct form of the words in parentheses. Use the correct word order.

1. _____ good for your health.
   (laugh / be)

2. My doctor _____ funny movies.
   (suggest / watch)

3. _____ jokes _____ your
   (tell / help)
   blood pressure.

4. One expert _____ too much coffee.
   (advise against / drink)

5. We _____ long walks.
   (enjoy / take)

6. What do you _____ in restaurants?
   (think about / smoke)

C | Find and correct seven mistakes. Remember to check punctuation.

1. You look great. Buying these bikes were a good idea.

2. I know. I'm happy about lose weight too. Didn't exercising was a bad idea.

3. It always is. Hey, I'm thinking of rent a movie. What do you suggest to see?

4. I've been looking forward to see *Grown Ups*. Have you seen it yet?

5. Not yet. Do you recommend it? You're so good at choose movies.

UNIT 24 Infinitives after Certain Verbs
FRIENDS AND FAMILY

STEP 1 GRAMMAR IN CONTEXT

Before You Read

Look at the advice column. Discuss the questions.

1. What kind of questions do you think Annie answers?
2. Do you think this is a good place to get advice? If no, why not?

Read

Read the newspaper advice column, Ask Annie.

Lifestyles	Section 4

ASK ANNIE

Dear Annie,

I've just moved to Seattle and started going to a new school. I **try to meet** people but nothing **seems to work**. A few weeks ago, I **agreed to have** dinner with someone from my English class. Bad idea. Right after we got to the restaurant, he **asked to borrow** money from me for the check. And he also **wanted to correct** my pronunciation (I'm from Louisiana). Obviously, I **decided not to see**[1] him again. Now my roommate **would like** me **to go out** with her brother. I **asked** her **not to arrange** anything because I really **don't want to date** anyone right now. First, I'**d** just **like to find** some friends to hang out with.[2] Do you have any suggestions?

Lonely in Seattle

Dear Lonely,

You **seem to have** the right idea about making new friends. A lot of people **try to solve** the problem of loneliness by falling in love. I usually **advise** them **to make** friends first. Perhaps you just **need to relax** a bit. Don't **expect to develop** friendships overnight because that takes time. Instead, do things that you'**d like to do** anyway. Join a sports club. **Learn to dance**.

Try not to focus so much on your problem. Just **remember to have** fun with your new activities. You'll interact with people who have similar interests. Even if you **fail to meet** your new best friends immediately, you will at least have a good time!

Don't give up!

Annie

---

[1] **see:** to go out socially with; to date
[2] **hang out with:** to spend free time with people

After You Read

A | Vocabulary: *Match the underlined words with the words in* **blue.**

_____ **1.** <u>It's easy to see that</u> they're going to be great friends.

_____ **2.** They have <u>almost the same</u> interests—dancing, for example.

_____ **3.** At school we <u>talk and work</u> with people from all over the world.

_____ **4.** <u>Keep your attention</u> on your work, and your grades will improve.

_____ **5.** Some people <u>find an answer to</u> their problem by writing to Annie.

a. interact

b. solve

c. obviously

d. similar

e. focus

B | Comprehension: *Check (✓)* **True** *or* **False.** *Correct the false statements.*

	True	False
1. "Lonely" has been successful in meeting people.	☐	☐
2. "Lonely" isn't asking for advice about dating.	☐	☐
3. Annie thinks making friends is a good idea.	☐	☐
4. Annie says that friendships develop quickly.	☐	☐
5. Annie thinks that "Lonely" ought to have some fun.	☐	☐

INFINITIVES AFTER CERTAIN VERBS

Statements				
Subject	**Verb**	**(Object)**	**Infinitive**	
I	**decided**		**(not) to write**	to Annie.
You	**advised**	John	**(not) to borrow**	money.
He	**asked**	(her)	**(not) to arrange**	a date.

GRAMMAR NOTES

1

An **infinitive** is *to* + **base form of the verb**.

Form the **negative** by placing *not* before the infinitive.

An infinitive can **follow certain verbs**.

- She decided **to join** a health club.

- She decided *not* **to join** the math club.

- I *agreed* **to have** dinner.
- He *wants* **to make** new friends.

2

Some **verbs**, such as the ones below, can be **followed directly by an infinitive**.

agree	forget	remember
attempt	hope	rush
begin	learn	seem
can't wait	manage	try
decide	plan	volunteer
fail	refuse	wait

VERB + INFINITIVE
- He *decided* **to take** a dance class.
- He *hoped* **to meet** new people.
- She *refused* **to go out** with him.
- She *tried* **not to be** late.

3

Some verbs, such as the ones below, need an **object** (noun or pronoun) **before the infinitive**.

advise	encourage	permit	tell
allow	force	persuade	urge
convince	invite	remind	warn

VERB + OBJECT + INFINITIVE
- I *invited* Mary **to eat** with us.
- I *reminded* her **to come**.
- She *told* me **to call** her.
- They *warned* us **not to forget**.

4

Some verbs, such as the ones below, can be **followed by**:
- **an infinitive**

  OR

- **an object + infinitive**

ask	need	promise
choose	pay	want
expect	prefer	would like

INFINITIVE
- I *asked* **to come** to the meeting.

OBJECT + INFINITIVE
- I *asked* them **to come** to the meeting.

REFERENCE NOTES

For a list of **verbs** that are **followed by infinitives**, see Appendix 14 on page A-7.

For a more complete list of **verbs** that need an **object before the infinitive**, see Appendix 16 on page A-7.

EXERCISE 1: Discover the Grammar

Read the diary entry. Underline *all the* **verb + infinitive** *and the* **verb + object + infinitive** *combinations.* Circle *the objects.*

Annie advised me to join a club or take a class, and I finally did it! I decided to join the school's Outdoor Adventure Club, and I went to my first meeting last night. I'm really excited about this. The club is planning a hiking trip next weekend. I can't wait to go. I hope it won't be too hard for my first adventure. Last night they also decided to go rafting in the spring. At first I didn't want to sign up, but the leader was so nice. He urged me not to miss this trip, so I put my name on the list. After the meeting, a group of people asked me to go out with them. We went to a coffee shop and talked for hours. Well, I hoped to make some new friends when I joined this club, but I didn't expect everyone to be so friendly. I'm glad Annie persuaded me not to give up.

EXERCISE 2: Verb (+ Object) + Infinitive

(Grammar Notes 1–4)

Complete the article. Use the correct form of the verbs in parentheses. Use the simple present or the imperative form for the first verb.

Most people make careful plans when they _____*decide to take*_____
                                                1. (decide / take)

a vacation. But when they _____ a mate, they depend on
                               2. (attempt / find)

luck. Edward A. Dreyfus, Ph.D., _____ love to chance.
                            3. (warn / single people / not leave)

He _____ his relationship plan when they search for a life partner.
           4. (urge / them / use)

Remember: When you _____, you _____.
                 5. (fail / plan)   **6. (plan / fail)**

STEP ONE: **Make a list.** What kind of person would you _____?
                                              7. (like / meet)

Someone intelligent? Someone who loves sports? List everything.

STEP TWO: **Make another list.** What kind of person are *you*? List *all* your characteristics (don't just focus on your good points!). _____ this list and comment on it.
                                      8. (ask / two friends / read)

_____ about hurting your feelings. The two lists should match.
        9. (tell / them / not worry)

(continued on next page)

Step Three: Increase your chances. _____ in activities you like.

10. (begin / participate)

That way you'll interact with people who have similar interests.

Step Four: _____ **introductions.** Dr. Dreyfus always

11. (ask / friends / arrange)

_____ embarrassed. After all, almost everyone

12. (advise / people / not feel)

_____ a matchmaker!

13. (want / be)

EXERCISE 3: Object or No Object

(Grammar Notes 1–4)

Write a summary sentence for each conversation. Use the correct form of a verb from the box followed by an infinitive or an object + infinitive.

agree	encourage	forget	invite	need	remind	~~would like~~

1. **KAREN:** *(yawn)* Don't you have a meeting tomorrow? Maybe you should go home now.

    TOM: It's only nine o'clock. And *Lost* is on in five minutes!

    SUMMARY: Karen _would like Tom to go home_____.

2. **KURT:** Hey, honey, did you get any stamps?

    LILY: Oh, I forgot. I'll stop at the post office on the way home.

    SUMMARY: Kurt _____.

3. **JOHN:** We're going out for coffee. Would you like to join us?

    MARY: I'd love to.

    SUMMARY: John _____.

4. **DAD:** I expect you to come home by 10:30. Do you understand? If you don't, I'm

    grounding you for two weeks—no parties, no friends, no telephone. Understand?

    JASON: OK, OK. Take it easy, Dad. I'll be home by 10:30.

    SUMMARY: Jason _____.

5. **DON:** You didn't go to the staff meeting. We missed you.

    JEFF: Oh, no! The staff meeting!

    SUMMARY: Jeff _____.

6.   LISA: I hate to ice skate. I always fall down.

         MOM: Don't be scared, sweetie. Just try once more. You'll love it.

SUMMARY: Lisa's mom _____.

7.   BRAD: Are you using the car tonight?

       TERRY: Well, I have a lot of shopping to do. And I promised Susan I'd give her a ride.

SUMMARY: Terry _____.

EXERCISE 4: Editing

Read the article from an online how-to site. There are nine mistakes in the use of infinitives.
The first mistake is already corrected. Find and correct eight more.

The things you need to know!
How to Make New Friends

               make
You'd like to ~~making~~ some new friends. Maybe you're at a new school or job, or, possibly, you

have changed and the "new you" wants meet new people. First, I strongly advise to turn off

your computer and TV. "Friending" people on Facebook just isn't the same as making real

friends. And those people on that old show "Friends" aren't YOUR friends. You need go out

and interact with real people. Decide right now to don't refuse invitations. When a classmate

or co-worker invites you for coffee, just say "Yes." Join a club and volunteer to doing

something. That responsibility will force you to attend the meetings. By doing these things, you

will manage meeting a lot of new people. But don't rush to become close friends with

someone right away. Learn to listen. Encourage the person to talks by asking questions. Allow

each relationship develops naturally, and soon you'll have a group of people you're really

comfortable with.

EXERCISE 5: Listening

A | *Read the statements about a blended family.[1] Then listen to a couple talk to a family counselor about their family. Listen again to their conversation and check (✓)* **True** *or* **False***. Correct the false statements.*

	True	False

                                       first

1. The woman has a daughter from her ~~second~~ marriage.   ☐   ☑

2. The man finally stopped arguing with his stepdaughter.   ☐   ☐

3. The woman was surprised about the problems with her daughter.   ☐   ☐

4. The girl stopped talking to her stepfather for a while.   ☐   ☐

5. The adults weren't interested in the girl's feelings.   ☐   ☐

6. The man invited his stepdaughter to go on a family vacation.   ☐   ☐

7. The family hasn't solved all their problems.   ☐   ☐

[1] **blended family:** a family that includes children from one parent's or both parents' earlier marriages

B | *Read the pairs of statements. Then listen again to the conversation and circle the letter of the statements you hear.*

1. a. I really wanted to discuss their problems.

    (b.) I really wanted them to discuss their problems.

2. a. I finally learned to argue with my stepdaughter.

    b. I finally learned not to argue with my stepdaughter.

3. a. I expected to have problems with my daughter.

    b. I expected you to have problems with my daughter.

4. a. Sometimes I just wanted to leave the house for a few hours.

    b. Sometimes I just wanted her to leave the house for a few hours.

5. a. After all, she didn't choose to live with us.

    b. After all, she chose to live with us.

6. a. Then one day, Brenda asked to go on a family vacation.

    b. Then one day, Brenda asked me to go on a family vacation.

7. a. We wanted to enjoy being together as a family

    b. We wanted her to enjoy being together as a family.

EXERCISE 6: Pronunciation

A | *Read and listen to the Pronunciation Note.*

Pronunciation Note
In sentences with **infinitives**:
• We usually **stress** the **main verb** and the **base form** of the verb in the infinitive.
• We do NOT usually stress **to** or a pronoun object.
EXAMPLES: She **expected to go** on vacation.
She **expected me to go** on vacation.

B | *Listen to the sentences. Put a dot (●) over the words or parts of words that are stressed.*

1. She **advised me to stay**.

2. They **prefer to study** at home.

3. Would you **like to leave**?

4. We **encouraged her to join** a club.

5. My parents **expect me to call** them tonight.

6. He **said to park** here.

C | *Listen again and repeat the sentences.*

EXERCISE 7: What About You?

A | *Work in pairs. Tell each other about your childhood relationship with your parents or other adults.*

- What did they encourage you to do?
- How did they encourage you to do that?
- What didn't they allow you to do?
- What did they force you to do?
- What would they like you to do?

- What did they advise you to do?
- Why did they advise you to do that?
- What do they expect you to do?
- What would you prefer to do?
- Why would you prefer to do that?

EXAMPLE: My parents encouraged me to learn other languages.

B | *Add your own questions.*

_____

_____

_____

EXERCISE 8: Cross-Cultural Comparison

As a class, discuss how people in your culture socialize. Do young men and women go out together? If so, do they go out in couples or in groups? What are some ways people meet their future husbands or wives?

EXAMPLE:
A: In Brazil, young people usually prefer to go out together in groups. They like to go to clubs or to the movies.

B: In Germany, families allow young people to go out on dates.

C: In Thailand . . .

EXERCISE 9: Writing

A | *Write emails to two or three friends and invite them to join you for an event that a group of your friends is going to attend. Remember to use infinitives.*

EXAMPLE:
Hi Ari,
Some classmates and I plan to see *Avatar* at the Regis Cineplex on Saturday. Would you like to come with us? We want to go to the 7:00 P.M. show. After the movie, we'll probably go out for pizza. I hope to see you Saturday.
It's going to be fun!
Liv

B | *Check your work. Use the Editing Checklist.*

Editing Checklist

Did you . . . ?
☐ use infinitives after the correct verbs
☐ form the negative with **not** + **infinitive**
☐ use **verb** + **object** + **infinitive** correctly

A | Complete each sentence with the infinitive form of the correct verbs from the box.

| call | finish | get | go | meet | play |

1. Sorry. I forgot _____ milk on the way home.

2. I've heard so much about you. I can't wait _____ you!

3. Did you manage _____ your paper on time?

4. Where did you decide _____ on your next vacation?

5. I love the piano. I want to learn _____.

6. Remember _____ when you get home.

B | Unscramble the words to complete the sentences.

1. I _____.
   (visit / Mary / invited / us / to)

2. She _____.
   (come / to / agreed)

3. She _____.
   (to / wants / new friends / make)

4. I _____.
   (early / her / to / told / come)

5. I _____.
   (Tom / not / decided / invite / to)

6. He _____.
   (his project / to / needs / finish)

C | Find and correct eight mistakes.

1. **A:** I want invite you to my party.

   B: Thanks. I'd love coming.

2. **A:** I plan to not get there before 8:00.

   B: Remember getting the soda. Don't forget!

3. **A:** Sara asked I to help her.

   B: I agreed helping her too.

4. **A:** I promised pick up some ice cream.

   B: OK. But let's do it early. I prefer don't arrive late.

More Uses of Infinitives
SMART PHONES

Before You Read

Look at the photo and the title of the article. Discuss the questions.

1. Why is the article called "The World in Your Pocket"?
2. What can you use a smart phone for?
3. Do you have a smart phone or a cell phone? How do you use it?

Read

Read the article about smart phones.

The World in Your Pocket

What's **smart enough to get** you all the information you'll ever need but **small enough to fit** inside your pocket? A smart phone! And it's getting smarter and smaller all the time. When smart phones first came out, people used them for three major purposes: **to make** calls, **to check** email, and **to connect** to the Internet. Today, people of all ages and walks of life[1] are using them for a lot more. Here's what some happy users report:

"I use my smart phone **to play** games, **listen** to music, and **watch** videos. It's awesome!"
— *Todd Miller, 16, high school student*

"I use it **to translate** words I don't understand."
— *Lian Chang, 21, nurse*

"When I'm considering buying a book in a bookstore, (sounds old-fashioned, doesn't it?) I use it **to look up** reviews."
—*Rosa Ortiz, 56, accountant*

"I travel a lot. When I'm on the road, I use it **to avoid** traffic jams. And if I get lost, I use it **to get** directions."
—*Brad King, 32, reporter*

It's **easy to see** why these multipurpose devices are so popular. They combine the functions of a phone, GPS,[2] camera, computer, calculator, organizer, and much more. But they have a downside too. Although the phones have become cheaper, when you add the monthly service charges, they are still **too expensive** for many people **to afford**. And there's another cost. When you are available 24/7,[3] people expect you to work and be reachable all the time. For a lot of people, that price may be **too high to pay**.

---

[1] *walks of life:* occupations

[2] *GPS:* Global Positioning System, a device that tells you where you are and gives you directions

[3] *24/7:* twenty-four hours a day, seven days a week

A | **Vocabulary:** *Circle the letter of the word or phrase that best completes each sentence.*

1. An **old-fashioned** idea is NOT _____.

   a. good

   b. modern

   c. interesting

2. A **device** is a small _____.

   a. phone

   b. machine

   c. video

3. If something is **multipurpose**, it has many _____.

   a. uses

   b. pieces

   c. meanings

4. If you **combine** several things, you _____.

   a. separate them

   b. clean them

   c. bring them together

5. Another word for **function** is _____.

   a. information

   b. purpose

   c. computer

6. A **major** reason is a reason that is very _____.

   a. popular

   b. expensive

   c. important

B | **Comprehension:** *Check (✓) True or False. Correct the false statements.*

	True	False
1. Today's smart phones are not very big.	☐	☐
2. People mostly use them to make calls.	☐	☐
3. Only young people use them.	☐	☐
4. Todd Miller uses one to have fun.	☐	☐
5. Lian Chang uses one to take pictures.	☐	☐
6. Rosa Ortiz uses one to read books on.	☐	☐
7. Brad King uses one on his way to work.	☐	☐
8. Many people like using them.	☐	☐
9. They are very cheap to own.	☐	☐
10. People are totally happy with them.	☐	☐

INFINITIVES

Infinitives of Purpose

Affirmative	Negative
I use it **to call** my friends.	I left at 9:00 **in order not to be** late.

Infinitives after Adjectives and Adverbs

With *Too*				
	(Too)	**Adjective / Adverb**	**(*For* + Noun / Object Pronoun)**	**Infinitive**
It's	**(too)**	**hard**		**to use**.
It's not		**expensive**	for Todd	**to buy**.
She spoke	**too**	**quickly**	for him	**to understand**.
They worked		**slowly**		**to finish**.

With *Enough*				
	Adjective / Adverb	**(*Enough*)**	**(*For* + Noun / Object Pronoun)**	**Infinitive**
It's	**easy**	**(enough)**		**to use**.
It's	**cheap**		for Todd	**to buy**.
She spoke	**slowly**	**enough**	for him	**to understand**.
They didn't work	**quickly**			**to finish**.

GRAMMAR NOTES

1 Use an **infinitive** (*to* + **base form of verb**) to explain the **purpose** of an action. It often answers the question *Why?*

A: *Why* did you go to the mall?
B: I went there **to buy** a new phone.

USAGE NOTES:

a. In conversation, you can answer the question *Why?* with an <u>incomplete sentence</u> beginning with *to*.

A: *Why* did you go to the mall?
B: **To buy** a new camera phone.

b. We usually <u>do NOT repeat *to*</u> when we give more than one purpose.

• I went to the mall **to buy** a phone, **eat** lunch, and **see** a movie.
  NoT: I went to the mall to buy a phone, ~~to~~ eat lunch, and ~~to~~ see a movie.

2

In **formal writing** we often use:

a. *in order to* + **base form of verb** to explain a <u>purpose</u>

b. *in order not to* + **base form of verb** to explain a <u>negative purpose</u>

USAGE NOTE: In everyday <u>spoken English</u>, we often express a negative purpose with *because* + **a reason**.

FORMAL: He acquired it **in order to stay** connected to the world.

INFORMAL: He got it **to stay** in touch with his friends.

• They use a GPS **in order not to get** lost.

• I use a GPS *because I don't want to get lost*.

3

You can use the infinitive **after adjectives and adverbs**.

Sometimes we use *for* + **noun / pronoun** <u>before</u> the infinitive.

Use *too* <u>before</u> the adjective or adverb to show the reason something is **not possible**.

Use *enough* <u>after</u> the adjective or adverb to show the reason something is **possible**.

Notice the **word order** in sentences with:
• *too* + adj. + *for* + noun/pro. + infinitive
• adj. + *enough* + *for* + noun/pro. + infinitive

REMEMBER: We **don't need the infinitive** when the meaning is clear.

ADJECTIVE
• It's *easy* to use.

ADVERB
• We worked *hard* to finish on time.

• It's **easy** *for Todd* to use.
• It's **easy** *for him* to use.

• It was *too expensive* to buy.
   (It was expensive, so I couldn't buy it.)

• It was *cheap enough* to buy.
   (It was cheap, so I could buy it.)
   NOT: It was ~~enough cheap~~ to buy.

• It's **too hard** *for my son* to understand.
• It's **easy enough** *for Jana* to use.

A: Did you buy a smart phone?
B: Yes. It's finally **cheap enough** *for me*!
   (It's cheap enough for me to buy.)

EXERCISE 1: Discover the Grammar

Read about changes in the telephone. Underline all the infinitives of purpose and infinitives after adjectives or adverbs.

PHONE TALK

The telephone has really changed a lot in less than a century. From the 1920s through the 1950s, there was the good old-fashioned rotary phone. It had just one function, but it wasn't that convenient to use. Callers had to turn a dial to make a call. And it was too big and heavy to move from place to place. (Besides, there was that annoying cord connecting it to the wall!). The 1960s introduced the touch-tone phone. It was much faster to place a call with it. You just pushed buttons in order to dial. With cordless phones, introduced in the 1970s, callers were free to move around their homes or offices while talking. Then came a really major change—hand-held cell phones. These were small enough to carry with you and you didn't even have to be inside to talk to your friends. But it wasn't until the invention of the camera phone that people began to use the phone to do more than just talk. And, that was nothing compared to today's multipurpose smart phones. People use them to do almost everything. What will the newest technology bring to the phone? It's hard to predict. But one thing is certain: It will be faster and smaller. And, as always, people will find uses for it that are difficult to imagine today.

EXERCISE 2: Affirmative and Negative Purposes

(Grammar Notes 1–2)

A | *Match the actions with their purposes.*

Action

___b___ 1. She bought a smart phone because she

_____ 2. He took the bus because he

_____ 3. We turned our phone off because we

_____ 4. She recorded her favorite TV show because she

_____ 5. She went to the electronics store because she

Purpose

a. didn't want to get calls.

b. wanted to check email.

c. wanted to buy a new phone.

d. didn't want to be late.

e. didn't want to miss it.

B | *Now combine the sentences. Use the infinitive of purpose.*

1. *She bought a smart phone to check email.*

2. _____

3. _____

4. _____

5. _____

EXERCISE 3: Affirmative Statements

(Grammar Note 1)

On a *moblog, you can post pictures, videos, and text from your camera phone directly to the Web for millions of people to see. Look at this moblog. Complete the sentences with the correct words from the box. Use the infinitive of purpose.*

buy fruit and vegetables	**pass it**	**exchange money**
communicate with her	**get more gas**	~~**take my own picture**~~
drive to Montreal	**have coffee**	

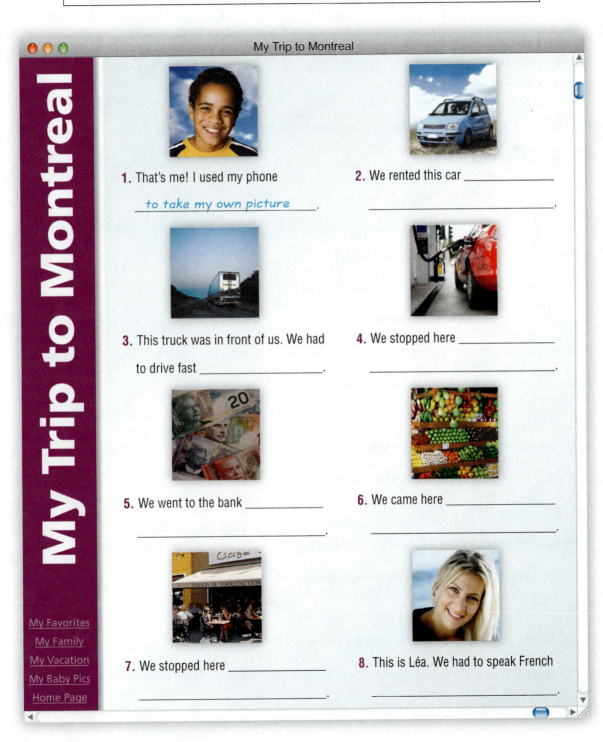

My Trip to Montreal

My Trip to Montreal

1. That's me! I used my phone
   to take my own picture .

2. We rented this car _____
   _____.

3. This truck was in front of us. We had
   to drive fast _____.

4. We stopped here _____
   _____.

5. We went to the bank _____
   _____.

6. We came here _____
   _____.

7. We stopped here _____
   _____.

8. This is Léa. We had to speak French
   _____.

My Favorites
My Family
My Vacation
My Baby Pics
Home Page

EXERCISE 4: Infinitive after Adjectives

(Grammar Note 3)

Complete the responses to an online survey. Use the infinitive form of the verbs from the box.

| carry | find out | ~~have~~ | own | spend | use | watch |

SURVEY

2-10-2012

Are you going to buy the latest and greatest smart phone?

2-10-2012

BobG: Yes. I think it's important _____ *to have* _____ the latest technology. And, it's cool!
1.

2-10-2012

Finefone: I don't know. I'm always a little nervous about buying a new device. I hope it

isn't too difficult for me _____ .
2.

2-10-2012

YIKES: No. I'm just not ready _____ the money on a new phone. It's a major
3.

expense. I'll wait until the prices come down.

2-11-2012

LilaX: Definitely! I love the fact that it's easy _____ around. It fits right in
4.

your pocket and it has so many functions. It sure beats having to take a phone, a PDA, a GPS,

and a laptop computer everywhere you go!

2-11-2012

Cat2: I'm not sure. I want one for videos, but I'm afraid it's not going to be comfortable

_____ them on such a small screen.
5.

2-11-2012

TimeOut: Not yet. I think I'll wait until the next one comes out. It'll be interesting

_____ what new features it'll have—and how much it'll cost.
6.

2-12-2012

Rosy: No thanks! Call me old-fashioned, but I don't think it's necessary _____
7.

all these multipurpose devices. Give me a phone, a laptop computer, a paperback book,

a radio—and I'll be happy.

EXERCISE 5: Infinitive after Adjectives and Adverbs

(Grammar Note 3)

*Complete the conversations. Use the words in parentheses and **too** or **enough**.*

1. **A:** Did you buy the new smart phone?

   B: No. Right now it's still _____ *too expensive for me to buy* OR *too expensive for me* _____.
   (expensive / for me)

2. **A:** Can we call Alicia now?

   B: Sure. It's _____.
   (early)

3. **A:** What did Mrs. Johnson just say? I didn't understand her.

   B: Me neither. She always speaks _____.
   (quickly / for me)

4. **A:** Did Dan ever pass his driving test?

   B: Yes. The last time he drove _____.
   (well)

5. **A:** Does he have enough money to get that used car?

   B: It's only $300. I think it's _____.
   (cheap / for him)

6. **A:** Do you want to go to a movie tonight?

   B: Sorry. I'm _____.
   (busy)

EXERCISE 6: Editing

Read the online bulletin board about smart phones. There are ten mistakes in the use of the infinitive of purpose and infinitives after adjectives. The first mistake is already corrected. Find and correct nine more.

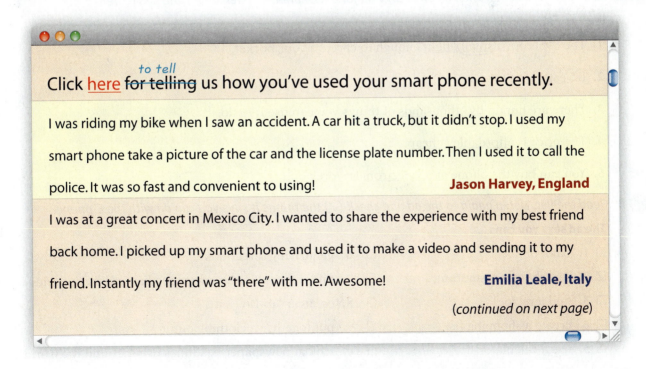

Click here <s>for telling</s> *to tell* us how you've used your smart phone recently.

I was riding my bike when I saw an accident. A car hit a truck, but it didn't stop. I used my smart phone take a picture of the car and the license plate number. Then I used it to call the police. It was so fast and convenient to using!   **Jason Harvey, England**

I was at a great concert in Mexico City. I wanted to share the experience with my best friend back home. I picked up my smart phone and used it to make a video and sending it to my friend. Instantly my friend was "there" with me. Awesome!   **Emilia Leale, Italy**

(continued on next page)

I sell houses. I always use my phone in order no waste my customers' time. When I see an interesting house, I immediately send a photo. Then, if they are interested, I make an appointment for them. Without a smart phone, my job would be to hard to do.

Andrea Cook, U.S.

Last night I used it to helping me make dinner. First, I searched online for a recipe. It was in grams, so I used a program to converts it to ounces. Then I used another program to create a shopping list. When I returned home from shopping, I set the phone's timer to reminded me when to take the food out of the oven. While dinner was baking, I used the phone to listen to my favorite songs. I love this thing! It combines functions for work and play, and it's enough smart to do almost everything. Too bad it can't do the dishes too!

Kim Soo-Min, South Korea

STEP 4 COMMUNICATION PRACTICE

EXERCISE 7: Listening

A | *Read the statements. Then listen to a TV ad for a new phone. Listen again and circle the correct information.*

1. The E-phone is (small) / light enough to carry in your pocket.

2. It's easy / fun to use.

3. There are hundreds / thousands of things you can use it to do.

4. The price is affordable / cheap.

5. You can buy the phone at an electronics store / online.

B | *Read the list. Listen again to the ad and check (✓) the things it says you can do with the E-phone.*

The ad says you can . . .

☐ 1. bank online
☑ 2. search for a restaurant
☐ 3. find a recipe
☐ 4. create a shopping list
☐ 5. use a calculator

☐ 6. get driving directions
☐ 7. find information in encyclopedias and dictionaries
☐ 8. create a "To Do" list
☐ 9. put together a clothing outfit
☐ 10. look at newspaper headlines from around the world

EXERCISE 8: Pronunciation

A | *Read and listen to the Pronunciation Note.*

> **Pronunciation Note**
>
> In sentences with **adjective + infinitive**, we usually **stress** the **adjective** and the **verb in the infinitive**.
>
> EXAMPLES: It's **nice to know**. She's **easy to understand**.
>
> It's **too expensive to buy**. He's **smart enough to learn** it.

B | *Listen to the sentences. Put a dot (•) over the words or parts of words that are stressed.*

1. It's easy to use.

2. It's good to know.

3. It's cheap enough to buy.

4. It's light enough to carry.

5. She's available to work.

6. It's too hard to understand.

C | *Listen again and repeat the sentences.*

EXERCISE 9: Survey

Work in small groups. Complete the sentences with infinitives to give your opinion. Compare your opinions. Give reasons or examples.

1. The smart phones are (not) easy . . .

   EXAMPLE: **A:** The smart phones are easy to use.
   B: I don't agree. They're not easy enough for *me* to use yet!
   C: I only use mine to make calls!
   D: Yes, but, it's easy enough to learn the new features.

2. The price is (not) low enough . . .

3. New technology is important . . .

4. People over age 80 are (not) too old . . .

5. Teens are responsible enough . . .

6. English is (not) difficult . . .

7. Radio and TV broadcasters speak (or don't speak) clearly enough . . .

8. Time goes by too quickly . . .

EXERCISE 10: For or Against

A | *Work in small groups. Look at the cartoon. Do you feel the same as the woman? If yes, which features don't you like? Why? Discuss the pros and cons of new technology.*

> EXAMPLE: **A:** I agree with the woman. Phones with a lot of features are too difficult to use. But everyone should have a cell phone for emergencies.
>
> **B:** I think people get too involved with their phones. They don't spend enough time with other people.
>
> **C:** I don't agree with the woman . . .

B | *You've just gotten a new smart phone. What will you use it for? What won't you use it for? Discuss your answers with a partner. Give reasons for your answers.*

> EXAMPLE: **A:** I'll use it to send emails with photos, or to watch videos . . .
>
> **B:** I won't use it to watch videos! The screen isn't big enough.
>
> **A:** I disagree. I think . . .

Do you have a phone that doesn't do too much?

EXERCISE 11: Problem Solving

A | *Work in small groups. Think of uses for these everyday objects. Use the infinitive of purpose and your imagination! Share your ideas with other groups.*

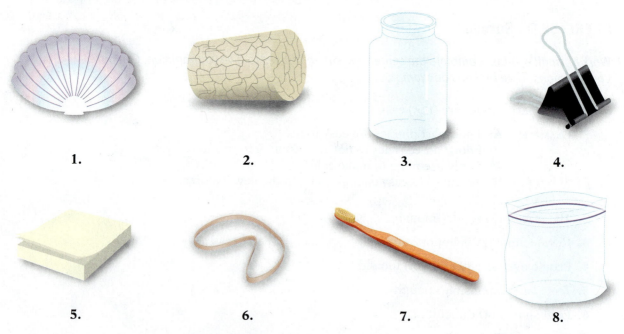

1.   2.   3.   4.

5.   6.   7.   8.

> EXAMPLE: **A:** You can use a shell to hold coins.
>
> **B:** Right. You can also use it to keep soap in.
>
> **C:** You can even use it to eat with—like a spoon.

B | *Which item is the most useful? Why?*

EXERCISE 12: Discussion

A | *Read the ad for a smart phone.*

The SMART Phone 1000

Use the Smart Phone 1000 to operate systems in your Smart House. Turn lights on and off, control appliances, and get text messages from your house about what's going on. It's easy and convenient to use. So, get smart, get the Smart Phone 1000.

Home
Messages
Lights
Appliances
Stereo
Basement
Outdoor
Security

B | *Work in small groups. Imagine that your smart phone will control everything in your house—not only electronic equipment. What will you use it for?*

EXAMPLE: **A:** I'll use it to turn on the shower.
B: I'll use it to open and close the windows.
C: I think I'll use it to . . .

EXERCISE 13: Writing

A | *Write a post for the online bulletin board in Exercise 6 on page 351. How have you used your phone (or another device) recently?*

EXAMPLE: I was at a family party last week. I used my phone to take a picture of my little nephew and send it to my mother in Argentina. It was great to be able to share the event with her . . .

B | *Check your work. Use the Editing Checklist.*

Editing Checklist

Did you use . . . ?
☐ infinitives of purpose
☐ **adjective or adverb + infinitive**
☐ ***too*** or ***enough*** **+ adjective or adverb + infinitive**

UNIT 25 Review

Check your answers on page UR-6.
Do you need to review anything?

A | Circle the correct words to complete the sentences.

1. Todd uses his smart phone to <u>get / gets</u> directions when he travels.

2. I set the alarm early <u>in order not / not in order</u> to miss my train.

3. In order <u>for taking / to take</u> photographs with your phone, first press this button.

4. It's <u>too / to</u> dark to read in here. Could you turn on a light?

5. It was raining hard. We couldn't see <u>clearly enough / too clearly</u> to drive.

B | Unscramble the words to complete the conversation. Use the infinitive form of the verbs.

A: How do you like your new phone? Was it _____?
   1. (enough / easy / figure out)

B: Yes. Luckily, this one isn't _____.
   2. (hard / too / use / for me)

A: Where's Kim's place? She was talking _____.
   3. (fast / too / understand / for me)

B: It's about 20 blocks from here. Is that _____?
   4. (too / for us / far / walk)

A: If you're worried, we could take the bus _____.
   5. (in order / be / late / not)

B: It's only 6:00. I think it's _____.
   6. (for us / enough / early / walk)

A: Let's cross at the light. The traffic is _____ safely here.
   7. (heavy / cross / too / for us)

B: I think we're lost. Let's use _____.
   8. (get / directions / my phone)

A: You didn't speak _____. Let me try.
   9. (clearly / for it / enough / work)

B: We're pretty far away. Let's take _____.
   10. (save / a taxi / time)

C | Find and correct five mistakes.

Is 16 too young for drive? It's really hard to saying. Some kids are mature enough to drive at 16, but some aren't. I think most 16-year-olds are still too immature drive with friends in the car, though. It's for them easy to forget to pay attention with a lot of kids in the car. In order preventing accidents, some families have a "no friends" rule for the first year. I think that's a reasonable idea.

STEP 1 GRAMMAR IN CONTEXT

Before You Read

Look at the cartoon and the title of the article. Discuss the questions.

1. What is procrastination?
2. What types of things do you put off doing?
3. Why do people procrastinate?

Read

Read the excerpt from a magazine article about procrastinating.

STOP PROCRASTINATING—NOW!

It's a beautiful day. Eva doesn't **feel like spending** it at the library. She goes to the park instead. She **keeps telling** herself she'll work better the next day.

Todd **planned to make** an appointment with the dentist, but he **decided to wait** another week, or maybe two.

Procrastinating—**putting off** until tomorrow things you **need to do** today—is a universal problem. College students are famous **for procrastinating**, but we all do it sometimes. Why do people put off important tasks? Read what the experts say.

UNPLEASANT TASKS • **It's** not always fun **to do** a lot of the things on our "To Do" lists. Most people **prefer to do** enjoyable things.

POOR TIME MANAGEMENT[1] • **Having** too little time for a task is discouraging. **It's** hard **to get** started on a project when you feel that you can't finish it.

FEAR • An important test can make you feel so anxious that you **put off studying**.

PERFECTIONISM • The belief that you must do a perfect job can prevent you **from starting** or **finishing** a task.

As you can see, people often procrastinate because they **want to avoid** bad feelings. But procrastinators **end up feeling** even worse because of their procrastination. The only solution: **Stop procrastinating**. Now!

Did you **finish writing** your paper on procrastination?

No. I'll do it tomorrow.

---

[1] *time management:* the skills for using your time well when you are trying to reach a goal

A | Vocabulary: *Complete the sentences with the words from the box.*

anxious	discouraging	project	put off	task	universal

1. Have you finished your class _____ yet?

2. The problem is _____. People all over the world experience it.

3. I get very _____ before a test.

4. Don't _____ writing your essay. Do it today!

5. Shopping for dinner is my least favorite _____.

6. It's _____, but I won't give up hope!

B | Comprehension: *Check (✓) the reasons the article gives for procrastination.*

☐ **1.** being lazy

☐ **2.** not enjoying the task

☐ **3.** not understanding something

☐ **4.** feeling anxious about the task

☐ **5.** not having enough time

☐ **6.** not getting enough sleep

☐ **7.** feeling depressed

☐ **8.** thinking your work has to be perfect

STEP 2 GRAMMAR PRESENTATION

GERUNDS AND INFINITIVES

Gerunds	Infinitives
Eva **enjoys going** to the park.	Eva **wants to go** to the park.
She **prefers taking** long breaks.	She **prefers to take** long breaks.
She **stopped studying**.	She **stopped to study**.
Starting a project is hard.	**It's** hard **to start** a project.
She's worried **about finishing** her paper.	

GRAMMAR NOTES

1	Some **verbs**, such as the ones below, are **followed by a gerund** (base form + -*ing*). avoid deny keep consider enjoy postpone delay finish quit	• Eva *avoids* **doing** her work. • She *doesn't enjoy* **studying**. • She *keeps* **making** excuses.
2	Some **verbs**, such as the ones below, are **followed by an infinitive** (*to* + base form). agree expect* plan arrange fail promise* choose* need* want* decide offer would like* *These verbs can also be **followed by**: object + infinitive **USAGE NOTE:** We usually <u>do NOT repeat *to*</u> when there is more than one infinitive.	• Todd *arranged* **to leave** work early. • He *decided* **not to keep** his appointment. • He *plans* **to make** another one next week. • We **expect to start** the project soon. • We **expect** *them* **to start** the project soon. • He *plans* **to watch** TV, **read** the paper, and **call** his friends. Not: He plans to watch TV, ~~to~~ read the paper, and ~~to~~ call his friends.
3	Some **verbs**, such as the ones below, can be **followed by a gerund or an infinitive**. They have the <u>same meaning</u>. begin hate prefer can't stand like start continue love	• Jeff *hates* **studying**. OR • Jeff *hates* **to study**.
4	**BE CAREFUL!** Some **verbs**, such as the ones below, can be **followed by a gerund or an infinitive**, but they have a very <u>different meaning</u>. stop remember forget	• Eva *stopped* **taking** breaks. (*She doesn't take breaks anymore.*) • Eva *stopped* **to take** a break. (*She stopped an activity in order to take a break.*) • Todd *remembered* **reading** the story. (*First he read the story. Then he remembered that he did it.*) • Todd *remembered* **to read** the story. (*First he remembered. Then he read the story. He didn't forget.*) • Jeff *forgot* **meeting** Dana. (*Jeff met Dana, but afterwards he didn't remember the event.*) • Jeff *forgot* **to meet** Dana. (*Jeff had plans to meet Dana, but he didn't meet her because he forgot about the plans.*)

(continued on next page)

5	A **gerund** is the only verb form that can **follow a preposition or a phrasal verb.**		
		PREPOSITION	
		• He's worried **about** writing it.	
		PREPOSITION	
		• He's looking forward **to finishing** it.	
		PREPOSITION	
		• Jeff doesn't feel **like** working on his paper.	
		PHRASAL VERB	
		• He won't **put off** starting it anymore.	

6	To make **general statements**, you can use:	
	• **gerund as subject**	• **Writing** a paper is hard.
	OR	OR
	• **it** + infinitive	• **It**'s hard **to write** a paper.
	They have <u>the same</u> meaning.	

REFERENCE NOTES

For a more complete list of **verbs followed by a gerund**, see Appendix 13 on page A-7.
For a more complete list of **verbs followed by an infinitive**, see Appendix 14 on page A-7.
For a more complete list of **verbs followed by a gerund or an infinitive**, see Appendix 15 on page A-7.
For more on **gerunds after prepositions**, see Unit 23 on page 324, and Appendices 17 and 18 on pages A-7 and A-8.
For a list of **transitive phrasal verbs**, see Appendix 4 on page A-3.

STEP 3 FOCUSED PRACTICE

EXERCISE 1: Discover the Grammar

A | *Read the paragraph. Circle the gerunds. Underline the infinitives.*

Like many students, Eva is a procrastinator. She keeps putting off her schoolwork. When she studies, she often stops to go for a walk in the park. She wants to improve her study habits, but she isn't sure how. Eva decided to make a list every day of tasks she needs to do. She always remembers to make her list, but she often forgets to read it. It's very discouraging, and Eva is worried about getting bad grades. Last night Eva remembered reading an article in the school newspaper about a support group for procrastinators. She thinks being in a group is a good idea. She likes sharing ideas with other students. Maybe it will help.

B | Now read the statements. Check (✓) True or False. Correct the false statements.

	True	False
puts off doing 1. Eva ~~never does~~ her school work.	☐	☑
2. She quit going for walks in the park.	☐	☐
3. She'd like to be a better student.	☐	☐
4. Eva makes a list every day.	☐	☐
5. She always reads her list.	☐	☐
6. She read about a support group.	☐	☐
7. She thinks it's good to be in a group.	☐	☐
8. She likes to share ideas with others.	☐	☐

EXERCISE 2: Gerund or Infinitive

(Grammar Notes 1–5)

Read the quiz. Circle the correct form of the verbs. In some cases, both forms are correct.

Are You a Procrastinator?

☐ When I don't feel like to do / (doing) something, I often put off to start / starting it.
     1.   **2.**

☐ I sometimes start to study / studying the night before a test.
                  3.

☐ I sometimes start a job but then postpone to finish / finishing it.
                                          4.

☐ I often delay to make / making difficult decisions.
                 5.

☐ I find excuses for not to do / doing things I dislike.
                       6.

☐ When a task seems too difficult, I often avoid to work / working on it.
                                              7.

☐ I prefer to do / doing easy tasks first.
           8.

☐ I often promise myself to work / working on a project but then fail to do / doing it.
                        9.   **10.**

☐ I worry about to make / making mistakes or about not to be / being perfect.
                   11.   **12.**

☐ I often choose to do / doing other tasks instead of the most important one.
                     13.

☐ I want to improve / improving, but I keep to put / putting it off.
             14.   **15.**

EXERCISE 3: Gerund or Infinitive

(Grammar Notes 1–5)

Complete the tips from a website. Use the correct form of the verbs in parentheses.

Some Tips for _____Stopping_____ Procrastination
1. (stop)

- If you have a large project to work on, break it into small tasks. Finish

  _____ one small task before _____ the next.
  2. (do)   **3. (start)**

- Choose _____ the hardest task first. You'll get it out of the way, and
  4. (do)

  you'll feel better about yourself.

- Promise yourself _____ at least 15 minutes on a task even if you don't
  5. (spend)

  really feel like _____ it. You'll be surprised. You can get a lot done in
  6. (do)

  15 minutes—and you'll often keep _____ even longer.
  7. (work)

- Stop _____ short breaks—but for no longer than 10 minutes at a time.
  8. (take)

- Arrange _____ yourself a reward when you succeed in _____
  9. (give)   **10. (finish)**

  a task. Do something you enjoy _____.
  11. (do)

- Consider _____ a support group for procrastinators.
  12. (join)

EXERCISE 4: General Statements: Gerund and Infinitive

(Grammar Note 6)

Eva and Todd are talking. They agree on everything. Read one person's opinion and write the other's. If the first person uses the gerund, use the infinitive. If the first person uses the infinitive, use the gerund.

1. **Eva:** It's hard to start a new project.

   Todd: I agree. _Starting a new project is hard._____

2. **Todd:** Taking short breaks is helpful.

   Eva: You're right. _It's helpful to take short breaks._____

3. **Eva:** It's difficult to work on a long project.

   Todd: That's true. _____

4. **Todd:** Completing a job on time feels great.

   Eva: You're right. _____

5. TODD: Rewarding yourself for finishing a project is a good idea.

   EVA: I agree. _____

6. EVA: Being in a support group is very helpful.

   TODD: Yes. _____

7. EVA: It's good to meet people with the same problem.

   TODD: I feel the same way. _____

EXERCISE 5: Gerund or Infinitive

(Grammar Notes 1–4)

Read the conversations that took place at a procrastinators' support group meeting.
Complete the summary statements. Use the gerund or the infinitive.

1. **JEFF:** Hi, Todd. Did you bring the soda?

   TODD: Yes. Here it is.

   SUMMARY: Todd remembered _to bring the soda_____.

2. **LEE:** Eva, do you remember Todd?

   EVA: Oh, yes. We met last year.

   SUMMARY: Eva remembers _____.

3. **EVA:** Todd, will Miriam be here tonight? I haven't seen her in ages!

   TODD: Yes, she's coming later.

   SUMMARY: Todd expects Miriam _____.

4. **JEFF:** You take too many breaks.

   TODD: No, I don't!

   SUMMARY: Todd denied _____.

5. **EVA:** What do you do in your free time, Kay?

   KAY: I listen to music a lot.

   SUMMARY: Kay likes _____.

6. **UTA:** I'm tired. Let's go home.

   KAY: OK. Just five more minutes.

   SUMMARY: Uta wants _____.

(continued on next page)

7.   **Uta:** Eva, can we give you a ride home?

        Eva: Thanks, but I think I'll stay a little longer.

   SUMMARY: Uta offered _____.

             Eva decided _____.

8.   **Pat:** Good night. Please drive carefully.

        Uta: Don't worry. I will.

   SUMMARY: Uta promised Pat _____.

EXERCISE 6: Editing

Read Eva's blog entry. There are eight mistakes in the use of the gerund and infinitive. The first mistake is already corrected. Find and correct seven more.

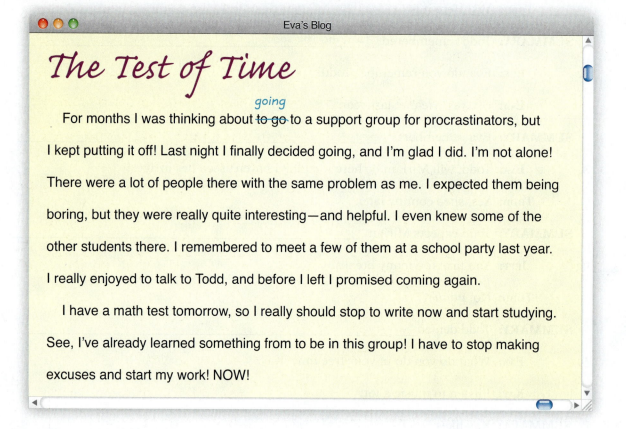

The Test of Time

                      going

For months I was thinking about ~~to go~~ to a support group for procrastinators, but I kept putting it off! Last night I finally decided going, and I'm glad I did. I'm not alone! There were a lot of people there with the same problem as me. I expected them being boring, but they were really quite interesting—and helpful. I even knew some of the other students there. I remembered to meet a few of them at a school party last year. I really enjoyed to talk to Todd, and before I left I promised coming again.

     I have a math test tomorrow, so I really should stop to write now and start studying. See, I've already learned something from to be in this group! I have to stop making excuses and start my work! NOW!

EXERCISE 7: Listening

A | *The school newspaper is interviewing Eva about her study habits. Read the statements. Then listen to the interview. Listen again and check (✓) **True** or **False**. Correct the false statements.*

	True	False
has joined a support group 1. Eva ~~is trying to find a solution to the problem on her own~~.	☐	☑
2. She has had a problem with procrastination.	☐	☐
3. Eva says the problem was discouraging.	☐	☐
4. She feels very anxious before tests.	☐	☐
5. The interviewer says Eva has good time management skills.	☐	☐
6. Eva gets good grades.	☐	☐

B | *Read the list of activities. Then listen again to the interview and check (✓) the things Eva does and doesn't do now when she is studying for a test.*

	Things Eva Does	Things Eva Doesn't Do
1. clean her work area	☑	☐
2. start the night before the test	☐	☐
3. study the hardest thing first	☐	☐
4. make a "To Do" list	☐	☐
5. take long breaks	☐	☐
6. do relaxation exercises	☐	☐
7. reward herself for finishing	☐	☐

EXERCISE 8: Pronunciation

A | *Read and listen to the Pronunciation Note.*

> **Pronunciation Note**
>
> In **conversation**:
>
> We usually pronounce the preposition **to** and the **to** in the infinitive /tə/.
>
> **EXAMPLES:** She looks forward **to** taking a break.   We plan **to** meet after class today.
> We're used **to** studying late.   I'd like you **to** help me with this paper.
>
> We pronounce the prepositions **for** /fɚ/ and **on** /ən/.
>
> **EXAMPLES:** I'm sorry **for** not calling today.   She plans **on** going to college.
> She has a good excuse **for** being late.   Can we count **on** seeing you next week?

B | *Listen to the short conversations. Notice the pronunciation of* **to,** *for,* **and on.**

1. **A:** Would you like **to** walk in the park today?
   B: I can't. I need **to** study.

2. **A:** You need **to** take a break.
   B: I plan **on** going **to** the movie at school tonight.
   A: Good. I look forward **to** seeing you there.

3. **A:** Thanks **for** lending me that book.
   B: It helped me. It's hard **to** change, but it's possible.

4. **A:** I'm sorry **for** being late today.
   B: It's OK, but I insist **on** starting class at 9:00.

C | *Listen again. Then practice the conversations with a partner.*

EXERCISE 9: Brainstorming

A | *Taking short breaks can help you work more effectively. Work in small groups. Brainstorm ideas for 10-minute work breaks.*

> **EXAMPLE:**   **A:** I enjoy . . .
>   **B:** It's relaxing . . .
>   **C:** You could consider . . .
>   **D:** I recommend . . .

B | *Share your ideas with the rest of your classmates.*

EXERCISE 10: Information Gap: At the Support Group

Work in pairs (A and B). **Student A,** *follow the instructions on this page.* **Student B,** *turn to page 370 and follow the instructions there.*

1. Look at the picture below. Ask your partner questions to complete what people said at the support group meeting.

   EXAMPLE: **A:** What does Eva remember doing?
   B: She remembers meeting Todd.

2. Answer your partner's questions.

   EXAMPLE: **B:** What does Todd hope to do?
   A: He hopes to see Eva again.

When you are done, compare your pictures. Are they the same?

EXERCISE 11: Quotable Quotes

Read the quotes about procrastination. Discuss them with a partner. What do they mean?
Do you agree with them?

1. Never put off till tomorrow what you can do today.
   —*Lord Chesterfield (British politician, 1694–1773)*

   EXAMPLE: **A:** Lord Chesterfield advises doing things right away.
   B: I think that's not always possible because . . .

2. Procrastination is the art of keeping up with yesterday.
   —*Don Marquis (U.S. author, 1878–1937)*

3. Procrastination is the thief of time.
   —*Edward Young (British poet, 1683–1765)*

4. When there is a hill to climb, don't think that waiting will make it smaller.
   —*Anonymous[1]*

5. Putting off an easy thing makes it hard, and putting off a hard one makes it impossible.
   —*George H. Lorimer (U.S. magazine editor, 1868–1937)*

6. Procrastination is like a credit card: It's a lot of fun until you get the bill.
   —*Christopher Parker (British actor, 1983–)*

---

[1] **anonymous:** The writer's name is not known

EXERCISE 12: Problem Solving

A | *Look at the picture. Like procrastination, clutter is a universal problem. What are some solutions to the problem? Work in groups. Brainstorm ways of stopping clutter. You can use the verbs from the box.*

avoid   decide   don't forget   keep   need   plan   remember   start   stop

EXAMPLE: **A:** You need to put away your things every night.
B: Plan on . . .
C: Remember to . . .

B | *Compare your ideas with the rest of the class.*

EXERCISE 13: Writing

A | *Writing a goals worksheet is a good way to help prevent procrastination. First, complete the worksheet. List three goals for this month in order of importance (1 = the most important goal).*

This Month's Goals	
Goal 1:	Complete by:
Goal 2:	Complete by:
Goal 3:	Complete by:

B | *Write three paragraphs (one for each goal) on how you plan to accomplish your goals.*

EXAMPLE: I want to finish writing my English paper by March 28. First, I plan to . . .

C | *Check your work. Use the Editing Checklist.*

Editing Checklist

Did you use . . . ?
- ☐ correct **verbs** + **gerunds**
- ☐ correct **verbs** + **infinitives**
- ☐ **prepositions** + **gerunds**
- ☐ gerunds as subjects
- ☐ *it* + **infinitive**

1. Look at the picture below. Answer your partner's questions.

> EXAMPLE: **A:** What does Eva remember doing?
> **B:** She remembers meeting Todd.

2. Ask your partner questions to complete what people said at the support group meeting.

> EXAMPLE: **B:** What does Todd hope to do?
> **A:** He hopes to see Eva again.

When you are done, compare your pictures. Are they the same?

A | Circle the correct words to complete the sentences.

1. Don't put off to start / starting your project.

2. I expect you to finish / finishing on time.

3. I keep to try / trying to improve my study habits.

4. Did you decide to join / joining our study group?

5. I look forward to see / seeing you there.

6. Don't forget to call /calling me the night before.

7. To study / Studying together can help.

B | Complete the conversation with the correct form of the verbs in parentheses.

A: Have you finished _____ your homework?
$\qquad$ **1. (do)**

B: No, not yet. I decided _____ a break.
$\qquad$ **2. (take)**

A: Already? You just started _____.
$\qquad$ **3. (work)**

B: I know. But I'm tired of _____ at my desk.
$\qquad$ **4. (sit)**

A: Well, _____ a short break is OK, I guess.
$\qquad$ **5. (take)**

B: Don't worry. I promise _____ it done before dinner.
$\qquad$ **6. (get)**

A: OK. I know you hate _____, but it's important.
$\qquad$ **7. (study)**

B: I agree.

C | Find and correct six mistakes.

It's difficult to study in a foreign country, so students need preparing for the experience. Most people look forward to living abroad, but they worry about don't feel at home. They're afraid of not understanding the culture, and they don't want making mistakes. It's impossible to avoid to have some problems at the beginning. No one escapes from feeling some culture shock, and it's important realizing this fact. But soon most people stop to feel uncomfortable and start to feel more at home in the new culture.

From Grammar to Writing

COMBINING SENTENCES WITH *AND, BUT, SO, OR*

You can combine two sentences with **and**, **but**, **so**, and **or**. The new longer sentence is made up of **two main clauses**.

EXAMPLE: Commuting to school is hard. I prefer to live in the dorm. ➜

MAIN CLAUSE   MAIN CLAUSE
Commuting to school is hard, **so** I prefer to live in the dorm.

The clause starting with **and**, **but**, **so**, or **or** always comes second. Notice that a **comma** comes after the first clause.

1 | *Circle the correct words to complete the email.*

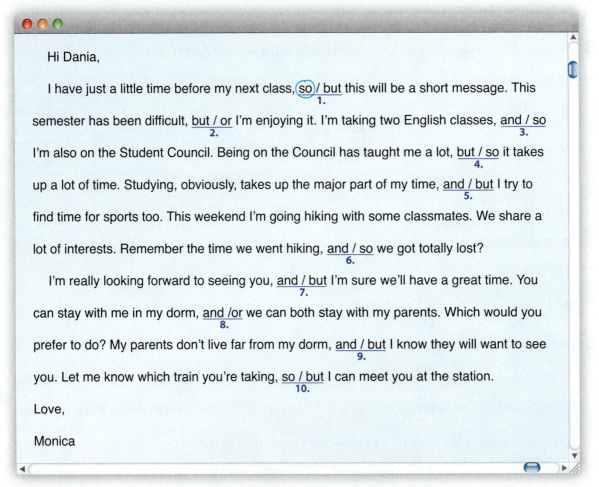

Hi Dania,

I have just a little time before my next class, (so) / but this will be a short message. This
1.
semester has been difficult, but / or I'm enjoying it. I'm taking two English classes, and / so
2.   **3.**
I'm also on the Student Council. Being on the Council has taught me a lot, but / so it takes
4.
up a lot of time. Studying, obviously, takes up the major part of my time, and / but I try to
5.
find time for sports too. This weekend I'm going hiking with some classmates. We share a
lot of interests. Remember the time we went hiking, and / so we got totally lost?
6.
    I'm really looking forward to seeing you, and / but I'm sure we'll have a great time. You
7.
can stay with me in my dorm, and /or we can both stay with my parents. Which would you
8.
prefer to do? My parents don't live far from my dorm, and / but I know they will want to see
9.
you. Let me know which train you're taking, so / but I can meet you at the station.
10.

Love,

Monica

There are many ways to close a personal email. Here are a few popular choices.

- *Love* or *Love you,* for family and close friends
- *Bye for now* or *Take care,* for friends
- *Best, Best wishes,* or *Best regards,* for colleagues and acquaintances

2 | Complete the rules for using **and**, **but**, **so**, and **or**. Look at the email in Exercise 1 for help.

1. Use _____*and*_____ when the second sentence adds information.

2. Use _____ when the second sentence gives a choice.

3. Use _____when the second sentence gives a contrasting idea.

4. Use _____ when the information in the second sentence is a result of the

information in the first sentence.

3 | Complete the sentences with your own ideas.

1. It has started to rain, but _____.

2. I don't really want to study tonight, so _____.

3. This weekend my friends and I will go to a movie, or _____.

4. I'm reading a lot of books in English, and _____.

5. After class I'm going shopping, so _____.

6. I used to go dancing a lot, but _____.

7. I'm looking forward to graduating, and _____.

8. Ed is too young to vote, but _____.

9. We can take a train, or _____.

10. Dan is tired of staying home evenings, so _____.

4 | Before you write . . .

Talk to a partner about your life these days. Answer some of these questions.
- What are you doing these days?
- What do you enjoy doing?
- What can't you stand?
- What do you plan to do next semester?
- What are you looking forward to?

5 | Write an email to a friend describing your present life. Use the email in Exercise 1 as a model. Include some of your ideas from Exercise 4. Use **and**, **but**, **so**, and **or**.

6 | Exchange emails with a new partner. Answer your partner's email.

PART VIII

PRONOUNS AND PHRASAL VERBS

I hate parties.

Reflexive and Reciprocal Pronouns
SELF-TALK

STEP 1 GRAMMAR IN CONTEXT

Before You Read

What do you think self-talk *is? Look at the examples of self-talk in the photos. Discuss the questions.*

1. Which examples are positive?
2. Which examples are negative?
3. What are some other examples of positive and negative self-talk?

Read

Read the article from a psychology magazine.

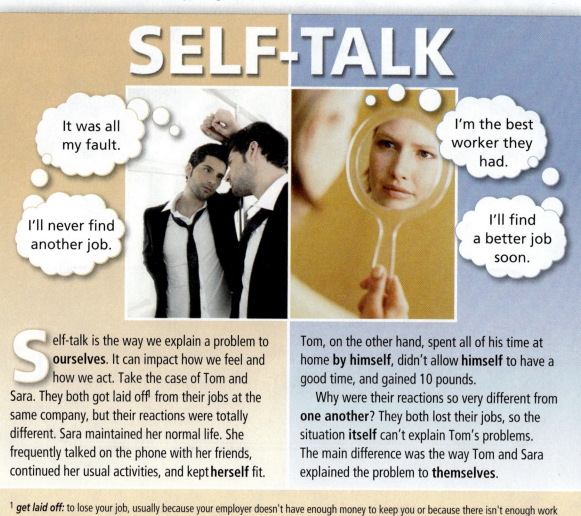

SELF-TALK

> It was all my fault.

> I'll never find another job.

> I'm the best worker they had.

> I'll find a better job soon.

Self-talk is the way we explain a problem to **ourselves**. It can impact how we feel and how we act. Take the case of Tom and Sara. They both got laid off[1] from their jobs at the same company, but their reactions were totally different. Sara maintained her normal life. She frequently talked on the phone with her friends, continued her usual activities, and kept **herself** fit.

Tom, on the other hand, spent all of his time at home **by himself**, didn't allow **himself** to have a good time, and gained 10 pounds.

Why were their reactions so very different from **one another**? They both lost their jobs, so the situation **itself** can't explain Tom's problems. The main difference was the way Tom and Sara explained the problem to **themselves**.

[1] ***get laid off:*** to lose your job, usually because your employer doesn't have enough money to keep you or because there isn't enough work

SELF-TALK

Sara told **herself** that the problem was temporary and that she herself could change it. Tom saw **himself** as completely helpless and likely to be unemployed forever.

Tom and Sara both got their jobs back. Their reactions when they talked to **each other** were, again, very different. For his part, Tom grumbled, "Oh, I guess they were really desperate." Sara, on the other hand, smiled and said, "Well! They finally realized that they need me!"

After You Read

A | **Vocabulary:** *Complete the sentences with the words from the box.*

fault	finally	impact	maintain	reaction	realize

1. I waited for more than an hour before I _____ got the call.

2. What was your _____ when you heard the news? Were you surprised?

3. At first, I didn't _____ that the problem was serious.

4. Everyone needs exercise and sleep in order to _____ good health.

5. It wasn't your _____. You didn't do anything wrong.

6. The company had to lay off 50 employees, but that didn't _____ John's job.

   He still works there.

B | **Comprehension:** *Check (✓) the correct answers.*

Who . . . ?	Tom	Sara	Tom and Sara
1. stayed in good physical condition	☐	☐	☐
2. spent a lot of time alone	☐	☐	☐
3. thought the problem was temporary	☐	☐	☐
4. felt helpless	☐	☐	☐
5. had a conversation back at work	☐	☐	☐

REFLEXIVE AND RECIPROCAL PRONOUNS

Reflexive Prounouns				Reciprocal Pronouns		
Subject Pronoun		**Reflexive Pronoun**		**Subject Pronoun**		**Reciprocal Pronoun**
I		**myself**				
You		**yourself**				
He		**himself**				
She	looked at	**herself**	in the mirror.	We	looked at	**each other.**
It		**itself**		You		**one another.**
We		**ourselves**		They		
You		**yourselves**				
They		**themselves**				

GRAMMAR NOTES

1	Use a **reflexive pronoun** when the subject and object refer to the <u>same people or things</u>.	SUBJECT = OBJECT • **Sara** looked at **herself** in the mirror. *(Sara looked at her own face.)* SUBJECT = OBJECT • **They** felt proud of **themselves**. *(They were proud of their own actions.)* SUBJECT = OBJECT • My **office light** turns **itself** off. *(It turns off automatically.)*
2	In **imperative sentences** with reflexive pronouns, use: • *yourself* when the subject is <u>singular</u> • *yourselves* when the subject is <u>plural</u> **REMEMBER:** In imperative sentences, the subject is *you*, and *you* can be either singular or plural.	• "Don't push **yourself** so hard, **Tom**," Sara said. *(talking to one friend)* • "Don't push **yourselves** so hard, **guys**," Sara said. *(talking to several friends)*
3	Use a reflexive pronoun to **emphasize a noun**. The reflexive pronoun usually <u>follows the noun</u> directly.	• Tom was upset when he lost his job. The **job itself** wasn't important to him, but he needed the money. • **Sara herself** didn't get depressed, but her co-workers felt terrible.

4	*By* + **a reflexive pronoun** means *alone* or *without any help*.	• Sara lives **by herself**. *(Sara lives alone.)* • We finished the job **by ourselves**. *(No one helped us.)*
	Be + **a reflexive pronoun** means *act in the usual way*.	• Just **be yourself** at your interview.

5	Use a **reciprocal pronoun** when the subject and object of a sentence refer to the <u>same people</u>, and these people have a <u>two-way</u> relationship.	
	• Use *each other* for <u>two</u> people.	SUBJECT = OBJECT • **Tom and Sara** met **each other** at work. *(Tom met Sara, and Sara met Tom.)*
	• Use *one another* for <u>more than two</u> people.	SUBJECT = OBJECT • **We all** told **one another** about our jobs. *(Each person exchanged news with every other person.)*
	USAGE NOTE: Many people use *each other* and *one another* in the **same way**.	• **Sara and Tom** talked to **each other**. OR • **Sara and Tom** talked to **one another**.
	BE CAREFUL! Reciprocal pronouns and plural reflexive pronouns have **different meanings**.	• Fred and Jane blamed **each other**. *(Fred blamed Jane, and Jane blamed Fred.)* • Fred and Jane blamed **themselves**. *(Fred blamed himself, and Jane blamed herself.)*
	Reciprocal pronouns have **possessive forms**: *each other's*, *one another's*	• Tom and Sara took **each other's** number. *(Tom took Sara's number, and Sara took Tom's.)*

REFERENCE NOTE

For a list of **verbs and expressions that often take reflexive pronouns**, see Appendix 3 on page A-2.

EXERCISE 1: Discover the Grammar

Read the rest of the article about self-talk. Underline the reflexive pronouns once and the reciprocal pronouns twice. Draw an arrow to the words that the pronouns refer to.

SELF-TALK *(continued)*

Positive self-talk can affect our thoughts, feelings, and actions. It can even make the difference between winning and losing. Top athletes not only compete against one another, they also compete against themselves when they try to improve their performances. Many athletes use self-talk to maintain their self-confidence and help themselves reach new goals. If you've asked yourself how Korean Olympic gold

Kim Yu-Na

winner Kim Yu-Na can do those perfect jumps under so much stress, now you know it's probably because she's telling herself, "I can, I will, I am."

One sports psychologist believes that Olympic athletes are not very different from one another —they are all the best in their sports. When two top athletes compete against each other, the winner is the one with the most powerful positive "mental movies."

According to psychologists, ordinary people themselves can use these techniques too. We can create "mental movies" to help ourselves succeed in difficult situations.

EXERCISE 2: Reflexive or Reciprocal Pronouns   *(Grammar Notes 1–5)*

Tom and Sara's company had an office party. Choose the correct reflexive or reciprocal pronouns to complete the conversations.

1. **A:** Listen, guys! The food and drinks are over here. Don't be shy. Please come and help

   _____ *yourselves* _____.
   (yourselves / themselves)

   B: Thanks. We will.

2. **A:** Isn't that the new head of the accounting department over there?

   B: I think so. Let's go over and introduce _____.
   (himself / ourselves)

3. **A:** I'm really nervous about my date with Nicole after the party. I actually cut

   _____ twice while shaving, and then I lost my car keys.
   (herself / myself)

   B: Come on. This is a party. Just relax and be _____.
   (yourself / yourselves)

   You'll do just fine.

4. A: What are you giving your boss for the holidays this year?

   B: We always give _____ the same holiday gifts. Every
   (ourselves / each other)

   year I give him a book, and he gives me a box of candy. I realize that this doesn't sound

   very exciting, but I _____ am quite happy with the
   (myself / ourselves)

   arrangement. It makes things easy that way.

5. A: What's your department's reaction to the new computer program?

   B: I'm not sure. We're still teaching _____ how to use it.
   (ourselves / themselves)

6. A: Jessica looks upset. Didn't she get a promotion?

   B: No, and she keeps blaming _____. She thinks it's all her
   (herself / himself)

   fault. Of course it isn't.

7. A: The Aguayos are finally going to Japan on vacation this year.

   B: That's wonderful. They really need one. Are they going by _____
   (each other / themselves)

   or with a tour group?

8. A: This was a great party.

   B: Yeah. We really enjoyed _____.
   (ourselves / myself)

EXERCISE 3: Reflexive or Reciprocal Pronouns   (Grammar Notes 1–5)

*Read the interview with George Prudeau, a high school French teacher. Complete the
interview. Use the correct reflexive or reciprocal pronouns.*

INTERVIEWER: How did you become a teacher?

   GEORGE: When I got laid off from my 9:00 to 5:00 job, I told _____*myself*_____, "Here's my
                                                                    1.

   chance to finally do what I really want." One of the great things about teaching is the

   freedom I have. I run the class by _____—just the way I want to. I also
                                        2.

   like the way my students and I learn from _____. My teaching impacts
                                               3.

   my students' lives, but they teach me a lot too.

INTERVIEWER: What about maintaining discipline? Is that a problem?

   GEORGE: We have just a few rules. I tell my students, "Keep _____ busy. Discuss
                                                                  4.

   the lessons, but don't interfere with _____'s work."
                                          5.

   (continued on next page)

INTERVIEWER: What do you like to teach best?

GEORGE: I love French, but the subject _____ really isn't all that important. A
6.

good teacher helps students learn by _____ and encourages them not to
7.

give up when they have problems. For instance, John, one of my students, just taught

_____ how to bake French bread. The first few loaves were failures. His
8.

first reaction was to give up, but I encouraged him to use positive self-talk, and in the

end he succeeded.

INTERVIEWER: What teaching materials do you use?

GEORGE: Very simple ones. I pride _____ on the fact that I can teach anywhere,
9.

even on a street corner.

INTERVIEWER: What do you like least about your job?

GEORGE: The salary. I teach French culture, but I can't afford to travel to France. I have to

satisfy _____ with trips to French restaurants!
10.

EXERCISE 4: Verbs with Reflexive or Reciprocal Pronouns   *(Grammar Notes 1, 4–5)*

*Sara and Tom went to an office party. Look at each picture and write a sentence describing
what happened. Use the correct form of a verb from the box with a reflexive or reciprocal
pronoun. You will use one verb more than once.*

buy	cut	drive	greet	introduce	smile at	talk to

1. _____*Sara bought herself a new dress.*_____   2. _____

3. _____

4. _____

5. _____

6. _____

7. _____

8. _____

EXERCISE 5: Editing

Read the woman's diary. There are seven mistakes in the use of reflexive and reciprocal pronouns. The first mistake is already corrected. Find and correct six more.

> Jan's birthday was Wednesday, and I forgot to call him. I reminded ~~me~~ *myself* all day, and then
>
> I forgot anyway! I felt terrible. My sister Anna said, "Don't be so hard on yourselves."
>
> But I myself didn't believe her. She prides herself on remembering everything. Then I
>
> finally remembered the article on self-talk. It said that people can change the way they
>
> explain problems to theirselves. Well, I listened to the way I talked to me, and I realized
>
> it sounded really insulting — like the way our high school math teacher used to talk to
>
> us. I thought, Jan and I are good friends, and we treat each other's well. One mistake
>
> shouldn't impact our friendship that much. In fact, he forgave myself for my mistake
>
> right away. And I forgave him for forgetting our dinner date two weeks ago. Friends
>
> can forgive themselves, so I guess I can forgive myself.

EXERCISE 6: Listening

A | *Employees are at an office party. Read the sentences. Then listen to the conversations. Then listen again and circle the pronouns that you hear.*

1. They should be really proud of <u>themselves</u> / (<u>each other</u>).

2. You know Ed blames <u>him / himself</u> for everything.

3. Are you going by <u>yourself / yourselves</u> or with a tour?

4. The doctor <u>herself / himself</u> called me this morning.

5. Megan keeps asking <u>herself / her</u> if she can do the job.

6. In our department, we're still teaching <u>each other / ourselves</u> how to use it.

7. I'm glad you enjoyed <u>yourself / yourselves</u>.

B | *Listen again to the conversations and choose the correct answer to complete the statements.*

1. The people in Mark's department probably work _____ a lot.
   a. alone   b. together

2. Ed blames _____ for everything.
   a. himself   b. Jeff

3. The woman plans to travel _____.
   a. alone   b. with other people

4. The doctor called _____.
   a. the woman   b. the man

5. Megan isn't sure if _____ can do the job.
   a. Jennifer   b. she herself

6. The man _____ new computer system.
   a. wants to buy a   b. is still learning to use the

7. The woman went to the party _____.
   a. by herself   b. with other people

EXERCISE 7: Pronunciation

A | *Read and listen to the Pronunciation Note.*

> **Pronunciation Note**
>
> We usually **stress -self** or **-selves** in reflexive pronouns.
>
> **EXAMPLE:** Did you enjoy **yourselves** at the party?
>
> We **stress other** or **another** in reciprocal pronouns.
>
> **EXAMPLE:** Yes. We spoke to **each other** for hours.

B | *Listen to the sentences. Put a dot (•) over the parts of the reflexive and reciprocal pronouns that are stressed.*

1. Sara looked at herself in the mirror.
2. They felt proud of themselves.
3. The job itself wasn't important to him.
4. They met each other at work.
5. We all told one another about our jobs.
6. Tom helped himself to the food.

C | *Listen again and repeat the sentences.*

EXERCISE 8: Questionnaire

A | *Test yourself by completing the questionnaire.*

Are you an optimist or a pessimist?

Optimists see bad situations as temporary or limited. Pessimists see them as permanent. What's *your* reaction when things go wrong? What do you tell yourself? Check (✓) your most likely self-talk for each situation below. Then find out if you're an optimist or a pessimist.

1. Your boss doesn't say good morning to you.
   - ☐ **a.** She isn't herself today.
   - ☐ **b.** She doesn't like me.

2. Your family forgets your birthday.
   - ☐ **a.** Next year we should keep in touch with one another more.
   - ☐ **b.** They only think about themselves.

3. You gain 10 pounds.
   - ☐ **a.** I promise myself to eat properly from now on.
   - ☐ **b.** Diets never work for me. I'll never maintain a healthy weight.

4. Your boyfriend or girlfriend decides to go out with other people.
   - ☐ **a.** We didn't spend enough time with each other.
   - ☐ **b.** We're wrong for each other.

5. You're feeling tired lately.
   - ☐ **a.** I pushed myself too hard this week.
   - ☐ **b.** I never take care of myself.

6. Your friend forgets an appointment with you.
   - ☐ **a.** He sometimes forgets to read his appointment book.
   - ☐ **b.** He never reminds himself about important things.

Score your questionnaire

All the **a** answers are optimistic, and all the **b** answers are pessimistic. Give yourself **0** for every **a** answer and **1** for every **b** answer.

If You Scored	You Are
0–2	very optimistic
3–4	somewhat optimistic
5–6	pessimistic

B | *Discuss your questionnaire with a partner. Which is more useful—optimistic or pessimistic self-talk? Why?*

C | *Now interview five classmates and find out how they answered the questions. Report the results to another group.*

> **EXAMPLE:** For question 1, three people checked "She isn't herself today."
> Two people checked "She doesn't like me."

EXERCISE 9: Game: Who remembers more?

A | *Work with a partner. First look at the picture carefully for 30 seconds. Then shut your books and do the following.*

1. Write down as many things as you can remember about what the people are doing.

2. Then compare your notes. Use reciprocal and reflexive pronouns in your description.

    EXAMPLE: **A:** Two men are waving at each other.
                       B: No, I think two women are waving at each other.

B | *When you are finished, open your books and check your answers. Who remembered the most? What did you leave out?*

EXERCISE 10: Picture Discussion

Look at the picture again. With your partner, imagine the self-talk of some of the people at the party.

    EXAMPLES: The man at the mirror: "I'll never give myself a haircut again."
                      The woman on the couch: "I don't know many people here.
                      Should I introduce myself to that couple?"

EXERCISE 11: Problem Solving

A | *Work in small groups. Discuss two or three of the situations in the list below. How do you make yourself feel better?*

- You're going to take a big test.
- You're stuck in traffic.
- You have a roommate you don't like.
- You're going to compete in a sports event.
- You're having an argument with a friend or relative.
- You forgot something important, and you're very angry at yourself.

EXAMPLE: **A:** When I'm going to take a big test, I tell myself that I usually get a good grade.
B: Me too. I tell myself that I've studied enough to do well.
C: I remind myself that . . .

B | *Report to the class. Make a class list of some of the best self-talk for each situation.*

EXAMPLES: When they're going to take a big test, Donna and Yuri remind themselves that they usually get very good grades.

When she's having an argument with a friend or a relative, Jana tells herself that the situation is temporary. Nobody stays angry forever.

When Javier is upset with his roommate, he always talks to his brother, and they cheer each other up.

EXERCISE 12: Writing

A | *Imagine that you write an Internet advice column called "Help Yourself with Self-Talk." A reader writes that he or she is not doing well at school and is having problems with a boyfriend or a girlfriend. Complete the advice column. You can use some of these phrases:*

- Some people tell themselves . . .
- One person I know tells herself/himself . . .
- Friends can remind each other that . . .
- I never tell myself . . .

Help Yourself with Self-Talk

Dear _____,

    I'm sorry you're having trouble at school. The best advice I can give you is to change your self-talk! What positive things can you say to yourself in this situation? What negative self-talk can you avoid? For example, some people tell themselves . . .

B | *Check your work. Use the Editing Checklist.*

A | Circle the correct pronouns to complete the sentences.

1. Emily and I see <u>each other / ourselves</u> at the gym every week.

2. My friend Lan teaches an exercise class there. He <u>itself / himself</u> is very fit.

3. The people in his class all know <u>themselves / one another</u>. They've been in his class for years.

4. Emily likes to exercise alone. She works out by <u>herself / oneself</u> every day.

5. I told her about Lan's class. I <u>myself / ourselves</u> wasn't attending his class, but I knew about it.

6. We decided to try it out <u>themselves / ourselves</u>, so we went to Lan's class together.

7. Lan told both of us, "You're pushing <u>yourself / yourselves</u> too hard. Slow down a little."

8. The class <u>itself / himself</u> isn't so different from other classes, but we like how Lan teaches.

B | Complete the sentences with the correct form of the verbs in parentheses and the correct pronouns.

1. Karl and Ana are good friends. They _____ every day.
   (talk to)

2. Ina and Eva always _____ with a kiss.
   (greet)

3. Lee, please _____ to some more cake.
   (help)

4. Rita and Tom are reading in the library. They're really _____.
   (enjoy)

5. Tania _____ to the party last night.
   (drive)

C | Find and correct seven mistakes.

When I first met Nicole, I told myself, "I'm not going to like working with herself." I was really wrong. Nicole has helped myself out with so many things. When she oneself didn't know something, she always found out for me. That way, both of ourselves learned something. After I learned the job better, we helped each other's out. Now the job themselves isn't that challenging, but I'm really enjoying myself. Everyone here likes each another. That makes it a great place to work. I feel lucky to be here.

Phrasal Verbs
ANIMAL INTELLIGENCE

STEP 1 GRAMMAR IN CONTEXT

Before You Read

Look at the picture. Discuss the questions.

1. Do you know who the man is?
2. What do you think he is famous for?
3. Why do you think people call him "The Dog Whisperer"?
4. Do people in your country have pets? If so, what kinds?

Read

Read the article about Cesar Millan.

When He Whispers, They Tune In[1]

What do you do when your dog **takes over** the dog park and attacks other dogs? Or when it gets lazy and won't **get up** and take a walk? When pet owners are ready to **give up**, many of them call Cesar Millan, the Dog Whisperer.

Millan is famous for **helping out** celebrities[2] like Oprah when they have problems with their pets. He also works with the problem pets of ordinary people. He usually goes into their homes to **figure out** the problem. Sometimes he can't help the dog at its home, so he brings it to his ranch outside Los Angeles. There, Millan works with animals with more serious problems. His training **turns** their lives **around**.

But what if you don't live in LA? No problem! Just **turn on** the TV. Fans of Millan's show *The Dog Whisperer* watch every week as Millan **straightens out** a "bad" dog and its owner.

When Millan rings the doorbell, he learns about the dog and its family for the first time. By the end of the show, a miracle[3] has happened: the angry or frightened dog now obeys its owner's commands to **get off** the couch, walk quietly, and **sit down**.

Not everybody admires Millan. Some believe that his ideas about dog psychology[4] are too simple. Others say that real change doesn't happen in an hour. These critics haven't stopped Millan's fans, however. They **keep on tuning in** for the weekly miracles.

---

[1] ***When he whispers, they tune in:*** When he speaks very quietly, the dogs listen.

[2] ***celebrity:*** a famous person, usually someone in movies or on TV

[3] ***miracle:*** a very positive, surprising event

[4] ***psychology:*** the study of the mind and how it works

After You Read

A | Vocabulary: *Match the phrasal verbs with their meanings.*

_____ 1. **figure out**   **a.** to change bad behavior

_____ 2. **turn on**   **b.** to quit

_____ 3. **give up**   **c.** to solve

_____ 4. **keep on**   **d.** to get control

_____ 5. **straighten out**   **e.** to start (a machine)

_____ 6. **take over**   **f.** to continue

B | Comprehension: *Check (✓) the boxes to complete the sentences. Check **all** the true information from the reading.*

1. Owners get upset when their dogs _____.
   - ☐ attack other dogs
   - ☐ won't leave the dog park
   - ☐ get lazy

2. In his business, Millan helps dogs _____.
   - ☐ of celebrities
   - ☐ with serious problems
   - ☐ only in people's homes

3. Millan helps dogs _____.
   - ☐ in their homes
   - ☐ on his ranch
   - ☐ on his TV program

4. On his show, Millan works with _____.
   - ☐ dogs he already knows
   - ☐ frightened dogs
   - ☐ the dogs' owners

5. People who disagree with Millan think that _____.
   - ☐ dog psychology is complicated
   - ☐ change takes time
   - ☐ Millan makes miracles happen

PHRASAL VERBS: TRANSITIVE AND INTRANSITIVE

Transitive Phrasal Verbs			
Subject	**Verb**	**Particle**	**Object (Noun)**
He	**figured**	**out**	the problem.
	helped	**out**	the owners.

Subject	**Verb**	**Object (Noun / Pronoun)**	**Particle**
He	**figured**	the problem	**out**.
		it	
	helped	the owners	**out**.
		them	

Intransitive Phrasal Verbs			
Subject	**Verb**	**Particle**	
She	**gave**	**up**.	
He	**sat**	**down**	quickly.
They	**get**	**up**	early.

GRAMMAR NOTES

1

Phrasal verbs (also called *two-word verbs*) are made up of a **verb** + **particle**.

On, *off*, *up*, *down*, *in*, and *out* are common particles.

Particles and prepositions look the same. However, particles are part of the verb phrase, and they often <u>change the meaning</u> of the verb.

VERB + PARTICLE
- He **turned on** the TV.

VERB + PARTICLE
- Cesar **helps out** pet owners.

VERB + PREPOSITION
- She's **looking up** at the sky.
  (*She's looking in the direction of the sky.*)

VERB + PARTICLE
- She's **looking up** the word.
  (*She's searching for the word in the dictionary.*)

2

Many **phrasal verbs** and **one-word verbs** have <u>similar meanings</u>.

USAGE NOTE: Phrasal verbs are often <u>less formal</u>, and they are <u>more common</u> in everyday speech.

PHRASAL VERB (less formal)	ONE-WORD VERB (more formal)
figure out	solve
give up	quit
hand in	submit
help out	assist
keep on	continue

(continued on next page)

3 Phrasal verbs can be **transitive or intransitive**.

a. Transitive phrasal verbs <u>have objects</u>.

Most transitive phrasal verbs are **separable**. This means that the object can come:

- <u>after</u> the verb + particle

  OR

- <u>between</u> the verb and its particle

BE CAREFUL! When the object is a **pronoun**, it must come <u>between</u> the verb and the particle.

b. Intransitive phrasal verbs do <u>NOT have</u> <u>objects</u>.

PHRASAL VERB + OBJECT
- He **turned on** *the TV*.

VERB + PARTICLE + OBJECT
- He **helped out** *the students*.

  OR

VERB + OBJECT + PARTICLE
- He **helped** *the students* **out**.

OBJECT
- He **helped** *them* **out**.
  Not: He ~~helped out them~~.

- Cesar Millan **grew up** in Mexico.
- He never **gives up**.

REFERENCE NOTES
For a list of **transitive phrasal verbs** and their meanings, see Appendix 4 on page A-3.
For a list of **intransitive phrasal verbs** and their meanings, see Appendix 5 on page A-4.

STEP 3 FOCUSED PRACTICE

EXERCISE 1: Discover the Grammar

A | *Read the article. Underline the phrasal verbs. Circle the objects of the transitive phrasal verbs.*

Cesar Millan puts (his running shoes) on as soon as he gets up in the morning. Then he wakes his dogs up, and they all set out on their daily four-hour walk. The exercise is part of Millan's dog therapy.[1] Most of these dogs were once dangerous, but now they are a "family" that teaches problem dogs how to fit in and get along in a group.

Millan's dream began on the farm in Mexico where he grew up. There, he found out he had a special ability with animals (his family called him "El Perrero"[2]). When Millan was 13, he told his mother, "I'm going to be the best dog trainer in the world." A few years later, Millan went to the United States. He was homeless for a while, but he never gave up his dream. Finally, he found a job as a dog groomer.[3] On the job, Millan showed owners some ways to calm their dogs down. Jada Pinkett (wife of actor Will Smith) hired him and also paid for his English lessons. After that, he was able to set up his own business. Today the Dog Whisperer lives and works on a 40-acre ranch with his pack of around 50 dogs and many other kinds of animals.

[1] *therapy:* the treatment of an illness or mental problem over a fairly long period of time
[2] *"El Perrero":* (*Spanish*) The Dog Boy
[3] *dog groomer:* someone who washes dogs and cuts their hair and nails

B | *Match the underlined words with the phrasal verbs.*

___f___ **1.** Millan and his dogs <u>start</u> on their walk early in the morning.   **a.** found out

_____ **2.** The dogs never fight because they all <u>have a good relationship</u>.   **b.** calm down

_____ **3.** Millan <u>became an adult</u> in Mexico.   **c.** grew up

_____ **4.** On the farm, he first <u>discovered</u> that he had a special ability.   **d.** set up

_____ **5.** He showed owners how to help their dogs <u>become less excited</u>.   **e.** get along

_____ **6.** Millan <u>started</u> his business after he learned English.   **f.** set out

EXERCISE 2: Particles   *(Grammar Notes 1–2)*

Circle the correct particle to complete each phrasal verb. Go to Appendices 4 and 5 on pages A-3 and A-4 for help.

VICKY: Hi. Carla? I'm Vicky Chang, the dog trainer.

CARLA: Come <u>back /(in)</u>, Vicky! Please call me Carla. And say hello to Mitzi.
                  1.

VICKY: She's really excited! I'll greet her when she calms <u>up / down</u>, OK?
                                                                                      2.

CARLA: Come <u>on / by</u>, Mitzi! Stop jumping!
                    3.

VICKY: Do you mind if I sit <u>into / down</u> here next to Mitzi?
                                        4.

CARLA: Please go <u>ahead / through</u>. Sorry, she always takes <u>on / over</u> the couch.
                      5.   **6.**

VICKY: Thanks. Today, I'd like to find <u>up / out</u> what problems you're having.
                                                  7.

CARLA: Well, Mitzi jumps on people. Also, sometimes she doesn't get <u>along / away</u> with other dogs,
                                                                          8.

but sometimes she does. I can't figure it <u>up / out</u>.
                                            9.

VICKY: Maybe she's frightened. At the park, pick <u>out / up</u> small dogs for her to play with.
                                                        10.

CARLA: Good idea. I'll try that <u>out / over</u> the next time we're there. Anything else?
                                      11.

VICKY: Exercise always helps behavior. Do you walk her when you get <u>up / by</u> in the morning?
                                                                          12.

CARLA: Every day. But sometimes I'm too tired when I get <u>back / over</u> from work.
                                                              13.

VICKY: Don't worry. We'll straighten <u>out / down</u> Mitzi's problems. She's a very smart dog.
                                            14.

CARLA: Thanks. We're going to take her to my company picnic tomorrow. I hope it works <u>by / out</u>!
                                                                                            15.

VICKY: She'll love that. She'll probably fit <u>in / up</u> very well.
                                                  16.

EXERCISE 3: Transitive Phrasal Verbs and Pronouns

(Grammar Note 3)

Complete the conversations. Use phrasal verbs and pronouns.

1. **BEN:** It looks like rain. I hope they don't call off the picnic.

    CARLA: Well, if they _____ *call it off* _____, we can go for a ride in the car.

2. **BEN:** Remember to put on Mitzi's leash.

    CARLA: OK. I'll _____ now.

3. **BEN:** The car's really hot. How do you turn on the air conditioner?

    CARLA: You _____ with this knob.

4. **BEN:** That breeze feels good. I'm going to take off my hat.

    CARLA: Don't _____ yet. It'll help protect you from this hot sun.

5. **CARLA:** Uh-oh. Here comes another dog. I'll pick up Mitzi.

    BEN: She can handle it. Don't _____.

6. **CARLA:** Could someone wake up Ben and Mitzi? They're taking a nap under that tree.

    TRISH: No problem. I'll _____.

EXERCISE 4: Transitive and Intransitive Phrasal Verbs: Word Order

(Grammar Note 3)

Unscramble the words to make sentences. If more than one answer is possible, give both.

1. on / put / your lab coats   *Put your lab coats on.* OR *Put on your lab coats.*

2. the experiment / set / up   _____

3. out / it / carry   _____

4. down / sit / when you're done   _____

5. to page 26 / on / go   _____

6. up / your reports / write   _____

7. in / them / hand   _____

8. off / take / your lab coats   _____

9. them / put / away   _____

10. the lab / clean / up   _____

EXERCISE 5: Meaning of Phrasal Verbs

(Grammar Note 2)

Complete the article. Choose the phrasal verb from the box that is closest in meaning to the verbs in parentheses. Use the correct form of the phrasal verb. Go to Appendices 4 and 5 on pages A-3 and A-4 for help.

calm down	find out	go away	keep on	make up	pass on
carry out	get along	~~grow up~~	look up	pass away	turn on

Bird Brains
(They're Smarter Than You Think)

Some children grow up with dogs and cats. Irene

Pepperberg _____grew up_____ with birds. Like many
       1. (became an adult)

shy people, she sometimes _____
          2. (had a good relationship)

Irene Pepperberg with Alex and friends

with her pets better than with people. Pepperberg got a Ph.D. in chemistry from

Harvard, but she never lost her interest in animal intelligence. One day at home, she

_____ the TV and saw a show about communicating with dolphins.
   3. (started)

Why not birds? she thought. She _____ information about talking birds
          4. (searched books)

and _____ about African gray parrots. In 1977, she bought Alex. For 30
  5. (discovered information)

years Pepperberg _____ experiments with Alex in a lab full of colorful
       6. (conducted)

toys. Alex didn't just "parrot"[1] words. He learned the meaning of more than 100 words

and could understand ideas such as "different," "smaller," and "_____."
                  7. (relax)

He even _____ words such as "yummy bread" for cake. When he got
      8. (created)

bored with an experiment, he'd say "I'm gonna _____ now."
             9. (leave)

    In September 1999, Alex _____. It was a terrible loss for Pepperberg,
          10. (died)

but today she _____ working with her other parrots. To her students at
  11. (continues)

Harvard and Brandeis, she is _____ her love and respect for these
      12. (giving to others)

intelligent birds.

---

[1] *parrot:* to repeat someone else's words or ideas without understanding them

EXERCISE 6: Editing

Service dogs help out people with disabilities. Read the entry from a website about service dogs. There are ten mistakes in the use of phrasal verbs. The first mistake is already corrected. Find and correct nine more. Go to Appendices 4 and 5 on pages A-3 and A-4 for help.

Service Dogs

A Good Match

For a long time, I looked ^*for* the right service dog ~~for~~. I almost gave on, but as soon as I met Barnie, I knew he was the one. The trainer had four puppies, and I picked out Barnie right away. Actually, he picked out me. He walked over to my wheelchair and sat down next to me. After that, I didn't have to think it down at all. I just said, "Come by, Barnie, let's go home."

When I started to train him, I was surprised at how fast he caught back. He learned to pick my keys up from the floor when he was only nine weeks old. Once I fell out of bed, so he started to wake on before me. Now he stands next to me while I get up and get into my chair.

When we started school, he figured my schedule through right away. After the first week, he would go to the right classroom and lie down. He stands up just before the bell rings. (How does he know how to do that?) When I need a book, he opens my book bag and takes out it for me! He really loves to take care of me.

Today, the famous Dr. Pepperberg dropped into my animal behavior class and brought an African gray parrot. At first, Barnie looked a little excited, but he calmed back right away. I know I can always count on him.

EXERCISE 7: Listening

A | *Some college students are taking a science class. Read the conversations. Then listen and circle the phrasal verbs that you hear. Listen again and check your answers.*

1. **A:** Did you see Dr. Pepperberg in class today?

   B: Yes. She (brought up) / brought back that DVD about Alex. Very interesting.

2. **A:** What's Terry doing?

   B: She's handing in / handing out some lab reports.

3. **A:** Are you done with your report, Rea?

   B: Almost. I just have to look up / look over some information.

4. **A:** Hey, guys. That music is disturbing us.

   B: Sorry. We'll turn it down / turn it off.

5. **A:** Jason is discouraged.

   B: I know. He says he can't keep on / keep up with the class.

6. **A:** Did you hear about Lila?

   B: Yes, we were all surprised when she dropped in / dropped out yesterday.

7. **A:** OK, class. It's time to take back / take off your lab coats.

   B: Oh, could we have a few more minutes? We're almost done.

8. **A:** Hi. Can I help you?

   B: Yes, thanks. I need to pick up / pick out a book for my biology report.

B | *Listen again and check (✓)* **True** *or* **False**. *Correct the false statements.*

	True	False
1. Professor Pepperberg ~~brought in~~ *talked about* a DVD.	☐	☑
2. Terry is giving some reports to the teacher.	☐	☐
3. Rea is going to look for some information in a reference book.	☐	☐
4. They're going to make the music lower.	☐	☐
5. Jason feels that the class is going too fast for him.	☐	☐
6. Lila visited the class yesterday.	☐	☐
7. It's time to return the lab coats.	☐	☐
8. He needs to choose a book for his report.	☐	☐

EXERCISE 8: Pronunciation

A | *Read and listen to the Pronunciation Note.*

Pronunciation Note

When the **object of a phrasal verb** is a **noun** that comes between the verb and its particle, **all three words** are usually **stressed**.

EXAMPLE: Could you **turn the lights off**?

When the object is a **pronoun**, the **particle** usually receives **stronger stress** than the verb. The pronoun is not stressed.

EXAMPLE: Sure. I'll **turn them off** in a minute.

B | *Listen to the short conversations. Put dots (• or •) over the phrasal verbs and their objects to show the stress on each part.*

1. **A:** What happens if you drop your keys?

   B: My service dog **picks them up**.

2. **A:** What are you doing?

   B: I'm **cleaning the lab up**.

3. **A:** How did Alex learn all those words?

   B: I can't **figure it out**. He was a genius, I guess.

4. **A:** I don't have your email address.

   B: I'll **write it down** for you.

5. **A:** I need some help planning the class party.

   B: OK. I'll **pick the music out**.

6. **A:** I failed the quiz today. I'm really upset.

   B: When that happens, I take my dog for a walk. It always **calms me down**.

C | *Listen again to the conversations and repeat the responses. Then practice the conversations with a partner.*

EXERCISE 9: Making Plans

Work in groups. Imagine that you are going to take a class field trip. Decide where to go—for example, the zoo, a museum, a park. Then assign tasks and make a list. Try to include some of the phrasal verbs from the box. Go to Appendices 4 and 5 on pages A-3 and A-4 for help.

call up	figure out	look over	make up	pick out	talk over
clean up	hand out	look up	pass out	pick up	write down

EXAMPLE: **A:** I'll write down the "To Do" list.
B: Good idea. I'll call the zoo up to find out the hours.
C: I can pick up a bus schedule.

EXERCISE 10: For or Against

What are some reasons for and against owning a pet? Work in groups to discuss the question. Use some of the phrasal verbs from the box. Go to Appendices 4 and 5 on pages A-3 and A-4 for help.

calm down	chew up	get along	get up	play around
cheer up	clean up	get off	go away	wake up

EXAMPLE: **A:** A pet can calm you down when you're upset.
B: But what do you do with your pet when you go away on vacation?

EXERCISE 11: Writing

A | *How intelligent are animals? Write a paragraph about a pet or an animal you've read about or observed in a zoo or on a TV show. Use phrasal verbs.*

EXAMPLE: I think animals have a lot of intelligence. They can figure out how to solve problems and some of them even use tools. For example, my cat always sleeps on top of the TV. She can turn it on so that it heats up and keeps her warm . . .

B | *Check your work. Use the Editing Checklist.*

Editing Checklist

Did you . . . ?
☐ use phrasal verbs
☐ use the correct particles
☐ put pronoun objects between the verb and the particle

A | *Circle the correct words to complete the sentences.*

1. Have you figured <u>in / out</u> the homework problem yet?

2. Not yet, but I won't give <u>up / back</u>.

3. I'm going to keep <u>away / on</u> trying.

4. Let me know if I can help you <u>out / over</u>.

5. I need to look <u>down / up</u> some information.

6. Maybe you can look <u>out / over</u> my answers when I'm finished.

B | *Unscramble the words to make sentences. Give two answers when possible.*

1. _____
   (early / Joe / up / gets)

2. _____
   (on / the TV / turns / he)

3. _____
   (he / down / with Ana / sits)

4. _____
   (get / well / they / along)

5. _____
   (his schedule / over / they / look)

6. _____
   (talk / over / they / it)

7. _____
   (they / put / away / it)

8. _____
   (put / on / their coats / they)

C | *Find and correct six mistakes.*

As soon as Ina wakes up, she finds Abby's leash and puts it away her. Then the two of them set

for their morning walk out. They keep up walking until they get to the park, where there are a lot

of other dogs and their owners. Abby is a very friendly animal, and she gets well along with other

dogs. Ina loves dogs and always had one when she was growing over. There is a saying that "A

dog is a man's best friend," but Ina knows it's a woman's best friend too. "I enjoy playing with

Abby," she says, "and just being with her cheers up me." Abby obviously enjoys being with Ina

too. The two have become really good friends and have improved each other's lives a lot.

PART VIII

From Grammar to Writing
USING PRONOUNS FOR COHERENCE

When you write a paragraph, it is usually better to use **pronouns** than to repeat the same noun. Pronouns can make your writing smoother and more connected.

EXAMPLE: **My apartment** is pretty cozy. I hope you enjoy staying in **my apartment**. ➜
My apartment is pretty cozy. I hope you enjoy staying in **it**.

1 | *Read the email from Ted, thanking Felicia in advance for house-sitting. Circle all the pronouns. Above each pronoun, write the noun that it refers to.*

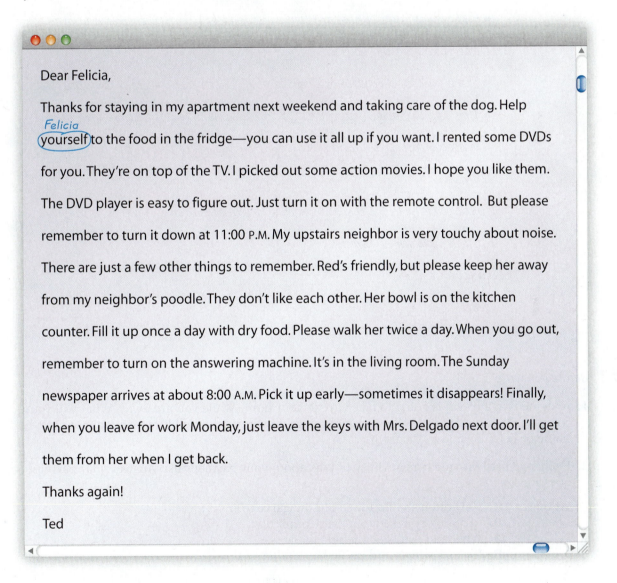

Dear Felicia,

Thanks for staying in my apartment next weekend and taking care of the dog. Help

Felicia
yourself to the food in the fridge—you can use it all up if you want. I rented some DVDs

for you. They're on top of the TV. I picked out some action movies. I hope you like them.

The DVD player is easy to figure out. Just turn it on with the remote control. But please

remember to turn it down at 11:00 P.M. My upstairs neighbor is very touchy about noise.

There are just a few other things to remember. Red's friendly, but please keep her away

from my neighbor's poodle. They don't like each other. Her bowl is on the kitchen

counter. Fill it up once a day with dry food. Please walk her twice a day. When you go out,

remember to turn on the answering machine. It's in the living room. The Sunday

newspaper arrives at about 8:00 A.M. Pick it up early—sometimes it disappears! Finally,

when you leave for work Monday, just leave the keys with Mrs. Delgado next door. I'll get

them from her when I get back.

Thanks again!

Ted

| *Read the note. Change the nouns to pronouns when you can. With phrasal verbs, remember to put the pronoun between the main verb and the particle.*

Dear Dara,

Welcome! I hope you enjoy staying here this week. Here are a few things to keep in mind:

- The mail is delivered every day around noon. You'll find ~~the mail~~ *it* in the mailbox on the ground floor. Please pick up the mail and put the mail on the dining room table.

- Feel free to use the air conditioner, but please turn off the air conditioner when you leave the house.

- There's plenty of food in the refrigerator! Please feel free to use up the food.

- I'm expecting a few phone calls. If you're home, could you please take a message? Just write down the message on the yellow pad in the top left desk drawer.

I think you'll find that the apartment is pretty comfortable. Enjoy the apartment and make yourself at home!

See you in a week.

Rachel

3 | *Before you write . . .*

1. Imagine that a friend is going to take care of your home while you are away. What will your friend's responsibilities be? What special things do you need to tell him or her about your home or neighborhood? Make a list.

2. Exchange lists with a partner. Ask questions about your partner's list. Answer your partner's questions.

   EXAMPLE: **A:** How often should I take out the garbage?
   B: Oh, you can take it out every other day.
   A: Where do you keep the dog food?
   B: It's in the cupboard under the kitchen sink.

4 | *Write a note to your friend. Use your own paper. Give instructions about taking care of your home. Include answers to your partner's questions in Exercise 3. Use pronouns and phrasal verbs.*

5 | *Exchange notes with a different partner. Complete the chart.*

1. Did the writer use pronouns where necessary?   **Yes** ☐   **No** ☐

2. Put a question mark **(?)** over each pronoun you think is in the wrong place.

3. Complete this chart of daily tasks with information from your partner's note. If you have a question ask your partner, and write the answer on the chart.

   EXAMPLES: Sunday: water the plants, feed the pets, pick up the newspaper
   Monday: feed the pets, pick up the mail and put it on the hall table

   Day   **Tasks**

   _____   _____

   _____   _____

   _____   _____

   _____   _____

   _____   _____

   _____   _____

   _____   _____

6 | *Work with your partner. Discuss each other's editing questions from Exercise 5. Then rewrite your note. Make any necessary changes in your use of pronouns. Add information that your partner requested.*

MORE MODALS
AND SIMILAR EXPRESSIONS

UNIT	GRAMMAR FOCUS	THEME
29	Necessity: *Have (got) to, Must, Don't have to, Must not, Can't*	Transportation
30	Expectations: *Be supposed to*	Wedding Customs
31	Future Possibility: *May, Might, Could*	Weather
32	Conclusions: *Must, Have (got) to, May, Might, Could, Can't*	Mysteries

29 Necessity: *Have (got) to, Must, Don't have to, Must not, Can't*

TRANSPORTATION

Before You Read

Look at the title and the illustration. Discuss the questions.

1. Have you ever traveled to a different country?
2. How did you prepare for your trip?
3. What did you need to know?

Read

Read the article about some rules for international travel.

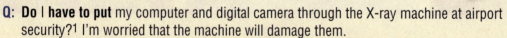

KNOW BEFORE YOU GO

What do international travelers **have to know** before they go? This week's column answers some questions from our readers.

Q: **Do** I **have to put** my computer and digital camera through the X-ray machine at airport security?[1] I'm worried that the machine will damage them.

A: It probably won't, but you **don't have to put** them through the X-ray equipment. An agent **must inspect** them, though. Ask for someone to inspect them by hand.

Q: My passport is going to expire in three months. Can I use it for a short trip to Asia next month?

A: For many countries, your passport **must be** valid for at least six months after you enter the country. Renew your passport before you leave, or you**'ll have to check** the rules of each country you plan to visit.

Q: I'm a French citizen. Last month I visited the United States, and I brought some gifts for friends. Why did U.S. Customs take the cheese?

A: You **can't bring** most types of cheese into the U.S. without a special permit. Many governments have strict rules about bringing food into their countries. To avoid problems, don't bring gifts of fresh food, and eat your snacks on the plane.

Q: I'm from Australia. My family and I are planning a trip to Europe and North America. We'd like to rent cars in a few places. **Do** I **have to get** an International Driver's Permit (IDP)?

A: Regulations differ: In Germany you **must not drive** without an IDP (unless you have a European Union driving license); in Canada you **don't have to have** one, but it's recommended. For a world tour, you really should get an IDP to avoid problems and disappointment.

[1] *airport security:* the area at the airport where they inspect your carry-on bags to make sure they are safe

KNOW BEFORE YOU GO

Q: I'm planning a trip from Toronto to New Delhi. There's a new nonstop flight, but it's more expensive, and it's about 14 hours long! What do you recommend?

A: Several airlines are now offering super-long flights. They provide more comfortable seats, wireless computers, and lots of entertainment. They cost a bit more, but you **won't have to make** as many connecting flights. That saves you time and hassles. But remember: To stay healthy on long flights you**'ve got to get up** and **move** around. You also **must drink** plenty of water. On a long flight these are "musts," not "shoulds"!

After You Read

A | Vocabulary: *Cross out the one word that does NOT belong in each category.*

1.	They must be **valid**:	passports	licenses	computers
2.	Agents **inspect** them at airports:	teeth	luggage	tickets
3.	They can be **hassles**:	cars	flights	movies
4.	There are **regulations** for them:	sleeping	driving	traveling
5.	They can be **strict**:	books	laws	parents
6.	They are **equipment**:	cameras	X-ray machines	bottles

B | Comprehension: *Check (✓) True or False. Correct the false statements.*

	True	False
1. Passengers must put computers and cameras through security X-ray equipment.	☐	☐
2. A passport is always valid.	☐	☐
3. Travelers are not allowed to bring cheese into the United States without permission.	☐	☐
4. You can't eat cheese on the plane.	☐	☐
5. Most international visitors need an IDP to drive in Germany.	☐	☐
6. You must have an IDP to drive in Canada.	☐	☐
7. To stay healthy on long flights, passengers must stay in their seats.	☐	☐

NECESSITY: *HAVE (GOT) TO, DON'T HAVE TO*

Affirmative Statements			
Subject	Have to / Have got to	Base Form of Verb	
I You We They	**have to** **have got to**	**leave**	now.
He She It	**has to** **has got to**		

Negative Statements*				
Subject	Do not	Have to	Base Form of Verb	
I You We They	**don't**	**have to**	**leave**	now.
He She It	**doesn't**			

*There is no negative form for *have got to*.

Contractions*		
have got to	=	**'ve got to**
has got to	=	**'s got to**

*There are no contractions for *have to* and *has to*.

Yes / No Questions			
Do	Subject	Have to	Base Form of Verb
Do	I you we they	**have to**	**leave**?
Does	he she it		

Short Answers					
Affirmative			Negative		
Yes,	you I / we you they	**do.**	**No,**	you I / we you they	**don't.**
	he she it	**does.**		he she it	**doesn't.**

Wh- Questions				
Wh- Word	Do	Subject	Have to	Base Form of Verb
When	**do**	I you we they	**have to**	**leave**?
	does	he she it		

NECESSITY: *MUST, MUST NOT, CAN'T*

Must*			
Subject	***Must (not)***	**Base Form of Verb**	
I You He She It We They	**must**	**leave**	very early.
	must not	**arrive**	too late.

Can't*			
Subject	***Can't***	**Base Form of Verb**	
You He They	**can't**	**sit**	over there.

*Must and *can't* are modals. Modals have only one form. They do not have *-s* in the third-person singular.

GRAMMAR NOTES

1 Use *have to*, *have got to*, or the modal *must* to show that something is **necessary**.

a. *Have to* is the most common expression in everyday speaking and writing.

b. You can also use *have got to* in conversation and informal writing.

c. *Must* is not very common in conversation. You will see *must* in formal writing and in official forms, signs, and notices. People also use it when they talk about laws and regulations.

USAGE NOTE: *Must* is much **stronger** than *have to*. In conversation, usually only people with power use it (parents, police, teachers, government leaders).

- You **have to carry** your passport when you travel to most countries.

- I**'ve got to apply** for a new passport right away!

- All passengers **must show** their passports when they check in.

MOTHER: Jess, you really **must pack** tonight.
JESSICA: OK, Mom.

(continued on next page)

2	You can use a form of ***have to*** for **past**, **present**, and **future** time.	• She **had to travel** a lot last year. *(past)* • He **has to travel** a lot for his job. *(present)* • We**'ll have to visit** them soon. *(future)*
	You can also use it with the **present perfect**.	• I **haven't had to drive**. *(present perfect)*
	Have got to and ***must*** have no past forms. Use ***had to*** for the **past**.	• We **had to work** last night. *(past)* NOT: We ~~had got to~~ work last night. NOT: We ~~must~~ work last night.
	Use ***have got to*** and ***must*** only for the **present** and the **future**.	• I**'ve got to turn off** my phone now. *(present)* • We **must be** at the airport an hour before tomorrow's flight. *(future)*
3	Use ***have to*** for most **questions**.	• **Did** you **have to renew** your passport? • **Do** you **have to leave** now?
	USAGE NOTE: We <u>almost never</u> use *must* in questions, and we do NOT use *have got to*.	NOT COMMON: Must I leave now? NOT: ~~Have I got to leave~~ right now?
4	**BE CAREFUL!** *Have (got) to* and *must* have similar meanings. However, ***don't have to*** and ***must not*** have very **different meanings**.	
	a. Use ***don't have to*** to show that something is **not necessary**. There is a <u>choice</u>.	• Tourists **don't have to have** an IDP in Canada. They can drive without one. • We **didn't have to show** our passports. • You **won't have to go** through customs.
	There is NO negative form of *have got to*.	NOT: Tourists ~~haven't got to have~~ an IDP in Canada.
	b. Use ***must not*** to show that something is **against the rules**. There is <u>no choice</u>.	• You **must not drive** without a license. It's against the law.
	USAGE NOTE: We often use ***can't*** instead of *must not* to express prohibition in spoken English.	• VERY COMMON: You **can't drive** without a license.
5	We sometimes use "**hafta**," "**hasta**," and "**gotta**" in <u>very informal</u> notes, emails, and text messages.	• **Gotta** go now. I **hafta** be at the dentist's office in five minutes. *(informal email)*
	BE CAREFUL! Do NOT use these forms in more <u>formal</u> writing.	NOT: Dear Mr. Smith, I ~~hafta~~ go to the dentist's office today, so I'll be late for class. *(formal note)*

REFERENCE NOTES

Have (got) to, ***must***, and ***can't*** are also used for **conclusions** (see Unit 32).

For a list of **modals and their functions**, see Appendix 19 on page A-8.

EXERCISE 1: Discover the Grammar

A | *Read Ben Leonard's telephone conversation with a clerk from the Italian consulate. Underline the words in their conversation that show that something is* **necessary,** **not necessary,** *or* **against the rules.**

BEN: Hello. I'm Australian, and I'm planning to spend several weeks in Europe with my family. I have some questions. First, <u>do we have to get</u> visas to visit Italy?

CLERK: Not for a short visit. But you can't stay for longer than 90 days without a visa. Australians also have to have a Permit to Stay for visits in Italy longer than eight days. You must apply for the permit at a local police station within eight days of your arrival. It's a hassle, but you've got to do it.

BEN: Can my wife and I use our Australian driver's licenses in Italy?

CLERK: You have to carry your Australian license, but you must also have a valid International Driver's Permit. And you've got to be at least 18 years old.

BEN: When do we have to get the IDPs? Is it possible to apply for them when we get to Europe?

CLERK: No, you must apply before you leave. The Australian Automobile Association can help you. You'll also have to get an International Insurance Certificate to show you have insurance. They're very strict about this, but you'll be able to get one at the car rental agency.

BEN: We'll be in Italy in January. We don't have a set schedule, so we haven't made any reservations. Is that going to be a problem?

CLERK: Yes. You've got to have reservations, even in January—especially in major cities like Rome, Florence, or Venice.

BEN: OK. Thanks a lot. You've been very helpful.

B | *Check (✓) the appropriate box for each instruction.*

	Necessary	Not Necessary	Against the Rules
1. Get a visa for a two-week visit.	☐	✓	☐
2. Get a Permit to Stay for visits longer than eight days.	☐	☐	☐
3. Apply for a Permit to Stay 10 days after arrival.	☐	☐	☐
4. Get a visa for a one-month visit.	☐	☐	☐
5. Use only an Australian driver's license.	☐	☐	☐
6. Apply for an IDP in Europe.	☐	☐	☐
7. Make hotel reservations.	☐	☐	☐

EXERCISE 2: Affirmative and Negative Statements: *Have to*   (Grammar Notes 1, 4)

The Leonards have checked off the things they've already done to get ready for their trip. Read the lists and write sentences about what the Leonards still **have to do** *and what they* **don't have to do.**

BEN
✔ make copies of passports and IDPs
buy euros
give the house keys to Nora

ANN
buy phone cards online
✔ call Pet Care
buy batteries for the digital camera
✔ stop the mail for two weeks

Sean and Maya
✔ pack clothes
choose DVDs and CDs for the trip
say good-bye to friends

Ben doesn't have to make copies of passports and IDPs.

He has to buy euros, and he . . .

Ann . . .

_____

_____

_____

_____

_____

_____

_____

EXERCISE 3: Questions and Statements: *Have (got) to* and *Can't*   (Grammar Notes 1–4)

Ben's family is traveling from Australia to Italy. Complete the conversations. Use the correct form of **have to**, **have got to**, *or* **can't** *and the verbs in parentheses. Use short answers.*

1. **BEN:** What time ____do____ we _____have to leave_____ tomorrow?
   a. (leave)

   ANN: We _____ later than 5:30. We _____
   b. (start)   **c. (check in)**
   with the airline by 7:00.

   SEAN: _____ we really _____ there so early? Our flight leaves at
   d. (get)
   10:00. We've got plenty of time.

   ANN: Yes, _____. It takes a long time to check in and get through
   e.
   airport security these days. They're very strict, and they inspect everything. It's a hassle,

   but they _____ it!
   f. (do)

   MAYA: And Mom _____ the car. That takes some time too!
   g. (park)

2. **BEN:** Maya, this bag _____ over 50 pounds, or we
   a. (weigh)

   _____ extra. _____ you _____
   b. (pay)   **c. (bring)**
   so many clothes?

   MAYA: Yes, _____. I _____ all my stuff! We'll
   d.   **e. (have)**
   be gone for weeks.

   ANN: Put some in my bag. And hurry. We _____!
   f. (go)

3. **BEN:** We _____ never _____ this long to check in before.
   a. (wait)
   ANN: I know. But we _____ much longer. We're next.
   b. (not wait)

4. **SEAN:** Look! They have computers and TV screens! I _____ Randy!
   a. (call)
   BEN: We _____ our cell phone on the plane. Send an email.
   b. (use)

5. **ANN:** We _____ around again. Come on, everybody, let's go.
   a. (walk)
   SEAN: Why _____ we _____ up all the time?
   b. (get)
   BEN: Remember our rules? We _____ for more than three hours.
   c. (sit)
   It's unhealthy.

6. **MAYA:** Are we there yet? This flight is endless!

   ANN: We _____ in here much longer. We're landing in an hour.
   a. (not be)

EXERCISE 4: Affirmative and Negative Statements: *Must*

(Grammar Notes 1, 4)

*Complete the rules for airline travel. Use **must** or **must not**.*

1. Passengers _____*must*_____ arrive three hours before an international flight.

2. They _____ keep their bags with them at all times.

3. Carry-on bags _____ be bigger than 45 inches (115 cm).

4. They _____ fit under the seat or in the overhead compartment of the airplane.

5. They _____ contain knives, scissors, or other dangerous items.

6. Checked bags _____ have labels with the passenger's name.

7. They _____ weigh more than 50 pounds, or there will be additional charges.

8. Travelers _____ show identification when they check in with the airline.

9. Everyone _____ have a ticket in order to go through security.

10. On board, passengers _____ get up when the seat belt sign is on.

11. On many flights, passengers _____ use cell phones when the plane is in the air.

EXERCISE 5: Negative Statements: *Must not* or *Don't have to*

(Grammar Note 4)

*Read the sign at the Casa Luciani swimming pool. Complete each statement. Use **must not** or **don't have to**.*

Swimming Pool Rules and Regulations

Pool Hours 10:00 A.M. – 10:00 P.M.

Children under 12 years NOT ALLOWED
in pool without an adult.

Towels available at front desk.

- NO radio
- NO diving
- NO ball playing
- NO glass bottles
- NO alcoholic beverages

1. Children under age 12 _____*must not swim*_____
   (swim)
   without an adult.

2. You _____ your own towel.
   (bring)

3. You _____ ball in or around
   (play)
   the pool.

4. You _____ into the pool.
   (dive)

5. Teenagers _____ with an adult.
   (swim)

6. You _____ the pool before
   (enter)
   10:00 A.M.

7. You _____ the swimming pool
   (leave)
   at 8:00 P.M.

8. You _____ in the pool past
   (stay)
   10:00 P.M.

EXERCISE 6: Editing

Read Sean's email to his friend. There are seven mistakes in expressing necessity. The first mistake is already corrected. Find and correct six more.

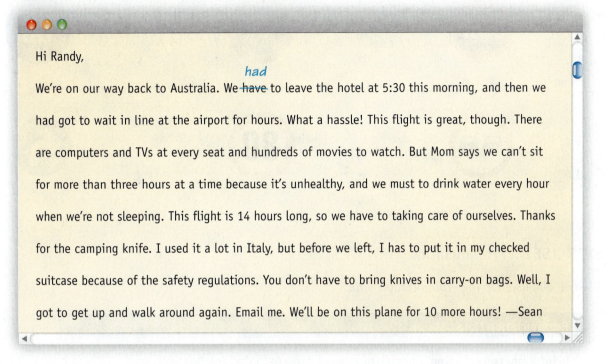

Hi Randy,

                         had

We're on our way back to Australia. We ~~have~~ to leave the hotel at 5:30 this morning, and then we

had got to wait in line at the airport for hours. What a hassle! This flight is great, though. There

are computers and TVs at every seat and hundreds of movies to watch. But Mom says we can't sit

for more than three hours at a time because it's unhealthy, and we must to drink water every hour

when we're not sleeping. This flight is 14 hours long, so we have to taking care of ourselves. Thanks

for the camping knife. I used it a lot in Italy, but before we left, I has to put it in my checked

suitcase because of the safety regulations. You don't have to bring knives in carry-on bags. Well, I

got to get up and walk around again. Email me. We'll be on this plane for 10 more hours! —Sean

---

STEP 4 COMMUNICATION PRACTICE

EXERCISE 7: Listening

A | Read the statements. Then listen to the conversations. Listen again and mark each statement **True** or **False**. Correct the false statements.

	True	False
left **1.** The young man has to turn ~~right~~.	☐	☑
2. The young woman must drive slower.	☐	☐
3. The woman has to stop.	☐	☐
4. The man is driving too fast.	☐	☐
5. The young woman was not preparing to stop.	☐	☐
6. The woman has to pass.	☐	☐

B | *Listen again to the conversations and write the number of each conversation next to the appropriate sign.*

a. ____

b. ____

c. ____

d. ____

e. ____

f. _1_

EXERCISE 8: Pronunciation

A | *Read and listen to the Pronunciation Note.*

Pronunciation Note

In **informal conversation**, we often pronounce ***have to*** "hafta" and ***has to*** "hasta."

EXAMPLES: I **have to** drive Bob to the airport. → "I **hafta** drive Bob to the airport."
He **has to** be there by 5:00. → "He **hasta** be there by 5:00."

For ***have got to***, we often pronounce ***got to*** "gotta," and we sometimes leave out ***have***.

EXAMPLE: You **have got to** turn left here. → "You**'ve gotta** turn left here." OR
"You **gotta** turn left here."

B | *Listen to the short conversations. Notice the pronunciation of* **have/has to,** *and* **have/has got to.**

1. **A:** John **has to** renew his passport. What about you?
   B: I don't **have to** renew mine yet. It's valid for another year.

2. **A:** When does he **have to** be at the airport?
   B: He **has to** be there by 8:00.

3. **A:** He**'s got to** leave now. Is he ready?
   B: Almost. He**'s got to** bring his bags downstairs, that's all.

4. **A:** Will we **have to** show our tickets before we board?
   B: Yes. And we'll **have to** show our passports too.

5. **A:** I**'ve got to** turn right here.
   B: No. You**'ve got to** turn left. You can't turn right here.

C | *Listen again. Then practice the conversations with a partner.*

EXERCISE 9: Picture Discussion

Work in pairs. Where can you find these signs? What do they mean? What do you have to do when you see each one? What can't you do? What do you think of the rules?

EXAMPLE: **A:** You can find this sign near train tracks.
B: Right. It means drivers have to slow down and look both ways before they continue . . .

EXERCISE 10: Game: Invent a Sign

*Draw your own sign to illustrate something people **have to do** or **must not do**. Show it to your classmates. See if they can guess the meaning. Decide where the sign belongs.*

EXAMPLE: **A:** I think that means you have to wear shoes.
B: Right! And where can you find a sign like this?
A: Near some poolside restaurants.
C: You can also find it . . .

EXERCISE 11: What About You?

A | *Work in small groups. Make a list of your most important tasks for this week. Check (✓) the things you've already done. Tell a partner what you still **have to do** and what you **don't have to do**.*

EXAMPLE: **Hamed:** I don't have to renew my driver's license. I've already done it.

B | *Report to the group.*

EXAMPLE: **Nadia:** Hamed doesn't have to renew his driver's license. He's already done it.

EXERCISE 12: Discussion: Rules and Regulations

A | *Work in small groups. Discuss your school's rules and regulations. What do you have to do? What don't you have to do? What can't you do?*

Some topics to consider:

- student cars and parking
- clothing
- cell or smart phones

- calculators
- class hours
- homework

- cigarettes
- food
- music

EXAMPLES: **A:** Our cars have to have a sticker for the student parking lot.
B: But we don't have to pay for parking.
C: We can't leave our cars in the parking lot overnight.

B | *Compare answers with your classmates. Complete a chart on the board like the one below.*

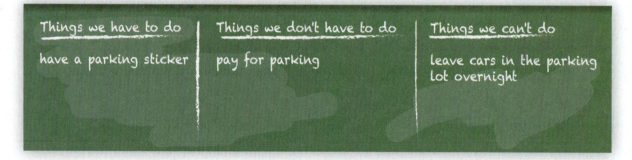

Things we have to do	Things we don't have to do	Things we can't do
have a parking sticker	pay for parking	leave cars in the parking lot overnight

EXERCISE 13: Writing

A | *Write about the application procedure for getting a driver's license, a passport, a work permit, citizenship, school admission, or a new job. What do you have to do? What don't you have to do? Use **have to**, **don't have to**, **must**, **must not**, or **can't**.*

EXAMPLE: To get a driver's license in my state, you must be at least 16 years and 3 months old. Drivers under the age of 19 also have to take a driver's education course. Then . . .

B | *Check your work. Use the Editing Checklist.*

Editing Checklist

Did you use . . . ?
- ☐ *must* or *have to* to show that something is necessary
- ☐ *don't have to* to show that something is not necessary
- ☐ *must not* or *can't* to show that something is against the rules.

Check your answers on page UR-7.

Do you need to review anything?

A | *Circle the correct words to complete the sentences.*

1. You <u>don't have to / must not</u> buy euros for the trip. I've already done it.

2. <u>Do / Does</u> Ken have to leave already? It's still early.

3. They said we <u>can't / don't have to</u> carry scissors onto the airplane.

4. We<u>'ve got to / can't</u> arrive at the airport by 9:00, or we won't be able to board.

5. Jake <u>has / had</u> to renew his passport before he left for Italy.

6. Tomorrow, Tara will <u>have / got</u> to take her driving test again. She failed the last time.

B | *Complete the sentences with* **can't** *or the correct form of* **have to** *and the verbs in parentheses.*

1. I've already downloaded several movies, so I _____ it before we leave.
   (do)

2. We forgot to get a gift for Uncle Fred. We _____ something at the airport.
   (pick up)

3. I _____ never _____ in line this long in my entire life.
   (stand)

4. Relax. We're next. We _____ much longer.
   (wait)

5. Sir, you _____ on any part of the plane, not even in the bathrooms.
   (smoke)

6. The passenger in 23B _____. She's in the wrong seat.
   (move)

7. Sorry. You _____ here. May I see the seat number on your boarding pass?
   (sit)

8. We _____ some French cheese at dinner tonight. I can't wait to try it.
   (have)

9. We _____ the cheese before landing. It isn't allowed into the country.
   (eat)

C | *Find and correct five mistakes.*

1. He can't boards the plane yet.

2. Passengers must not stay in their seats when the seat belt light is off.

3. Passengers: Please note that you gotta pay extra for luggage over 50 pounds.

4. You don't have got to show your passport right now, but please have it ready.

5. Paul will has to unpack some of his stuff. His suitcase is much too heavy.

Expectations: *Be supposed to*
WEDDING CUSTOMS

Before You Read

Look at the photo and the title of the book excerpt. Discuss the questions.

1. What do you think the letter to Ms. Etiquette is about?
2. Have you ever been to a wedding or been part of a wedding?
3. If yes, what special clothing did people wear? What special customs did they follow?

Read

Read the page from Ms. Etiquette's book, The Right Thing.

Wedding Wisdom

Dear Ms. Etiquette:

What **is** the maid of honor **supposed to do** in a wedding ceremony? My best friend is getting married soon. She has invited me to be her maid of honor. I was planning to buy a new dress to wear, but someone told me that the bride **is supposed to select** my dress. This surprised me. I'm new in this country, and I'm not sure what my friend expects of me.

Dear Reader:

First, you should be very proud. In the past, the bride's sister **was supposed to serve** as her maid of honor, and the groom's brother **was supposed to be** his best man. Today, however, the bride and groom can ask anyone they want. Your friend's invitation means that she values your friendship very highly.

You and the best man will play important roles before, during, and after the ceremony. The maid of honor is the bride's assistant, and the best man is the groom's. Before the wedding, these two **are supposed to help** the couple prepare for the ceremony. You might help the bride choose the bridesmaids' dresses and send the wedding invitations, for example. The day of the wedding, the best man **is supposed to drive** the groom to the ceremony. During the ceremony, the maid of honor holds the bride's flowers. After the wedding, the maid of honor and the best man **are** both **supposed to sign** the marriage certificate as witnesses.

After You Read

A | Vocabulary: *Circle the letter of the word or phrase that best completes each sentence.*

1. An **assistant** is someone who _____ you.
   a. helps
   b. teaches
   c. protects

2. A _____ is an example of a **ceremony**.
   a. new job
   b. graduation
   c. math test

3. A **certificate** will NOT show facts about your _____.
   a. birth
   b. marriage
   c. phone bill

4. If you know wedding **etiquette**, you can _____ at a wedding.
   a. behave correctly
   b. take good photos
   c. hold the bride's flowers

5. The best man's **role** is the _____ for the wedding.
   a. suit he wears
   b. job he does
   c. car he uses

6. If you **select** flowers for an event, you _____ them.
   a. choose
   b. water
   c. pay for

B | Comprehension: *Check (✓) the maid of honor's responsibilities.*

She has to . . .

☐ **1.** choose her own dress for the wedding

☐ **2.** help send wedding invitations

☐ **3.** choose the best man

☐ **4.** drive the groom to the ceremony

☐ **5.** hold the bride's flowers during the ceremony

☐ **6.** sign the marriage certificate as a witness

EXPECTATIONS: *BE SUPPOSED TO*

Statements					
Subject	*Be*	*(Not)*	*Supposed to*	Base Form of Verb	
I	am / was	(not)	supposed to	sign	the marriage certificate.
You We They	are / were				
He She	is / was				
It				be	a small wedding.

Yes / No Questions			
Be	Subject	*Supposed to*	Base Form of Verb
Am / Was	I	supposed to	stand?
Are / Were	you		
Is / Was	she		

Short Answers					
Affirmative			Negative		
Yes,	you	are. / were.	No,	you	aren't. / weren't.
	I	am. / was.		I	'm not. / wasn't.
	she	is. / was.		she	isn't. / wasn't.

Wh- Questions				
Wh- Word	*Be*	Subject	*Supposed to*	Base Form of Verb
Where	am / was	I	supposed to	stand?
	are / were	you		
	is / was	she		

GRAMMAR NOTES

1 Use the expression **be supposed to** + **base form** of the verb to talk about different kinds of <u>expectations</u>:

- **rules**

- **customs** (usual ways of doing things)

- **predictions**

- **hearsay** (what everyone says)

- **plans** or **arrangements**

- You**'re not supposed to park** over here. There's a No Parking sign.

- The groom **is supposed to arrive** at the ceremony early.

- The weather forecast says it**'s supposed to rain** tomorrow morning.

- The beaches in Aruba **are supposed to be** beautiful. Everyone says so.

- Let's hurry. We**'re supposed to pick up** the Smiths at 6:00. They're expecting us.

2 Use **be supposed to** only in the **simple present** or the **simple past**.

a. Use the **simple present** for the <u>present</u> or the <u>future</u>.

b. Use the **simple past** for <u>past</u> expectations.

USAGE NOTES:

Was/were supposed to and *was/were going to* can have <u>similar meanings</u>.

We often use *was/were supposed to* or *was/were going to* when something we expected to happen <u>did not happen</u>.

- The bride **is supposed to be** here *now*.
- I**'m supposed to be** at the wedding rehearsal *tomorrow evening*.
  Not: I ~~will be~~ supposed to be . . .

- They **were supposed to get** there by 6:00, so they took a taxi.

- The ceremony **was supposed to start** at 8:00.
- The ceremony **was going to start** at 8:00.

- Nathaniel **was supposed to get** here at noon, *but* his train was late.
- Nathaniel **was going to get** here at noon, *but* his train was late.

EXERCISE 1: Discover the Grammar

A | *Read the article. Underline the phrases that express expectations.*

Wheel2Wheel: A blog for cyclists

It wasn't supposed to be a big wedding.

For people who believe that serious cyclists only think about the newest equipment, here's a romantic story about my friends Bill and Beth Strickland.

The Stricklands wanted a small, quiet wedding—that's why they eloped[1] to Block Island, off the Atlantic Coast of the United States.

The ferry they took to their wedding site doesn't carry cars, so the Stricklands packed their bikes for the trip.

The couple found a lonely hill overlooking the ocean. The weather was supposed to be beautiful, so they asked the town mayor to marry them on the hill the next afternoon. They were going to have a small private ceremony in this romantic setting.

"When we got there, we found a crowd of cyclists admiring the view," laughed Beth Strickland.

When Bill kissed his bride, the audience burst into loud applause and rang their bicycle bells. "We weren't supposed to have 50 wedding guests, but we love biking, and we're not sorry," Bill said.

When they packed to leave the island the next day, Beth left her wedding bouquet at the hotel. She remembered it minutes before the ferry was going to leave. Bill jumped on his bike, recovered the flowers, and made it back to the ferry before it left.

"Cyclists are supposed to stay fast and fit," he said. "Now I know why."

---

[1] *elope*: to go away and get married secretly

B | *Read the article again. Check (✓) **True** or **False** for each statement. Correct the false statements.*

	True	False
1. The Stricklands planned a ~~big~~ *small* wedding.	☐	☑
2. The weather forecaster predicted rain.	☐	☐
3. The Stricklands wanted an outdoor wedding.	☐	☐
4. They didn't expect 50 guests.	☐	☐
5. Beth remembered her bouquet after the ferry left.	☐	☐
6. People expect cyclists to be in good shape.	☐	☐

EXERCISE 2: Questions and Statements

(Grammar Notes 1–2)

Complete the conversations. Use the verbs in parentheses and a form of **be supposed to.**

1. **Sophie:** Netta, Gary called while you were out.

   Netta: _____*Am*_____ I _____*supposed to call*_____ him back?

a. (call)

   Sophie: No, he'll call you later in the afternoon.

2. **Sophie:** The dress store called too. They delivered your wedding dress to your office this

   morning. _____ they _____ that?

a. (do)

   Netta: No, they weren't! They _____ it here. That's why I

b. (deliver)

   stayed home today.

3. **Sophie:** Let's get in line. The rehearsal _____ in a few minutes.

a. (start)

   Julia: We're bridesmaids. Where _____ we _____?

b. (stand)

   Sophie: Right here, behind Netta.

4. **Gary:** Hi. Where's Netta?

   Sophie: Gary! You _____ here!

a. (not be)

   Gary: Why not?

   Sophie: The groom _____ the bride on the day of the wedding

b. (not see)

   until the ceremony. It's bad luck.

5. **Netta:** Sophie, could I borrow your handkerchief, please?

   Sophie: Sure, but why?

   Netta: I _____ something old, something new, something

a. (wear)

   borrowed, and something blue. I don't have anything borrowed.

   Sophie: It _____ this afternoon. Maybe I should lend you my

b. (rain)

   umbrella instead.

6. **Julia:** Where are Gary and Netta going on their honeymoon?

   Sophie: Aruba.

   Julia: Oh, that _____ a really nice island.

a. (be)

7. **Julia:** How long are they going to be away?

   Sophie: They _____ 10 days, but they decided to stay two

a. (stay)

   weeks instead.

EXERCISE 3: *Was* or *Were going to*

(Grammar Note 2)

Look at the list of wedding plans. Write sentences describing the changes. Use **was/were going to**.

TASK	WHO	COMPLETED
1. select the bridesmaids' dresses	*Sophie* ~~Netta~~	✔
2. mail ~~180~~ *210* invitations	Netta's parents	✔
3. order a ~~vanilla~~ *chocolate!* cake	Netta	✔
4. hire a ~~rock~~ *jazz* band	Gary's parents	✔
5. give the bridal shower May ~~10~~ *20*	Sophie	✔
6. plan the rehearsal dinner	*Gary's parents* ~~Gary~~	✔
7. find a photographer	*Jack* ~~Netta~~	✔
8. rent a ~~limo~~ *red sports car*	Jack	✔
9. order flowers by ~~April 1~~ *April 15*	Sophie	✔
10. Buy ~~candles~~ *clocks* as bridesmaids' gifts	Netta's parents	✔
11. Send the wedding announcement to the newspaper	*Jack* ~~Gary~~	✔

1. *Netta was going to select the bridesmaids' dresses, but instead, Sophie selected them.*

2. _____

3. _____

4. _____

5. _____

6. _____

7. _____

8. _____

9. _____

10. _____

11. _____

EXERCISE 4: Editing

Read Jack's email to a friend. There are eight mistakes in the use of **be supposed to** *and* **was/were going to**. *The first mistake is already corrected. Find and correct seven more.*

Hi Cesar!

Remember my old college roommate Gary? He's getting married tomorrow, and I'm the best man!

He and his fiancée *were* supposed to have a small wedding, but they ended up inviting more than 200 people! As best man, my role is mostly to be Gary's assistant. For one thing, I'm supposing to make sure Gary gets to the wedding ceremony on time—not an easy job for me. At first we was going to hire a limousine and driver, but I decided to drive him there myself in a rented red sports car. I'm also supposed to hold the wedding rings during the ceremony. Then, at the end of the reception party, I'm supposed to helping the newlyweds leave quickly for their honeymoon. They're going straight to the airport. (I'm also suppose to hold the plane tickets for them.) They are going to go to Hawaii, but they changed their minds and are going to Aruba instead. Oh! I just looked at the clock. I'd better sign off now, or I'll be late for the rehearsal dinner. I going to leave five minutes ago! By the way, Sophie, the maid of honor, will be there too. I've never met her, but she supposes to be very nice. I'll let you know how it goes! —Jack

The bride and groom with their
maid of honor and best man

EXERCISE 5: Listening

A | *It's the day of the wedding. Read the statements. Then listen to the conversations. Listen again and check (✓) **True** or **False** for each statement. Correct the false statements.*

	True	False

      isn't

1. Netta ~~is~~ late. ☐ ☑

2. Netta decided to walk to the ceremony. ☐ ☐

3. The photographer isn't taking pictures. ☐ ☐

4. The families of the bride and groom don't sit together during the ceremony. ☐ ☐

5. The bridesmaids aren't wearing pink. ☐ ☐

6. The maid of honor comes in before the bride. ☐ ☐

7. Guests should say "congratulations" to the bride. ☐ ☐

8. Gary and Netta are signing the marriage certificate before the reception. ☐ ☐

9. Some people don't throw rice at weddings anymore. ☐ ☐

B | *Listen again to the conversations and circle the correct information.*

1. Netta is / (isn't) supposed to be at the church by 2:00.

2. Netta was / wasn't going to walk to the wedding.

3. The photographer is / isn't supposed to take pictures during the ceremony.

4. Members of the bride's family are / aren't supposed to sit on the right.

5. The bridesmaids were / weren't going to wear pink.

6. The maid of honor is / isn't supposed to walk behind the bride.

7. Guests are / aren't supposed to say "congratulations" to the groom.

8. Gary and Netta are / aren't supposed to sign the marriage certificate after the ceremony.

9. Guests are / aren't supposed to throw rice at the bride and groom these days.

EXERCISE 6: Pronunciation

A | *Read and listen to the Pronunciation Note.*

Pronunciation Note
We often pronounce **supposed to** "supposta" and **going to** "gonna."   **EXAMPLES:** The bride is **supposed to** be here. → "The bride is **supposta** be here."   I was **going to** walk, but it rained. → "I was **gonna** walk, but it rained."

B | *Listen to the short conversations. Notice the pronunciation of* **supposed to** *and* **going to.**

1. **A:** What time is the ceremony **supposed to** start?
   B: The invitation said 4:30.

2. **A:** I think the groom is **supposed to** arrive early.
   B: I've heard that too.

3. **A:** The weather was **supposed to** be great.
   B: Well, the ceremony will be indoors, so the rain won't matter.

4. **A:** I thought Rob was **going to** be the photographer.
   B: He was **supposed to** be, but he got sick.

5. **A:** We were **going to** go, but I had to work.
   B: That's too bad.

C | *Listen again to the conversations and repeat each question or statement with* **supposed to** *or* **going to.** *Then practice the conversations with a partner.*

EXERCISE 7: Discussion

Work with a partner. Discuss important plans that you had that changed. Were you happy or disappointed about the changes in your plans? What did you do instead? What was the result? Use **was/were supposed to** *and* **was/were going to.**

Use these ideas or your own:

- get married
- move to a different town or country
- attend a particular school or take a particular course
- go to or have a party or a celebration
- buy something (some new clothing, a camera, a car . . .)

EXAMPLE: **A:** We were going to get married in Mexico City because my family lives there, but my whole family ended up coming here instead.
B: So I guess it was a big wedding!

EXERCISE 8: Cross-Cultural Comparison

Work in small groups. Discuss these important events. What are people in your culture supposed to do and say at these times? Is there a ceremony? Are people expected to give certain gifts? Wear special clothing? What roles do certain family members and friends play? Report to the class.

- a wedding

- an important birthday

- a school graduation

- an engagement to be married

- an anniversary

- a birth

- a funeral

  EXAMPLE: In traditional Japanese weddings, the bride and groom are supposed to wear kimonos.

EXERCISE 9: Writing

A | *Write a short essay about one of the events listed in Exercise 8. Use **be supposed to** for customs and plans or arrangements.*

   EXAMPLE: In Mexico, a girl's 15th birthday is called the *quinceañera*. The quinceañera celebration is very special. The girl is supposed to wear a pink or white dress . . .

B | *Check your work. Use the Editing Checklist.*

Editing Checklist

Did you use . . . ?

☐ ***be supposed to*** for customs, rules, and plans

☐ only the present or past of ***be*** in ***be supposed to***

☐ ***was/were going to*** or ***was/were supposed to*** for things that people expected to happen but did not happen at a particular event

---

A | *Circle the letter of the correct answer to complete each sentence.*

1. Tomorrow is graduation, and we _____ supposed to be at school at 10:00.

   a. 're   **b.** 'll   **c.** do

2. The weather is _____ to be very nice.

   a. suppose   **b.** supposed   **c.** supposing

3. Jan and Stu _____ going to drive me, but they can't.

   a. are   **b.** was   **c.** were

4. The ceremony was _____ supposed to be outside, but it's going to be in the park.

   a. not   **b.** no   **c.** didn't

5. What time are we supposed _____?

   a. leave   **b.** leaving   **c.** to leave

B | *Complete the conversations with the correct form of* **be supposed to** *and the verbs in parentheses.*

- **A:** Hurry up! We _____ there in 10 minutes.

  1. (be)

  B: Don't worry. The ceremony _____ until 10:15.

  2. (not / start)

- **A:** Where _____ we _____?

  3. (sit)

  B: I think we _____ over there, on the right side.

  4. (go)

- **A:** Oh, no. Most men are wearing ties. _____ I _____ one?

  5. (wear)

  B: I think you _____ a jacket, but ties are optional. So, you're fine.

  6. (wear)

- **A:** It _____, but look at those clouds!

  7. (not / rain)

  B: I know. It _____ a beautiful day.

  8. (be)

C | *Find and correct seven mistakes.*

1. Dahlia was suppose to drive. She was supposed not to fly.

2. She is going to wear her blue dress, but she changed her mind.

3. What are we supposed to doing after the ceremony?

4. My parents will supposed to fly home tomorrow, but they're staying another day.

5. It was no supposed to be this cold, and it didn't suppose to rain.

Unit 30 Review: Expectations: *Be supposed to*   **433**

Future Possibility: *May, Might, Could*
WEATHER

Before You Read

Look at the map that forecasts weather for European cities. Discuss the questions.

1. Are the temperatures in Celsius or Fahrenheit?
2. What are the possible high and low temperatures for Ankara?
3. What's the weather forecast for Moscow? For London?

Read

Read the transcript of a weather report on British TV.

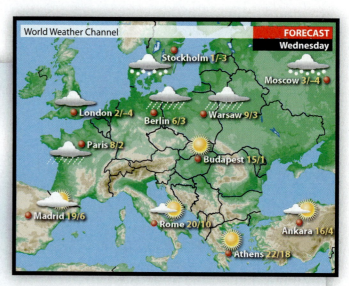

WEATHER WATCH

CAROL: Good morning. I'm Carol Johnson, and here's the local forecast for tomorrow, Wednesday, January 10. The cold front that has been affecting much of northern Europe is moving quickly toward Great Britain. Temperatures **may drop** as much as 11 degrees by late tomorrow afternoon. In London, expect a high of only 2 and a low of –4 degrees. We **might** even **see** some snow flurries[1] later on in the day. By evening, winds **could exceed** 40 miles per hour. So, bundle up; it's going to be a cold one! And now it's time for our travelers' forecast with Ethan Harvey. Ethan?

ETHAN: Thank you, Carol. Take your umbrella if you're traveling to Paris. Stormy conditions **may move** into France by tomorrow morning. Rain **could turn** into snow by evening when temperatures fall to near or below freezing. But look at the forecast for Italy! You **may not need** your coat at all if you plan to be in Rome, where we'll see partly cloudy skies with early morning temperatures around only 10 degrees on Wednesday. But later in the day, temperatures **could climb** to above 20 as skies clear up in the afternoon. The warming trend **could reach** the rest of western Europe by Thursday. But if not, it still looks like it will turn out to be a beautiful, sunny weekend in central Italy, Carol.

CAROL: Italy sounds great! Will you join me on a Roman holiday, Ethan?

ETHAN: I **might**!

[1] *flurries:* small amounts of light snow that fall and blow around

After You Read

A | Vocabulary: *Circle the letter of the word or phrase that best completes each sentence.*

1. A **forecast** tells you about _____ weather.

   a. foreign

   b. yesterday's

   c. tomorrow's

2. **Local** news gives you information about places that are _____ you.

   a. near

   b. far from

   c. interesting to

3. When the weather **affects** people, they always feel _____.

   a. better

   b. worse

   c. different

4. If you **bundle up**, you wear a lot of _____ clothes.

   a. warm

   b. new

   c. expensive

5. A **trend** is the way a situation _____.

   a. stays the same

   b. changes with time

   c. is right now

6. If winds **exceed** 30 miles per hour, they will be _____ 30 miles per hour.

   a. exactly

   b. less than

   c. more than

B | Comprehension: *Check (✓)* **True** *or* **False**. *Correct the false statements.*

	True	False
1. Temperatures will definitely drop 11 degrees in Great Britain.	☐	☐
2. Snow is possible in London.	☐	☐
3. There will definitely be stormy weather in France.	☐	☐
4. Snow is possible in Paris.	☐	☐
5. Western Europe is going to get colder.	☐	☐
6. Temperatures will definitely be above 20 degrees Celsius in Rome.	☐	☐

FUTURE POSSIBILITY: *MAY, MIGHT, COULD*

Statements			
Subject	**Modal***	**Base Form of Verb**	
You It They	**may (not)** **might (not)** **could**	**get**	cold.

*May, *might*, and *could* are modals. Modals have only one form. They do not have *-s* in the third-person singular.

Yes / No Questions		
Are you going to fly to Paris? Are you leaving on Monday?		
Are you going to Will you Is it possible you'll	**be**	there long?

Short Answers		
I	**may (not).*** **might (not).*** **could.**	
We	**may (not)*** **might (not)*** **could**	**(be).**

*May not and *might not* are not contracted.

Wh- Questions
When are you **going** to Paris?
How long are you going to **be** there?

Answers		
I	**may**	**go**	next week.
We	**could**	**be**	there a week.

GRAMMAR NOTES

1

Use the modals *may*, *might*, and *could* to talk about the **possibility** that something <u>will happen</u> in the **future**. The three modals have very similar meanings. You can use any one to talk about future possibility.

BE CAREFUL! *May be* and *maybe* both express possibility. Notice these differences:

- *May be* is a <u>modal + *be*</u>. It is always two words.

- *Maybe* is <u>not a modal</u>. It is an adverb. It is always one word, and it comes at the beginning of the sentence.

REMEMBER: Use a form of the **future** when you are <u>certain</u> that something <u>will happen</u>.

- It **may get** windy *tomorrow*.
- It **might get** windy *tomorrow*.
- It **could get** windy *tomorrow*.
  (It's possible that it will be windy, but we're not certain.)

- Demetrios **may be** late today.

- *Maybe* he'll take the train.
  NOT: He maybe take the train.

- It**'s going to rain** tonight.
  (I'm certain that it will rain.)

2	Use **may not** and **might not** to express the **possibility** that something <u>will not happen</u>. **BE CAREFUL!** We usually <u>do NOT contract</u> **might not**, and we never contract **may not**. **REMEMBER:** Use a form of the **future** when you are <u>certain</u> that something will <u>not happen</u>.	• There are a lot of clouds, but it **might not rain**. • You **may not** need a coat. NOT: You ~~mayn't~~ need a coat. • You **won't need** a coat. *(I'm certain that you will not need a coat.)*
3	**Questions** about possibility usually use the **future** (**will**, **be going to**, the present progressive, the simple present). They usually do not use *may*, *might*, or *could*. You can also use phrases such as **Do you think . . . ?** or **Is it possible that . . . ?** with the **future** or with *may*, *might*, or *could*. The **answers** to these questions often use *may*, *might*, or *could*. In **short answers** to *yes / no* questions, we usually use *may*, *might*, or *could* alone. **USAGE NOTE:** If *be* is the main verb, it is common to include *be* in the short answer.	• When **will** it **start** snowing? NOT COMMON: When ~~might~~ it start snowing? • **Do you think** it **will start** snowing? OR • **Do you think** it **could start** snowing? A: **Are** you **going to drive** to work? B: I don't know. I **may take** the bus. A: When **are** you **leaving**? B: I **might leave** in a few minutes. A: **Do you think** it**'ll snow** tomorrow? B: It **could stop** tonight. A: Will your office close early? B: It **may**. OR It **may not**. NOT: It may not ~~close~~. A: Will our flight **be** on time? B: It **might be**. OR It **might**. It **might not be**. OR It **might not**.

REFERENCE NOTES

Might is also used for **conclusions** (see Unit 32).
For a list of **modals and their functions**, see Appendix 19 on page A-8.

EXERCISE 1: Discover the Grammar

A | *Anna is a college student who works part-time; Cody is her husband. Read their conversation. Underline the words that express future possibility.*

ANNA: Are you going to drive to work tomorrow?

CODY: I don't know. I <u>might take</u> the car. Why?

ANNA: I just heard the local weather report. It may snow tonight.

CODY: Oh, then I may have to shovel snow before I leave. You know, I might just take the 7:30 train instead of driving. I have a 9:00 meeting, and I don't want to miss it. Do you have a class tomorrow morning?

ANNA: No, but I'm going to the library to work on my paper. Maybe I'll bundle up and take the train with you in the morning. And let's try to go home together too. Maybe we could meet at the train station at 6:00, OK? I'm taking the 6:30 train home.

CODY: I might not be able to catch the 6:30 train. My boss said something about working late tomorrow. I may be stuck there until 8:00. I'll call you tomorrow afternoon and let you know what I'm doing.

ANNA: OK. I'll get some takeout on the way home. Do you mind eating late?

CODY: No. I definitely want to have dinner together.

ANNA: Me too. Definitely.

B | *Read the conversation again. Check (✓) the appropriate box for each activity that they discuss.*

CODY	Certain	Possible
1. take car to work		✓
2. shovel snow		
3. take 7:30 A.M. train		
4. 9:00 meeting		
5. work until 8:00 P.M.		
6. call Anna		
7. dinner with Anna		

ANNA	Certain	Possible
1. go to library	✓	
2. work on paper		
3. ride train with Cody		
4. 6:00 P.M.—meet Cody		
5. take 6:30 train home		
6. buy takeout for dinner		
7. dinner with Cody		

EXERCISE 2: Affirmative and Negative Statements

(Grammar Notes 1–2)

Anna is graduating from college with a degree in meteorology.[1] Complete this entry in her diary. Choose the appropriate words in parentheses.

I just got the notice from my school. I _____ 'm going to _____ graduate in June, but I still don't
1. (might not / 'm going to)

have plans. Some TV stations hire students to help out their meteorologists, so I _____
2. (could / may not)

apply for a job next month. On the other hand, I _____ apply to graduate school and
3. (might / might not)

get my master's degree in atmospheric science. I'm just not sure, though—these past two years have

been really hard, and I _____ be ready to study for two more years. At least I *am* sure
4. (may / may not)

about my career. I _____ forecast the weather—that's certain. I made an appointment
5. ('m going to / might)

to discuss my grades with my advisor, Mrs. Humphrey, tomorrow. I _____ talk about
6. (maybe / may)

my plans with her. She _____ have an idea about what I should do.
7. (won't / might)

[1] *meteorology:* the scientific study of weather

EXERCISE 3: Statements: *May, Might, Be going to*

(Grammar Note 1)

*Look at Anna's schedule for Monday. She put a question mark (?) next to each item she wasn't sure about. Write sentences about Anna's plans for Monday. Use **may** or **might** (for things that are possible) and **be going to** (for things that are certain).*

MONDAY
1. call Cody at 9:00
2. buy some notebooks before class ?
3. go to the meeting with Mrs. Humphrey at 11:00
4. have coffee with Sue after class ?
5. go to work at 1:00
6. go shopping for snow boots ?
7. take the 7:00 train ?

1. *Anna is going to call Cody at 9:00.* _____

2. _____

3. _____

4. _____

5. _____

6. _____

7. _____

EXERCISE 4: Short Answers

(Grammar Note 3)

Read the questions. Write short answers. Use **could** *(for things that are possible) or* **won't** *(for things that are certain). Use* **be** *when possible.*

1. **A:** Do you think the roads will be dangerous? It's snowing really hard.

   B: ____*They could be*____. It's a big storm.

2. **A:** Will the schools stay open?

   B: I'm sure _____. It's too dangerous for school buses.

3. **A:** Will it be very windy?

   B: _____. The winds are very strong already. They might even exceed 40 miles

   per hour. So, bundle up!

4. **A:** Will it get very cold?

   B: _____. The temperature in Centerville is already below zero.

5. **A:** Is it possible that the storm will be over by tomorrow?

   B: _____. It's moving pretty quickly now.

6. **A:** Do you think it will be warmer on Tuesday?

   B: _____. There seems to be a warming trend. It's stopped snowing already.

EXERCISE 5: Editing

Read the student's report about El Niño. There are seven mistakes in the use of **may, might,** *and* **could.** *The first mistake is already corrected. Find and correct six more.*

Every few years, the ocean near Peru becomes warmer. This change is called El Niño. An El Niño
~~maybe~~ *may* cause big weather changes all over the world. The west coasts of North and South America
might have very heavy rains. On the other side of the Pacific, New Guinea might becomes very
dry. Northern areas could have warmer, wetter winters, and southern areas maybe become much
colder. These weather changes affect plants and animals. Some fish mayn't survive in warmer
waters. They may die or swim to colder places. In addition, dry conditions could causing crops to
die. When that happens, food may get very expensive. El Niño does not happen regularly. It may
happen every two years, or it might not come for seven years. Will El Niños get worse in the
future? They could be. Pollution will increase the effects of El Niño, but no one is sure yet.

EXERCISE 6: Listening

A | *Read the statements. Then listen to the weather forecast. Listen again and circle the correct information.*

1. This weather forecast is for the (weekend)/ week.

2. The report is <u>local / international</u>.

3. The weather is going to get <u>colder / warmer</u>.

4. On Saturday, you need to <u>bring a jacket / bundle up</u>.

5. On Sunday evening, the weather could affect <u>shopping / driving</u>.

6. The best day will probably be <u>Friday / Saturday / Sunday</u>.

B | *Look at the charts. Then listen again to the forecast and check (✓) **Certain** or **Possible** for each day.*

Friday

	Certain	Possible
Dry	✓	☐
Sunny	☐	☐
Low 50s	☐	☐

Saturday

	Certain	Possible
Sunny	☐	☐
62°	☐	☐
Windy	☐	☐

Sunday

	Certain	Possible
Cold	☐	☐
Windy	☐	☐
Snow flurries	☐	☐

EXERCISE 7: Pronunciation

 A | *Read and listen to the Pronunciation Note.*

Pronunciation Note

In **affirmative short answers** with *may, might,* or *could,* the **most stress** is on the **modal**.

EXAMPLE: **A:** Will you be home at 8:00?

                •

         B: I **might** be.

In **negative short answers** with *may, might,* or *could,* the **most stress** is on *not*.

EXAMPLE: **A:** Will it stop raining this afternoon?

                   •

         B: It **might not**.

 B | *Listen to the short conversations. Notice the word that has the most stress in each short answer. Put a dot (•) over it.*

1. **A:** Is it going to snow tomorrow?

   B: It could.

2. **A:** Do you think the roads will be dangerous?

   B: They could be.

3. **A:** Are you going to drive?

   B: I might not.

4. **A:** Are schools going to be open?

   B: They may not be.

5. **A:** Will you be able to catch the 8:00 train?

   B: I might be.

6. **A:** Will the train be late?

   B: It could be.

 C | *Listen again to the conversations and repeat the short answers. Then practice the conversations with a partner.*

EXERCISE 8: Conversation

Work with a partner. Talk about your weekend plans. Use **be going to** *or* **will** *for plans that are certain. Use* **may, might,** *or* **could** *for plans that are possible. Will the weather affect your plans?*

EXAMPLE: **A:** What are you doing this weekend?
B: I'm not sure. I might go to the park with some friends on Saturday.
A: The forecast says it may rain.
B: Well, in that case, I guess we could go to the movies instead. What about you?

EXERCISE 9: Problem Solving

A | *Look at the student profiles from a school newspaper. Work in small groups. Talk about what the students might do in the future. Use the information from the box or your own ideas.*

About Your Classmates

Name:	Nick Vanek
Major:	TV broadcasting
Activities:	Speakers Club, Sailing Club
Likes:	learning something new
Dislikes:	crowded places
Plans:	go to a four-year college
Dreams:	be a TV weather forecaster

Name:	Marta Rivera
Major:	Early Childhood Education
Activities:	Students' Association, school newspaper
Likes:	adventure, meeting new people
Dislikes:	snow, boring routines
Plans:	teach in a preschool
Dreams:	travel around the world

FUTURE POSSIBILITIES		
Occupations	**Hobbies**	**Achievements**
• weather forecaster	• dancing	• fly on space shuttle
• teacher	• skiing	• teach in Alaska
• manager, day-care center	• creative writing	• develop a new weather satellite

EXAMPLE: **A:** Marta is on the school newspaper. She might do creative writing as a hobby.
B: Nick dislikes crowded places. He might not be happy on the space shuttle.

B | *Now write your own profile. Discuss your future possibilities with your group.*

EXERCISE 10: Writing

A | *Think about your conversation in Exercise 8. Write an email to a friend about your weekend plans. What are you certain about? What things do you think are possible? How will the weather affect your plans?*

EXAMPLE: Hi, Erik. What are you doing this weekend? I'm afraid my plans aren't very exciting. I'm going to stay home and study for my science test. If the weather is nice, I might go for a bike ride. If I do that, maybe you could join me . . .

B | *Check your work. Use the Editing Checklist.*

Editing Checklist

Did you use . . . ?
- ☐ *will*, *be going to*, or the present progressive for things you are certain about or for questions about possibility
- ☐ *may*, *might*, or *could* for things you think are possible

Check your answers on page UR-8.

Do you need to review anything?

A | *Circle the correct words to complete the sentences.*

1. <u>Does / Will</u> it rain tomorrow?

2. It <u>might / might be</u>. I'm not sure.

3. When is Ileana <u>might / going to</u> leave for work?

4. She <u>maybe / may</u> not go to work today. She hasn't decided.

5. It could <u>get / gets</u> very cold tonight. Bundle up!

6. The train <u>will / could</u> be late because of bad weather. It's possible, but it doesn't happen often.

7. <u>Maybe / May be</u> I'll take the train with you this evening.

B | *Complete the conversations with the correct form of* **may, might, could,** *or* **be going to** *and the verbs in parentheses. Choose between affirmative and negative. Use short answers.*

- **A:** _____ you _____ to the game with us on Sunday?
  1. (go)
  B: I _____. There's a good chance. I just have to finish this paper.
  2.
- **A:** _____ Marta _____ at Trish's wedding on Saturday?
  3. (be)
  B: She _____. She and Trish had a big argument about something.
  4.
- **A:** How late _____ you _____ this evening?
  5. (work)
  B: I _____ until 6:00. I'll call and let you know, OK?
  6. (stay)
- **A:** Schools _____ tomorrow. They're predicting a lot of snow tonight.
  7. (open)
  B: Or they _____ late. They do that sometimes.
  8. (open)

C | *Read this review of the movie* Day After Tomorrow. *Find and correct five mistakes.*

Suddenly, weather forecasts all over the world are predicting terrible storms. Climatologist Jack Hall understands weather trends, and he thinks that a new ice age could to begin very quickly. His son Sam is in New York with his high school class. One student is sick and mayn't live without medicine. May those kids survive by themselves? They maybe not. Jack bundles up and starts walking to New York to save them. There might could be a happy ending. Or the world could end. You'll have to watch to find out!

Conclusions: *Must, Have (got) to, May, Might, Could, Can't*

MYSTERIES

Before You Read

Look at the photograph. Discuss the questions.

1. Who is Sherlock Holmes?
2. Have you ever read or watched a Sherlock Holmes mystery?
3. Do you like mystery stories? Why?
4. Who is your favorite detective?

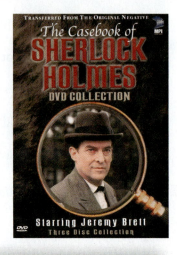

TRANSFERRED FROM THE ORIGINAL NEGATIVE
The Casebook of
SHERLOCK HOLMES
DVD COLLECTION
Starring Jeremy Brett
Three Disc Collection

Read

Read the first part of the Sherlock Holmes story.

THE RED-HEADED LEAGUE [1]
Adapted from a story by Sir Arthur Conan Doyle

When Dr. Watson arrived, Sherlock Holmes was with a visitor.

"Dr. Watson, this is Mr. Jabez Wilson," said Holmes. Watson shook hands with a fat man with red hair.

"Mr. Wilson **must write** a lot," Dr. Watson said immediately.

Holmes smiled. "You **could be** right. But why do you think so?"

"His right shirt cuff [2] looks very old and worn. And he has a small hole in the left elbow of his jacket. He probably rests his left elbow on the desk when he writes."

Wilson looked amazed. "Dr. Watson is correct," he told Holmes. "Your methods **may be** useful after all."

"Please tell Dr. Watson your story," said Holmes. Dr. Watson looked very interested.

"I have a small shop," began the red-headed man.

"I don't have many customers, so I was very interested in this advertisement. My clerk, Vincent, showed it to me." He showed Watson a newspaper ad that said:

> An American millionaire started the Red-Headed League to help red-headed men. The League now has one position open. The salary is £4 per week for four hours of work every day. The job is to copy the encyclopedia in our offices.

"They **couldn't pay** someone just for having red hair and copying the encyclopedia," Watson laughed. "This **has to be** a joke."

"It **might not be**," said Holmes. "Listen to Wilson tell the rest of his story."

"I got the job, and I worked at the League for two months. Then this morning I found a note on the door." Wilson gave Holmes the note . . .

(to be continued)

[1] *league:* a group of people with the same goal

[2] *cuff:* the end of a shirt sleeve, near the hand

A | Vocabulary: *Complete the conversations with the words from the box.*

> advertisement   amazed   encyclopedia   method   millionaire   position   salary

1. **A:** Your English is great—and you've only been studying a year. I'm _____!

   B: Well, I have a good teacher. His teaching _____ really works.

2. **A:** The bank has a(n) _____ available for a clerk. Why don't you apply?

   B: Do you know how much the _____ is?

   A: Here's the _____ in the newspaper. Check it out yourself.

3. **A:** You won the quiz show! You're a(n) _____! How did you do it?

   B: I studied the entire _____, from A to Z.

B | Comprehension: *Circle the letter of the word or phrase that best completes each sentence.*

1. Dr. Watson is probably Sherlock Holmes's _____.
   a. clerk   **b.** dentist   **c.** friend

2. _____ is heavy and has red hair.
   a. Holmes   **b.** Wilson   **c.** Watson

3. Watson thinks that Wilson writes a lot because of Wilson's _____.
   a. clothing   **b.** shop   **c.** red hair

4. Watson helps to solve crimes by _____.
   a. asking questions   **b.** looking at details   **c.** reading the encyclopedia

5. Wilson learned about the job from _____.
   a. Watson   **b.** his clerk Vincent   **c.** a note on his door

6. Wilson copied the encyclopedia in _____.
   a. his shop   **b.** Holmes's house   **c.** the Red-Headed League's office

CONCLUSIONS: *MUST, HAVE (GOT) TO, MAY, MIGHT, COULD, CAN'T*

Affirmative Statements

Subject	Modal*	Base Form of Verb	
I You He They	must may might could	be	wrong.

Negative Statements

Subject	Modal + *Not*	Base Form of Verb	
I You He They	must not may not might not couldn't can't	be	right.

Must, may, might, could, and *can't* are modals. Modals have only one form.
They do not have -*s* in the third-person singular.

Affirmative Statements with *Have (got) to*

Subject	*Have (got) to*	Base Form	
I You They	have (got) to	be	right.
He	has (got) to		

Yes / No Questions

Can / Could	Subject	Base Form	
Could Can	he	know	that?

Do	Subject	Base Form	
Does	he	know	that?

Short Answers

Subject	Modal
He	must (not). may (not). might (not). could(n't). has (got) to. can't.

Yes / No Questions with *Be*

Can / Could	Subject	Be	
Could Can	he	be	a detective?

Be	Subject	
Is	he	a detective?

Short Answers

Subject	Modal	Be
He	must (not) may (not) might (not) could(n't) has (got) to can't	be.

Wh- Questions with *Can* and *Could*

Wh- Word	Can / Could	Subject	Base Form
Who What	can could	it they	be? want?

GRAMMAR NOTES

1 We often make guesses and come to **conclusions** about present situations using the facts we have.

We use **modals** and similar expressions to show <u>how certain or uncertain</u> we are about our conclusions.

	MORE CERTAIN	
AFFIRMATIVE		**NEGATIVE**
must		can't, couldn't
have (got) to		must not
may, might, could		may not, might not
	LESS CERTAIN	

2 For **affirmative conclusions**, use these modals:

a. *must*, *have to*, or *have got to* if you are <u>very certain</u> about your conclusions

b. *may*, *might*, or *could* if you are <u>less certain</u> about your conclusions and you think something is **possible**

FACT	CONCLUSION
Wilson has only one clerk.	• His shop **must be** quite small.
Wilson applied for a position.	• He **has to need** money.
They pay men for having red hair.	• It**'s got to be** a joke.
Wilson has a hole in his sleeve.	• He **may write** a lot.
Vincent knows a lot about cameras.	• He **might be** a photographer.
Holmes solves a lot of crimes.	• His method **could be** a good one.

3 For **negative conclusions**, use these modals:

a. *can't* and *couldn't* when you are <u>almost 100 percent certain</u> that something is **impossible**

• He **can't be** dead! I just saw him!
• Vincent **couldn't be** dishonest. I trust him completely.

b. *must not* when you are <u>slightly less certain</u>

• He **must not earn** a good salary. He always needs money.

c. *may not* and *might not* when you are <u>even less certain</u>

• He **may not know** about the plan.
• His boss **might not tell** him everything. I don't think his boss trusts him.

BE CAREFUL! Do NOT use *have to* and *have got to* for negative conclusions.

• It **can't be** true!
  NOT: It ~~doesn't have to be~~ true!

(continued on next page)

4 Use *can* and *could* in **questions**.

- Someone's coming. Who **can** it **be**?
- **Could** Vincent **be** in the shop?

In **short answers**, use a <u>modal alone</u>.

A: Does she still work at Wilson's?
B: She **may not**. I saw a new clerk there.
NOT: She may not ~~work~~.

BE CAREFUL! Use *be* in short answers to questions with *be*.

A: *Is* Ron still with City Bank?
B: I'm not sure. He **might not be**.

REFERENCE NOTES

Must, *have to*, and *have got to* are also used for **necessity** (see Unit 29).
May, *might*, and *could* are also used for **future possibility** (see Unit 31).
For a list of **modals and their functions**, see Appendix 19 on page A-8.
For information about the **pronunciation and usage** of *have to* and *have got to*, see Unit 29.

STEP 3 FOCUSED PRACTICE

EXERCISE 1: Discover the Grammar

A | *Read the next part of "The Red-Headed League." Underline the verbs that express conclusions.*

THE RED-HEADED LEAGUE *(continued)*

Sherlock Holmes studied the note: *The Red-Headed League does not exist anymore.*

"This <u>could be</u> serious," Holmes told Wilson. "What can you tell us about your clerk Vincent?"

"Vincent couldn't be dishonest," replied Wilson. "In fact, he took this job for half the usual salary because he wanted to learn the business. His only fault is photography."

"Photography?" Holmes and Watson asked together.

"Yes," replied Wilson. "He's always running down to the basement to work with his cameras."

Wilson left soon after that.

"Wilson's clerk might be the key to this mystery," Holmes told Watson. "Let's go see him." An hour later, Holmes and Watson walked into Wilson's shop. The clerk was a man of about 30, with a scar on his forehead.

Holmes asked him for directions. Then he and Watson left the shop.

"My dear Watson," Holmes began. "It's very unusual for a 30-year-old man to work for half-pay. This clerk has to have a very special reason for working here."

"Something to do with the Red-Headed League?" Watson asked.

"Yes. Perhaps the clerk placed that ad in the newspaper. He may want to be alone in the shop. Did you look at his legs?"

"No, I didn't."

"He has holes in his trouser knees. He must spend his time digging a tunnel from Wilson's basement. But where is it?"

Holmes hit the ground sharply with his walking stick. "The ground isn't hollow, so the tunnel must not be here in front of the shop. Let's walk to the street in back of Wilson's shop."

B | *Read the second part of the story again. What does Sherlock Holmes believe about each of the statements? Check (✓) **Possible** or **Almost Certain** for each statement.*

	Possible	Almost Certain
1. Something serious is happening.	✓	☐
2. The clerk is the key to the mystery.	☐	☐
3. The clerk has a special reason for working in Mr. Wilson's shop.	☐	☐
4. He wants to be alone in the shop.	☐	☐
5. He's digging a tunnel from Wilson's basement.	☐	☐
6. The tunnel isn't in front of the shop.	☐	☐

EXERCISE 2: Affirmative and Negative Statements

(Grammar Notes 1–3)

Look at the illustration for the story "The Red-Headed League." Come to conclusions and circle the appropriate words.

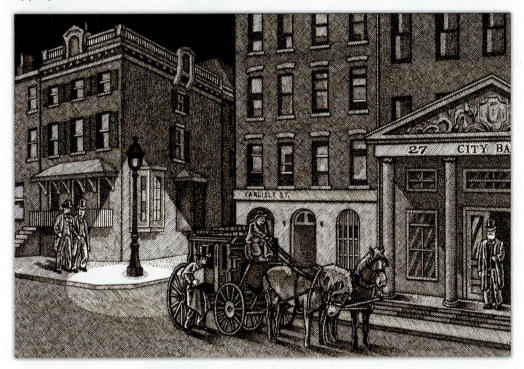

1. It **must** / could be nighttime.

2. It <u>must / must not</u> be hot outside.

3. Number 27 <u>might / can't</u> be a bank.

4. The delivery <u>couldn't / might</u> be for the bank.

5. The box <u>could / must not</u> contain gold.

6. The two men on the sidewalk <u>must not / could</u> notice the delivery.

7. The manager <u>might not / must</u> want people to know about this delivery.

8. Robbers <u>may / can't</u> know about it.

EXERCISE 3: *Must* and *Must Not*

(Grammar Notes 1–3)

Look at the poster and the map of Mr. Wilson's neighborhood. Write conclusions. Use the evidence and the words in parentheses with **must** *and* **must not**.

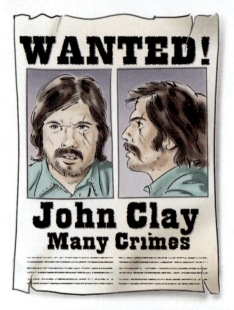

1. Wilson's clerk is the man on the poster.

   He must be a criminal.
   _____
   (he / be a criminal)

2. The man on the poster is named John Clay.

   _____
   (Vincent / be the clerk's real name)

3. Wilson trusts Vincent.

   _____
   (he / know about the poster)

4. Clay has committed a lot of crimes, but the police haven't caught him.

   _____
   (he / be very clever)

5. The address of the bank on the map and the address in the picture for Exercise 2 are the same.

   _____
   (number 27 Carlisle Street / be City Bank)

6. The hat shop and the drugstore don't make much money.

   _____
   (Vincent's tunnel / lead to those shops)

7. There's a lot of money in the bank, and it's very close to Wilson's shop.

   _____
   (Vincent's tunnel / lead to the bank)

8. The bank is expecting a shipment of gold.

   _____
   (the tunnel / be almost finished)

EXERCISE 4: *Have got to* and *Can't*

(Grammar Notes 1–3)

*Ann and Marie are buying hats in the shop on Carlisle Street. Read the conversation.
Rewrite the underlined sentences another way. Use **have got to** or **can't** and the word in
parentheses. Use contractions.*

ANN: Look at this hat, Marie. What do you think?

MARIE: Oh, come on. That's got to be a joke.

You can't be serious.
_____

1. (serious)

Anyway, it's much too expensive. Look at the price tag. I mean, I'm not a millionaire!

ANN: It's $100! That can't be right.

_____

2. (wrong)

MARIE: I know. It can't cost more than $50.

_____

3. (less)

Anyway, let's talk about it over lunch. I'm getting hungry.

ANN: It's too early for lunch. It has to be before 11:00.

_____

4. (after)

MARIE: Look at the time. I'm amazed! It's already 12:30.

ANN: Then let's go to the café on Jones Street. It can't be far.

_____

5. (nearby)

MARIE: Let's go home after lunch. I need a nap.

ANN: Oh, come on. You're fine. You must be hungry.

_____

6. (tired)

EXERCISE 5: Short Answers: *Might (not)* or *Must (not)*

(Grammar Note 4)

*Sherlock Holmes and Dr. Watson have been discussing the mystery all evening. Write a short
answer to each question. Use **might (not)** or **must (not)** and include **be** where necessary.*

WATSON: You sound terrible, Holmes. Are you sick?

HOLMES: I _____ *must be* _____. I have a headache, and my throat is starting to hurt.
        1.

WATSON: Hmm. This bottle is empty. Do you have more cough syrup?

HOLMES: I _____. I *think* it's the last bottle.
    2.

(continued on next page)

WATSON: I'll have to go get some. My patients like Pure Drops Cough Medicine. Does that work for you, Holmes?

HOLMES: It _____. It's worth a try.
3.

WATSON: I forgot to go to the bank today. Do you have any money?

HOLMES: I _____. Look in my wallet. It's on the table downstairs.
4.

WATSON: I found it. It's 6:45. Is Drake Drugstore still open?

HOLMES: It _____. Their advertisement says "Open 'til 7."
5.

WATSON: Do you think they sell chicken soup? Some drugstores carry food.

HOLMES: They _____. It's a very small store.
6.

WATSON: What about the café on Jones Street? Do they have soup?

HOLMES: They _____. They've got everything.
7.

EXERCISE 6: Questions and Statements With *Be*   (Grammar Notes 1-4)

Mr. and Mrs. Wilson are trying to get to sleep. Write questions and answers. Use **could be,** **couldn't be,** *or* **can't be.** *Choose between affirmative and negative .*

MRS. WILSON: Shh! I hear someone at the door. It's 9:30. Who ____*could*____ it __*be*__?
1.

MR. WILSON: It _____ a late customer. Mrs. Simms said she was going to stop by
2.
this evening.

MRS. WILSON: No, it _____ her. It's much too late. Maybe it's the cat.
3.

MR. WILSON: It _____. I put the cat out before we went to bed.
4.

MRS. WILSON: _____ it _____ Vincent? He's always down in the basement with
5.
his camera.

MR. WILSON: No, Vincent went out an hour ago. He _____ back this early. Wait a
6.
minute. It _____ Sherlock Holmes and Dr. Watson. They said they
7.
wanted to talk to me.

MRS. WILSON: _____ they really _____ here so late?
8.

MR. WILSON: No. You're right. It _____ them.
9.

MRS. WILSON: What _____ it _____ then?
10.

MR. WILSON: That door rattles whenever the wind blows. It _____ the wind.
11.

MRS. WILSON: That must be it. Let's go to sleep.

EXERCISE 7: Editing

Read the student's reading journal for a mystery novel. There are six mistakes in the use of **must, have (got) to, may, might, could,** *and* **can't**. *The first mistake is already corrected. Find and correct five more.*

> The main character, Molly Smith, is a college ESL teacher. She is trying to
> find her dead grandparents' first home in the United States. It may ~~being~~ ^{be}
> in a nearby town. The townspeople there seem scared. They could be have a
> secret, or they must just hate strangers. Molly found some letters hidden in
> an old encyclopedia that might lead her to the place. They are in Armenian,
> but one of her students mights translate them for her. They got to be
> important because the author mentions them right away. The letters must
> contain family secrets. I'm sure of it. Who is the bad guy? It couldn't be
> the student because he wants to help. It must be the newspaper editor in
> the town. That's a possibility.

STEP 4 COMMUNICATION PRACTICE

EXERCISE 8: Listening

A | *The Red-Headed League mystery continues. . . . Sherlock Holmes, Dr. Watson, and Captain Rogers meet in front of City Bank. Read the sentences. Then listen to their conversation. Listen again and number the sentences in order from what happens first (**1**) to what happens last (**6**).*

_____ **a.** John Clay arrives.

__1__ **b.** Holmes introduces Watson to Rogers.

_____ **c.** Rogers arrests Clay.

_____ **d.** Watson sits on a box of gold coins.

_____ **e.** Rogers finds Clay's tunnel.

_____ **f.** Holmes, Watson, and Rogers go to the storeroom.

B | *Read the statements. Then listen again to the conversation. How certain is each speaker? Check (✓) Possible, Almost Certain, or Fact for each statement.*

The speaker believes the statement is . . .	Possible	Almost Certain	Fact
1. Captain Rogers is from the police department.	☐	☐	☑
2. It's 10:00.	☐	☐	☐
3. There are 2,000 gold coins in one of the boxes.	☐	☐	☐
4. John Clay knows about the gold.	☐	☐	☐
5. An American millionaire didn't start the Red-Headed League.	☐	☐	☐
6. Clay ended the Red-Headed League.	☐	☐	☐
7. Clay's tunnel is finished.	☐	☐	☐
8. The tunnel is under the bank floor.	☐	☐	☐
9. Clay is dangerous.	☐	☐	☐
10. Clay is in the tunnel.	☐	☐	☐

EXERCISE 9: Pronunciation

A | *Read and listen to the Pronunciation Note.*

> **Pronunciation Note**
>
> When we express **conclusions**, we often **stress** the modals *must*, *may*, *might*, *can't*, and *could*.
>
> **EXAMPLE:** That **must** be George Clooney! He looks just like him.
>
> We also stress *have* and *has* in *have/has to* and *got* in *have/has got to*.
>
> **EXAMPLES:** The store **has to** be open. It's only 5:00.
>
> They**'ve got to** sell soup. They have everything.

B | *Listen to the short conversations. Notice the stressed modals. Then listen again and complete the conversations with the modals you hear.*

1. **A:** Look at the crowds!

   B: This _____ be a really popular movie.

2. **A:** Do you have the tickets?

   B: Yeah, I'm sure I put them in my pocket. They _____ be here somewhere.

3. A: This _____ be the best movie I've seen this year.

 B: Me too. George Clooney is so funny.

4. A: He _____ be the thief. He's already committed a lot of crimes.

 B: He _____ be. He's the star!

5. A: You _____ be right.

 B: I guess we'll know in a few minutes. It _____ be over soon.

6. A: That was a long movie. It _____ be after 10:00 by now.

 B: You're right. It's almost 10:30.

C | *Practice the conversations with a partner.*

EXERCISE 10: Picture Discussion

Work in small groups. Look at the pictures of Sandra Diaz and some things that she and her family own. Make guesses about the Diaz family. Give reasons for your guesses.

EXAMPLE: **A:** Sandra might be a construction worker. She's wearing a hard hat.
 B: Or she could be . . .
 C: She couldn't . . .

EXERCISE 11: Problem Solving

Read the situations. In pairs, discuss possible explanations for each situation. Then come to a conclusion. Discuss your explanations with the rest of the class. Use your imagination!

1. Yolanda lives alone, but she hears a noise in the house.

   EXAMPLE: **A:** It might be an open window. Maybe the wind is blowing.
   B: It couldn't be. She closed all the windows five minutes ago.
   A: Well, then, it could be the cat . . .

2. Stefan has been calling his sister on the phone for three days. She hasn't returned any of his messages.

3. Allan is on the street. He's asked a woman three times for the time. She hasn't answered.

4. Lili sees a neighbor with a 10-year-old. She's never seen the child before.

5. Julia and Claudio went on a picnic in the park. They ate strawberries and cheese. Now they are sneezing and their eyes are watering.

EXERCISE 12: Writing

A | *Agatha James, the mystery writer, starts a new novel by writing story outlines about each one of her characters. Read about the murder suspect's activities on the day of the crime.*

MARCH 1	MURDER SUSPECT'S ACTIVITIES
7:00–8:00	gym—aerobics class—talks to exercise instructor!
9:30	calls Dr. Lorenzo
11:00–1:00	hairdresser—changes hair color
1:30	pharmacy—picks up prescription
2:00	bank—withdraws $10,000
3:00	Mr. Jordan
4:30	calls travel agency—vegetarian meal?

B | *Work in small groups to make guesses and come to conclusions about the story and the characters. Consider questions like these:*

- Is the murder suspect a man or a woman?
- Who is Dr. Lorenzo?
- Why does the suspect need $10,000?
- Who is Mr. Jordan? What is his relationship with the suspect?

   EXAMPLE: **A:** The suspect must be a woman. She's going to the hairdresser.
   B: It could be a man. Men go to hairdressers too.

C | *Now write possibilities and conclusions about the story and the characters.*

EXAMPLE: The suspect must be a woman. Very few men take aerobics classes. She talked to the aerobics instructor, so she might . . .

D | *Check your work. Use the Editing Checklist.*

Editing Checklist
Did you use . . . ? ☐ modals that show how certain or uncertain you are of your conclusions ☐ *must*, *have (got) to*, *may*, *might*, and *could* for affirmative statements ☐ *can't*, *couldn't*, *must not*, *may not*, and *might not* for negative statements

32 Review

Check your answers on page UR-8.

Do you need to review anything?

A | *Circle the correct words to complete the sentences.*

1. Rosa got 100 on her test. She <u>may / must</u> be a good student.

2. It's a gold ring with a very large diamond. It <u>has got to / might</u> cost a lot of money.

3. I'm really not sure how old he is. He <u>has to / could</u> be 21.

4. Doug <u>can't / doesn't have to</u> be married. He's much too young!

5. <u>Could / May</u> Doug know Rosa?

6. The phone is ringing. It <u>must not / could</u> be Alexis. She sometimes calls at this time.

B | *Complete the conversations with the verbs in parentheses. Choose between affirmative and negative.*

- **A:** That _____ George's brother. He looks nothing like George.
  1. (could / be)

  B: He _____. Sometimes brothers don't look at all alike.
  2. (could / be)

- **A:** Someone's at the door. What _____ they _____ at this hour?
  3. (could / want)

  B: I don't know. _____ it _____ Leon?
  4. (could / be)

  A: No. It _____ Leon. Leon's in Spain.
  5. (can / be)

- **A:** _____ this road _____ to Greenville?
  6. (could / lead)

  B: I'm not sure. Ask Talia. She _____.
  7. (might / know)

C | *Find and correct seven mistakes.*

1. Jason has been coughing all morning. He might having a cold.

2. Diana must not likes fish. She left most of it on her plate.

3. May the package be from your parents?

4. That's impossible! It might not be true.

5. Is the bank still open? That's a good question. I don't know. It might.

6. She could be a thief! I trust her completely!

7. It's got be a joke. I don't believe it's serious.

From Grammar to Writing
COMBINING SENTENCES WITH
BECAUSE, ALTHOUGH, EVEN THOUGH

You can combine two sentences with *because*, *although*, and *even though*. In the new sentence, the clause that begins with *because*, *although*, or *even though* is the **dependent clause**. The other clause is the main clause.

EXAMPLE: It was my mistake. I think the cashier was rude. →

DEPENDENT CLAUSE   MAIN CLAUSE
Even though it was my mistake, I think the cashier was rude.

The dependent clause can come first or second. When it comes first, a **comma** separates the two clauses.

1 | *Circle the correct words to complete the business letter. Underline the main clauses once and the dependent clauses twice.*

> 23 Creek Road
> Provo, UT 84001
> September 10, 2011
>
> Customer Service Representative
> Hardy's Restaurant
> 12345 Beafy Court
> Provo, UT 64004
>
> Dear Customer Service Representative:
>
> I am writing this letter of complaint although / (because) one of your cashiers treated me rudely.
>
> Because / Even though I was sure I paid her with a $20 bill, I only received change for $10. I told her
>
> that there was a mistake. She said "You're wrong" and slammed the cash drawer shut. I reported the
>
> incident. Later the manager called. He said the cashier was right although / because the money in the
>
> cashier drawer was correct.
>
> Because / Even though the mistake was mine, I believe the cashier behaved extremely rudely.
>
> Although / Because I like Hardy's, I also value polite service. I hope I won't have to change
>
> restaurants although / because I can't get it there.
>
> Sincerely,
>
> *Ken Nelson*
>
> Ken Nelson

2 | Look at the letter in Exercise 1. Circle the correct words in the sentences to complete the rules about dependent clauses and business letters.

1. Use *because* to give a (reason) / contrasting idea.

2. Use *although* or *even though* to give a <u>reason / contrasting idea</u>.

3. When you begin a sentence with a dependent clause, use a <u>colon / comma</u> after it.

4. When a sentence has a dependent clause, it <u>must also / doesn't have to</u> have a main clause.

5. When a sentence has a main clause, it <u>must also / doesn't have to</u> have a dependent clause.

6. In a business letter, the <u>sender's / receiver's</u> address comes first.

7. The date comes <u>before / after</u> the receiver's address.

8. Use a <u>colon / comma</u> after the receiver's name.

3 | Before you write . . .

1. Work with a partner. Complete these complaints with dependent clauses and the correct punctuation. Use your own ideas.

   a. _____ I will not bring my car to your mechanic again.

   b. The server brought me a hamburger _____.

   c. My neighbor still won't turn down the TV _____.

2. Choose one of the above situations. Plan a role play about the conflict. Act out your role play for another pair of students.

3. Discuss what to write in a letter of complaint.

4 | Write a letter of complaint. Use information from your role play in Exercise 3.

5 | Exchange letters with a different partner. Complete the chart.

Did the writer . . . ?	Yes	No
1. use dependent clauses correctly	☐	☐
2. use modals correctly	☐	☐
3. give enough information about the complaint	☐	☐
4. use correct business-letter form	☐	☐

6 | Work with your partner. Discuss each other's editing questions from Exercise 5. Then rewrite your own letter and make any necessary corrections.

APPENDICES

1 Irregular Verbs

Base Form	Simple Past	Past Participle
arise	arose	arisen
awake	awoke	awoken
be	was/were	been
beat	beat	beaten/beat
become	became	become
begin	began	begun
bend	bent	bent
bet	bet	bet
bite	bit	bitten
bleed	bled	bled
blow	blew	blown
break	broke	broken
bring	brought	brought
build	built	built
burn	burned/burnt	burned/burnt
burst	burst	burst
buy	bought	bought
catch	caught	caught
choose	chose	chosen
cling	clung	clung
come	came	come
cost	cost	cost
creep	crept	crept
cut	cut	cut
deal	dealt	dealt
dig	dug	dug
dive	dived/dove	dived
do	did	done
draw	drew	drawn
dream	dreamed/dreamt	dreamed/dreamt
drink	drank	drunk
drive	drove	driven
eat	ate	eaten
fall	fell	fallen
feed	fed	fed
feel	felt	felt
fight	fought	fought
find	found	found
fit	fit/fitted	fit
flee	fled	fled
fling	flung	flung
fly	flew	flown
forbid	forbade/forbid	forbidden
forget	forgot	forgotten
forgive	forgave	forgiven
freeze	froze	frozen
get	got	gotten/got
give	gave	given
go	went	gone
grind	ground	ground
grow	grew	grown

Base Form	Simple Past	Past Participle
hang	hung	hung
have	had	had
hear	heard	heard
hide	hid	hidden
hit	hit	hit
hold	held	held
hurt	hurt	hurt
keep	kept	kept
kneel	knelt/kneeled	knelt/kneeled
knit	knit/knitted	knit/knitted
know	knew	known
lay	laid	laid
lead	led	led
leap	leaped/leapt	leaped/leapt
leave	left	left
lend	lent	lent
let	let	let
lie *(lie down)*	lay	lain
light	lit/lighted	lit/lighted
lose	lost	lost
make	made	made
mean	meant	meant
meet	met	met
pay	paid	paid
prove	proved	proved/proven
put	put	put
quit	quit	quit
read /rid/	read /rɛd/	read /rɛd/
ride	rode	ridden
ring	rang	rung
rise	rose	risen
run	ran	run
say	said	said
see	saw	seen
seek	sought	sought
sell	sold	sold
send	sent	sent
set	set	set
sew	sewed	sewn/sewed
shake	shook	shaken
shave	shaved	shaved/shaven
shine *(intransitive)*	shone/shined	shone/shined
shoot	shot	shot
show	showed	shown
shrink	shrank/shrunk	shrunk/shrunken
shut	shut	shut
sing	sang	sung
sink	sank/sunk	sunk
sit	sat	sat
sleep	slept	slept
slide	slid	slid

(continued on next page)

Base Form	Simple Past	Past Participle	Base Form	Simple Past	Past Participle
speak	spoke	spoken	swing	swung	swung
speed	sped/speeded	sped/speeded	take	took	taken
spend	spent	spent	teach	taught	taught
spill	spilled/spilt	spilled/spilt	tear	tore	torn
spin	spun	spun	tell	told	told
spit	spit/spat	spat	think	thought	thought
split	split	split	throw	threw	thrown
spread	spread	spread	understand	understood	understood
spring	sprang	sprung	upset	upset	upset
stand	stood	stood	wake	woke	woken
steal	stole	stolen	wear	wore	worn
stick	stuck	stuck	weave	wove/weaved	woven/weaved
sting	stung	stung	weep	wept	wept
stink	stank/stunk	stunk	win	won	won
strike	struck	struck/stricken	wind	wound	wound
swear	swore	sworn	withdraw	withdrew	withdrawn
sweep	swept	swept	wring	wrung	wrung
swim	swam	swum	write	wrote	written

2 Non-Action Verbs

Appearance	Emotions	Mental States		Possession and Relationship	Senses and Perceptions	Wants and Preferences
appear	admire	agree	know	belong	feel	desire
be	adore	assume	mean	come from (origin)	hear	hope
look (seem)	appreciate	believe	mind	contain	notice	need
represent	care	consider	presume	have	observe	prefer
resemble	detest	disagree	realize	own	perceive	want
seem	dislike	disbelieve	recognize	possess	see	wish
signify	doubt	estimate	remember		smell	
	envy	expect	see (understand)		sound	
Value	fear	feel (believe)	suppose		taste	
cost	hate	find (believe)	suspect			
equal	like	guess	think (believe)			
weigh	love	hesitate	understand			
	miss	hope	wonder			
	regret	imagine				
	respect					
	trust					

3 Verbs and Expressions Used Reflexively

allow yourself
amuse yourself
ask yourself
avail yourself of
be hard on yourself
be pleased with yourself
be proud of yourself
be yourself
behave yourself

believe in yourself
blame yourself
buy yourself
cut yourself
deprive yourself of
dry yourself
enjoy yourself
feel proud of yourself
feel sorry for yourself

forgive yourself
help yourself
hurt yourself
imagine yourself
introduce yourself
kill yourself
look at yourself
prepare yourself
pride yourself on

push yourself
remind yourself
see yourself
take care of yourself
talk to yourself
teach yourself
tell yourself
treat yourself
wash yourself

(s.o. = someone   s.t. = something)

PHRASAL VERB	MEANING
ask s.o. **over**	*invite to one's home*
blow s.t. **out**	*stop burning by blowing air on it*
blow s.t. **up**	*make explode*
bring s.o. or s.t. **back**	*return*
bring s.o. **up**	*raise (a child)*
bring s.t. **up**	*bring attention to*
burn s.t. **down**	*burn completely*
call s.o. **back**	*return a phone call*
call s.t. **off**	*cancel*
call s.o. **up**	*contact by phone*
calm s.o. **down**	*make less excited*
carry s.t. **out**	*complete (a plan)*
clean s.o. or s.t. **up**	*clean completely*
clear s.t. **up**	*explain*
close s.t. **down**	*close by force*
count on s.t. or s.o.	*depend on*
cover s.o. or s.t. **up**	*cover completely*
cross s.t. **out**	*draw a line through*
do s.t. **over**	*do again*
drink s.t. **up**	*drink completely*
drop in on s.o.	*visit by surprise*
drop s.o. or s.t. **off**	*take someplace in a car and leave there*
empty s.t. **out**	*empty completely*
figure s.o. **out**	*understand (the behavior)*
figure s.t. **out**	*solve, understand after thinking about it*
fill s.t. **in**	*complete with information*
fill s.t. **out**	*complete (a form)*
find s.t. **out**	*learn information*
get off s.t.	*leave (a bus, a couch)*
get over s.t.	*recover from*
give s.t. **back**	*return*
give s.t. **up**	*quit, abandon*
hand s.t. **in**	*give work (to a boss/teacher), submit*
hand s.t. **out**	*distribute*
hand s.t. **over**	*give*
help s.o. **out**	*assist*
keep s.o. or s.t. **away**	*cause to stay at a distance*
keep s.t. **on**	*not remove (a piece of clothing/ jewelry)*
keep s.o. or s.t. **out**	*not allow to enter*
lay s.o. **off**	*end employment*
leave s.t. **on**	1. *not turn off (a light/radio)* 2. *not remove (a piece of clothing/ jewelry)*
leave s.t. **out**	*not include, omit*
let s.o. **down**	*disappoint*
let s.o. or s.t. **in**	*allow to enter*
let s.o. **off**	*allow to leave (from a bus/car)*
light s.t. **up**	*illuminate*
look s.o. or s.t. **over**	*examine*
look s.t. **up**	*try to find (in a book/on the Internet)*

PHRASAL VERB	MEANING
make s.t. **up**	*create*
pass s.t. **on**	*give to others*
pass s.t. **out**	*distribute*
pass s.o. or s.t. **over**	*decide not to use*
pass s.o. or s.t. **up**	*decide not to use, reject*
pay s.o. or s.t. **back**	*repay*
pick s.o. or s.t. **out**	*choose*
pick s.o. or s.t. **up**	1. *lift* 2. *go get someone or something*
pick s.t. **up**	1. *get (an idea/a new book)* 2. *answer the phone*
point s.o. or s.t. **out**	*indicate*
put s.t. **away**	*put in an appropriate place*
put s.t. **back**	*return to its original place*
put s.o. or s.t. **down**	*stop holding*
put s.t. **off**	*delay*
put s.t. **on**	*cover the body (with clothes/lotion)*
put s.t. **together**	*assemble*
put s.t. **up**	*erect*
set s.t. **up**	1. *prepare for use* 2. *establish (a business)*
shut s.t. **off**	*stop (a machine/light)*
straighten s.o. **out**	*change bad behavior*
straighten s.t. **up**	*make neat*
switch s.t. **on**	*start (a machine/light)*
take s.o. or s.t. **back**	*return*
take s.t. **off/out**	*remove*
take over s.t.	*get control of*
talk s.o. **into**	*persuade*
talk s.t. **over**	*discuss*
tear s.t. **down**	*destroy*
tear s.t. **off**	*remove by tearing*
tear s.t. **up**	*tear into small pieces*
think s.t. **over**	*consider*
think s.t. **up**	*invent*
throw s.t. **away/out**	*put in the trash, discard*
try s.t. **on**	*put clothing on to see if it fits*
try s.t. **out**	*use to see if it works*
turn s.t. **around**	*make it work well*
turn s.o. or s.t. **down**	*reject*
turn s.t. **down**	*lower the volume (a TV/radio)*
turn s.t. **in**	*give work (to a boss/teacher), submit*
turn s.o. or s.t. **into**	*change from one form to another*
turn s.o. **off**	*[slang] destroy interest in*
turn s.t. **off**	*stop (a machine/light), extinguish*
turn s.t. **on**	*start (a machine/light)*
turn s.t. **up**	*make louder (a TV/radio)*
use s.t. **up**	*use completely, consume*
wake s.o. **up**	*awaken*
work s.t. **out**	*solve, find a solution to a problem*
write s.t. **down**	*write on a piece of paper*
write s.t. **up**	*write in a finished form*

5 Intransitive Phrasal Verbs

Phrasal Verb	Meaning
blow up	explode
break down	stop working (a machine)
burn down	burn completely
call back	return a phone call
calm down	become less excited
catch on	1. begin to understand
	2. become popular
clear up	become clear
close down	stop operating
come about	happen
come along	come with, accompany
come by	visit
come back	return
come in	enter
come off	become unattached
come on	do as I say
come out	appear
come up	arise
dress up	wear special clothes
drop in	visit by surprise
drop out	quit
eat out	eat in a restaurant
empty out	empty completely
find out	learn information
fit in	be accepted in a group

Phrasal Verb	Meaning
follow through	complete
fool around	act playful
get ahead	make progress, succeed
get along	have a good relationship
get away	go on vacation
get back	return
get by	survive
get through	finish
get together	meet
get up	get out of bed
give up	quit
go ahead	begin or continue to do something
go away	leave
go on	continue
grow up	become an adult
hang up	end a phone call
keep away	stay at a distance
keep on	continue
keep out	not enter
keep up	go as fast
lie down	recline
light up	illuminate

Phrasal Verb	Meaning
look out	be careful
make up	end a disagreement, reconcile
pass away	die
play around	have fun
run out	not have enough
set out	begin an activity or a project
show up	appear
sign up	register
sit down	take a seat
slip up	make a mistake
stand up	rise
start over	start again
stay up	remain awake
straighten up	make neat
take off	depart (a plane)
tune in	1. watch or listen to (a show)
	2. pay attention
turn up	appear
wake up	stop sleeping
watch out	be careful
work out	1. be resolved
	2. exercise

6 Irregular Plural Nouns

Singular	Plural
half	halves
knife	knives
leaf	leaves
life	lives
loaf	loaves
shelf	shelves
wife	wives

Singular	Plural
man	men
woman	women
child	children
foot	feet
tooth	teeth
goose	geese
mouse	mice

Singular	Plural
deer	deer
fish	fish
sheep	sheep
person	people

7 Non-Count Nouns

REMEMBER: Non-count nouns are singular.

Activities	Courses of Study	Food		Ideas and Feelings	Liquids and Gases	Materials	Very Small Things
baseball	archeology	bread	fruit	anger	air	ash	dust
biking	art	broccoli	ice cream	beauty	blood	clay	pepper
exploring	economics	butter	lettuce	fear	gasoline	cotton	rice
farming	English	cake	meat	freedom	ink	glass	salt
football	geography	cheese	pasta	friendship	milk	gold	sand
golf	history	chicken	pizza	happiness	oil	leather	sugar
hiking	mathematics	chocolate	salad	hate	oxygen	paper	
running	music	coffee	soup	hope	paint	silk	Weather
sailing	photography	corn	spaghetti	loneliness	smoke	silver	fog
soccer	psychology	fat	spinach	love	soda	stone	ice
swimming	science	fish	tea	truth	water	wood	rain
tennis		flour	yogurt			wool	snow
							wind

Names of Categories

clothing	(But: coats, hats, shoes . . .)
equipment	(But: computers, phones, TVs . . .)
food	(But: bananas, eggs, vegetables . . .)
furniture	(But: beds, chairs, lamps, tables . . .)
homework	(But: assignments, pages, problems . . .)
jewelry	(But: bracelets, earrings, necklaces . . .)
mail	(But: letters, packages, postcards . . .)
money	(But: dinars, dollars, euros, pounds . . .)
time	(But: minutes, months, years . . .)
work	(But: jobs, projects, tasks . . .)

Other

(Some non-count nouns don't fit into any list. You must memorize these non-count nouns.)

advice
garbage/trash
help
information
luggage
news
traffic

8 Proper Nouns

REMEMBER: Write proper nouns with a capital letter. Notice that some proper nouns use the definite article *the*.

People
• first names	Anne, Eduardo, Mehmet, Olga, Shao-fen
• family names	Chen, García, Haddad, Smith
• family groups	the Chens, the Garcias, the Haddads, the Smiths
• titles	Doctor, Grandma, President, Professor
• title + names	Mr. García, Professor Smith, Uncle Steve

Places
• continents	Africa, Asia, Australia, Europe, South America
• countries	Argentina, China, France, Nigeria, Turkey, the United States
• provinces/states	Brittany, Ontario, Szechwan, Texas
• cities	Beijing, Istanbul, Rio de Janeiro, Toronto
• streets	the Champs-Elysées, Fifth Avenue
• structures	Harrods, the Louvre, the Petronas Towers
• schools	Midwood High School, Oxford University
• parks	Central Park, the Tivoli Gardens
• mountains	the Andes, the Himalayas, the Pyrenees
• oceans	the Atlantic, the Indian Ocean, the Pacific
• rivers	the Amazon, the Ganges, the Seine
• lakes	Baikal, Erie, Tanganyika, Titicaca
• canals	the Suez Canal, the Panama Canal
• deserts	the Gobi, the Kalahari, the Sahara

Documents
the Bible, the Koran, the Constitution

Languages
Arabic, Chinese, Portuguese, Russian, Spanish

Nationalities
Brazilian, Japanese, Mexican, Saudi, Turkish

Religions
Buddhism, Christianity, Hinduism, Islam, Judaism

Courses
Introduction to Computer Sciences, Math 201

Product Brands
Adidas, Dell, Kleenex, Mercedes, Samsung

Time
• months	January, March, December
• days	Monday, Wednesday, Saturday
• holidays	Bastille Day, Buddha Day, Christmas, Hanukah, New Year's Day, Ramadan

9 Adjectives That Form the Comparative and Superlative in Two Ways

Adjective	Comparative	Superlative
cruel	crueler/more cruel	cruelest/most cruel
deadly	deadlier/more deadly	deadliest/most deadly
friendly	friendlier/more friendly	friendliest/most friendly
handsome	handsomer/more handsome	handsomest/most handsome
happy	happier/more happy	happiest/most happy
likely	likelier/more likely	likeliest/most likely
lively	livelier/more lively	liveliest/most lively
lonely	lonelier/more lonely	loneliest/most lonely
lovely	lovelier/more lovely	loveliest/most lovely
narrow	narrower/more narrow	narrowest/most narrow
pleasant	pleasanter/more pleasant	pleasantest/most pleasant
polite	politer/more polite	politest/most polite
quiet	quieter/more quiet	quietest/most quiet
shallow	shallower/more shallow	shallowest/most shallow
sincere	sincerer/more sincere	sincerest/most sincere
stupid	stupider/more stupid	stupidest/most stupid
true	truer/more true	truest/most true

10   Irregular Comparisons of Adjectives, Adverbs, and Quantifiers

ADJECTIVE	ADVERB	COMPARATIVE	SUPERLATIVE
bad	badly	worse	the worst
far	far	farther/further	the farthest/furthest
good	well	better	the best
little	little	less	the least
many/a lot of	—	more	the most
much*/a lot of	much*/a lot	more	the most

*Much is usually only used in questions and negative statements.

11   Participial Adjectives

-ed	-ing	-ed	-ing	-ed	-ing
alarmed	alarming	disturbed	disturbing	moved	moving
amazed	amazing	embarrassed	embarrassing	paralyzed	paralyzing
amused	amusing	entertained	entertaining	pleased	pleasing
annoyed	annoying	excited	exciting	relaxed	relaxing
astonished	astonishing	exhausted	exhausting	satisfied	satisfying
bored	boring	fascinated	fascinating	shocked	shocking
charmed	charming	frightened	frightening	surprised	surprising
confused	confusing	horrified	horrifying	terrified	terrifying
depressed	depressing	inspired	inspiring	tired	tiring
disappointed	disappointing	interested	interesting	touched	touching
disgusted	disgusting	irritated	irritating	troubled	troubling

12   Order of Adjectives Before a Noun

REMEMBER: We do not usually use more than three adjectives before a noun.

1. Order of Adjectives from Different Categories

Adjectives from different categories usually go in the following order. Do not use a comma between these adjectives.

OPINION	SIZE*	AGE	SHAPE	COLOR	ORIGIN	MATERIAL	NOUNS USED AS ADJECTIVES	
beautiful	enormous	antique	flat	blue	Asian	cotton	college	
comfortable	huge	modern	oval	gray	European	gold	flower	
cozy	little	new	rectangular	green	Greek	plastic	kitchen	+ NOUN
easy	tall	old	round	purple	Pacific	stone	mountain	
expensive	tiny	young	square	red	Southern	wooden	vacation	

*EXCEPTION: Big and small usually go first in a series of adjectives: a small comfortable apartment

EXAMPLES: I bought an **antique Greek flower** vase.   NOT: a ~~Greek antique~~ flower vase
She took some **easy college** courses.   NOT: some ~~college easy~~ courses
We sat at an **enormous round wooden** table.   NOT: a ~~wooden enormous round~~ table

2. Order of Adjectives from the Same Category

Adjectives from the same category do not follow a specific order. Use a comma between these adjectives.

EXAMPLES: We rented a **beautiful, comfortable, cozy** apartment. OR
We rented a **cozy, comfortable, beautiful** apartment. OR
We rented a **comfortable, cozy, beautiful** apartment.

13 Verbs Followed by Gerunds (Base Form of Verb + *-ing*)

acknowledge	can't help	discuss	feel like	limit	prevent	resent
admit	celebrate	dislike	finish	mention	prohibit	resist
advise	consider	endure	forgive	mind *(object to)*	put off	risk
allow	delay	enjoy	go	miss	quit	suggest
appreciate	deny	escape	imagine	permit	recall	support
avoid	detest	excuse	justify	postpone	recommend	tolerate
ban	discontinue	explain	keep *(continue)*	practice	report	understand

14 Verbs Followed by Infinitives (*To* + Base Form of Verb)

agree	can('t) afford	deserve	hurry	neglect	promise	threaten
aim	can't wait	expect	intend	offer	refuse	volunteer
appear	claim	fail	learn	pay	request	wait
arrange	choose	help	manage	plan	rush	want
ask	consent	hesitate	mean *(intend)*	prepare	seem	wish
attempt	decide	hope	need	pretend	struggle	would like

15 Verbs Followed by Gerunds or Infinitives

begin	continue	like	remember*	stop*
can't stand	forget*	love	regret*	try
	hate	prefer	start	

*These verbs can be followed by either a gerund or an infinitive, but there is a big difference in meaning *(see Unit 32)*.

16 Verbs Followed by Object + Infinitive

advise	convince	get	need*	persuade	require	want*
allow	encourage	help*	order	prefer*	teach	warn
ask*	expect*	hire	pay*	promise*	tell	wish
cause	forbid	invite	permit	remind	urge	would like*
choose*	force			request		

*These verbs can also be followed by an infinitive without an object (example: *ask to leave* or *ask someone to leave*).

17 Adjective + Preposition Combinations

accustomed to	bad at	curious about	good at	responsible for	sorry for/about
afraid of	bored with/by	different from	happy about	sad about	surprised at/about/by
amazed at/by	capable of	disappointed with	interested in	safe from	terrible at
angry at	careful of	excited about	nervous about	satisfied with	tired of
ashamed of	certain about	famous for	opposed to	shocked at/by	used to
aware of	concerned about	fond of	pleased about	sick of	worried about
awful at	content with	glad about	ready for	slow at/in	

18 Verb + Preposition Combinations

admit to
advise against
apologize for
approve of

believe in
choose between
complain about
count on

deal with
dream about/of
feel like
insist on

look forward to
object to
pay for
plan on

rely on
resort to
succeed in
talk about

thank someone for
think about
wonder about
worry about

19 Modals and Their Functions

FUNCTION	MODAL OR EXPRESSION	TIME	EXAMPLES
Ability	**can** **can't**	Present	• Sam **can swim**. • He **can't skate**.
	could **couldn't**	Past	• We **could swim** last year. • We **couldn't skate**.
	be able to* **not be able to***	All verb forms	• Lea **is able to run** fast. • She **wasn't able to run** fast last year.
Permission	**can** **can't** **could** **may** **may not**	Present or future	• **Can** I **sit** here? • **Can** I **call** tomorrow? • Yes, you **can**. • No, you **can't**. Sorry. • **Could** he **leave** now? • **May** I **borrow** your pen? • Yes, you **may**. • No, you **may not**. Sorry.
Requests	**can** **can't** **could** **will** **would**	Present or future	• **Can** you **close** the door, please? • Sure, I **can**. • Sorry, I **can't**. • **Could** you please **answer** the phone? • **Will** you **wash** the dishes, please? • **Would** you please **mail** this letter?
Advice	**should** **shouldn't** **ought to** **had better**** **had better not****	Present or future	• You **should study** more. • You **shouldn't miss** class. • We **ought to leave**. • We'**d better go**. • We'**d better not stay**.
Necessity	**have to*** **not have to***	All verb forms	• He **has to go** now. • I **had to go** yesterday. • I **will have to go** soon. • He **doesn't have to go** yet.
	have got to* **must**	Present or future	• He'**s got to leave**! • You **must use** a pen for the test.
Prohibition	**must not** **can't**	Present or future	• You **must not drive** without a license. • You **can't drive** without a license.

*The meaning of this expression is similar to the meaning of a modal. Unlike a modal, it has -s for third-person singular.
**The meaning of this expression is similar to the meaning of a modal. Like a modal, it has no -s for third-person singular.

Function	Modal or Expression	Time	Examples
Possibility	must must not have to*	Present	• This **must be** her house. Her name is on the door. • She **must not be** home. I don't see her car. • She **had to know** him. They went to school together.
	have got to* may may not might might not could	Present or future	• He's **got to be** guilty. We saw him do it. • She **may be** home now. • It **may not rain** tomorrow. • Lee **might be sick** today. • He **might not come** to class. • They **could be** at the library. • It **could rain** tomorrow.
Impossibility	can't	Present or future	• That **can't be** Ana. She left for France yesterday. • It **can't snow** tomorrow. It's going to be too warm.
	couldn't	Present	• He **couldn't be** guilty. He was away . . .

*The meaning of this expression is similar to the meaning of a modal. Unlike a modal, it has -s for third-person singular.

20 Spelling Rules for the Simple Present: Third-Person Singular (*He, She, It*)

1. Add -*s* for most verbs.

work	work**s**
buy	buy**s**
ride	ride**s**
return	return**s**

2. Add -*es* for verbs that end in -*ch*, -*s*, -*sh*, -*x*, or -*z*.

watch	watch**es**
pass	pass**es**
rush	rush**es**
relax	relax**es**
buzz	buzz**es**

3. Change the *y* to *i* and add -*es* when the base form ends in **consonant** + *y*.

study	stud**ies**
hurry	hurr**ies**
dry	dr**ies**

   Do not change the *y* when the base form ends in **vowel** + *y*. Add -*s*.

play	play**s**
enjoy	enjoy**s**

4. A few verbs have **irregular forms**.

be	**is**
do	**does**
go	**goes**
have	**has**

21   Spelling Rules for Base Form of Verb + -ing (Progressive and Gerund)

1. Add -ing to the base form of the verb.

read	read**ing**
stand	stand**ing**

2. If the verb ends in a **silent -e**, drop the final -e and add -ing.

leave	leav**ing**
take	tak**ing**

3. In **one-syllable** verbs, if the last three letters are a consonant-vowel-consonant combination (CVC), double the last consonant and add -ing.

C V C
↓ ↓ ↓
s i t   sit**ting**

C V C
↓ ↓ ↓
p l a n   plan**ning**

Do not double the last consonant in verbs that end in -w, -x, or -y.

sew	sew**ing**
fix	fix**ing**
play	play**ing**

4. In verbs of **two or more syllables** that end in a consonant-vowel-consonant combination, double the last consonant only if the last syllable is stressed.

admít	admit**ting**	*(The last syllable is stressed.)*
whísper	whisper**ing**	*(The last syllable is not stressed, so don't double the -**r**.)*

5. If the verb ends in -ie, change the ie to y before adding -ing.

die	d**ying**
lie	l**ying**

> **STRESS**
> ′ shows main stress.

22   Spelling Rules for Base Form of Verb + -ed (Simple Past and Past Participle of Regular Verbs)

1. If the verb ends in a **consonant**, add -ed.

return	return**ed**
help	help**ed**

2. If the verb ends in -e, add -d.

live	live**d**
create	create**d**
die	die**d**

3. In **one-syllable** verbs, if the last three letters are a consonant-vowel-consonant combination (CVC), double the last consonant and add -ed.

C V C
↓ ↓ ↓
h o p   hop**ped**

C V C
↓ ↓ ↓
g r a b   grab**bed**

Do not double the last consonant in verbs that end in -w, -x, or -y.

bow	bow**ed**
mix	mix**ed**
play	play**ed**

4. In verbs of **two or more syllables** that end in a consonant-vowel-consonant combination, double the last consonant only if the last syllable is stressed.

prefér	prefer**red**	*(The last syllable is stressed.)*
vísit	visit**ed**	*(The last syllable is not stressed, so don't double the -**t**.)*

5. If the verb ends in **consonant** + y, change the y to i and add -ed.

worry	worr**ied**
carry	carr**ied**

6. If the verb ends in **vowel** + y, add -ed. (Do not change the y to i.)

play	play**ed**
annoy	annoy**ed**

EXCEPTIONS:

lay	la**id**
pay	pa**id**
say	sa**id**

23 Spelling Rules for the Comparative *(-er)* and Superlative *(-est)* of Adjectives

1. With **one-syllable** adjectives, add *-er* to form the comparative. Add *-est* to form the superlative.

   | cheap | cheaper | cheapest |
   | bright | brighter | brightest |

2. If the adjective ends in *-e*, add *-r* or *-st*.

   | nice | nicer | nicest |

3. If the adjective ends in **consonant** + *y*, change *y* to *i* before you add *-er* or *-est*.

   | pretty | prettier | prettiest |

   EXCEPTION:

   | shy | shyer | shyest |

4. If a one-syllable adjective ends in a consonant-vowel-consonant combination (CVC), double the last consonant before adding *-er* or *-est*.

   C V C
   ↓ ↓ ↓
   | b i g | bigger | biggest |

   Do not double the consonant in adjectives ending in *-w* or *-y*.

   | slow | slower | slowest |
   | gray | grayer | grayest |

24 Spelling Rules for Adverbs Ending in *-ly*

1. Add *-ly* to the corresponding adjective.

nice	nicely
quiet	quietly
beautiful	beautifully

2. If the adjective ends in **consonant** + *y*, change the *y* to *i* before adding *-ly*.

   | easy | easily |

3. If the adjective ends in *-le*, drop the *e* and add *-y*.

   | possible | possibly |

   Do not drop the *e* for other adjectives ending in *-e*.

   | extreme | extremely |

   EXCEPTION:

   | true | truly |

4. If the adjective ends in *-ic*, add *-ally*.

   | basic | basically |
   | fantastic | fantastically |

25 Spelling Rules for Regular Plural Nouns

1. Add *-s* to most nouns.

book	books
table	tables
cup	cups

2. Add *-es* to nouns that end in *-ch*, *-s*, *-sh*, or *-x*.

watch	watches
bus	buses
dish	dishes
box	boxes

3. Add *-s* to nouns that end in **vowel** + *y*.

   | day | days |
   | key | keys |

4. Change the *y* to *i* and add *-es* to nouns that end in **consonant** + *y*.

baby	babies
city	cities
strawberry	strawberries

5. Add *-s* to nouns that end in **vowel** + *o*.

radio	radios
video	videos
zoo	zoos

6. Add *-es* to nouns that end in **consonant** + *o*.

   | potato | potatoes |
   | tomato | tomatoes |

   EXCEPTIONS: kilo—kilos, photo—photos, piano—pianos

26 Contractions with Verb Forms

1. SIMPLE PRESENT, PRESENT PROGRESSIVE, AND IMPERATIVE

Contractions with *Be*

I am	=	I'm
you are	=	you're
he is	=	he's
she is	=	she's
it is	=	it's
we are	=	we're
you are	=	you're
they are	=	they're

SIMPLE PRESENT	**PRESENT PROGRESSIVE**
I'm a student.	I'm **studying** here.
He's my teacher.	He's **teaching** verbs.
We're from Canada.	We're **living** here.

I am not	=	I'm **not**		
you are not	=	you're **not**	OR	you **aren't**
he is not	=	he's **not**	OR	he **isn't**
she is not	=	she's **not**	OR	she **isn't**
it is not	=	it's **not**	OR	it **isn't**
we are not	=	we're **not**	OR	we **aren't**
you are not	=	you're **not**	OR	you **aren't**
they are not	=	they're **not**	OR	they **aren't**

SIMPLE PRESENT	**PRESENT PROGRESSIVE**
She's **not** sick.	She's **not** reading.
He **isn't** late.	He **isn't** coming.
We **aren't** twins.	We **aren't** leaving.
They're **not** here.	They're **not** playing.

Contractions with *Do*

do not	=	**don't**
does not	=	**doesn't**

SIMPLE PRESENT	**IMPERATIVE**
They **don't live** here.	**Don't run!**
It **doesn't snow** much.	

2. SIMPLE PAST AND PAST PROGRESSIVE

Contractions with *Be*

was not	=	**wasn't**
were not	=	**weren't**

SIMPLE PAST	**PAST PROGRESSIVE**
He **wasn't** a poet.	He **wasn't** singing.
They **weren't** twins.	They **weren't** sleeping.
We **didn't** see her.	

Contractions with *Do*

did not	=	**didn't**

3. FUTURE

Contractions with *Will*

I will	=	I'll
you will	=	you'll
he will	=	he'll
she will	=	she'll
it will	=	it'll
we will	=	we'll
you will	=	you'll
they will	=	they'll

will not	=	**won't**

FUTURE WITH *WILL*
I'll **take** the train.
It'll **be** faster that way.
We'll **go** together.
He **won't come** with us.
They **won't miss** the train.

Contractions with *Be going to*

I am going to	=	I'm going to
you are going to	=	you're going to
he is going to	=	he's going to
she is going to	=	she's going to
it is going to	=	it's going to
we are going to	=	we're going to
you are going to	=	you're going to
they are going to	=	they're going to

FUTURE WITH *BE GOING TO*
I'm **going to buy** tickets tomorrow.
She's **going to call** you.
It's **going to rain** soon.
We're **going to drive** to Boston.
They're **going to crash!**

4. PRESENT PERFECT AND PRESENT PERFECT PROGRESSIVE

Contractions with *Have*

I have	=	I**'ve**
you have	=	you**'ve**
he has	=	he**'s**
she has	=	she**'s**
it has	=	it**'s**
we have	=	we**'ve**
you have	=	you**'ve**
they have	=	they**'ve**
have not	=	**haven't**
has not	=	**hasn't**

You**'ve** already **read** that page.
We**'ve been writing** for an hour.
She**'s been** to Africa three times.
It**'s been raining** since yesterday.
We **haven't seen** any elephants yet.
They **haven't been living** here long.

5. MODALS AND SIMILAR EXPRESSIONS

cannot or can not	=	**can't**
could not	=	**couldn't**
should not	=	**shouldn't**
had better	=	**'d better**
would prefer	=	**'d prefer**
would rather	=	**'d rather**

She **can't dance**.
We **shouldn't go**.
They**'d better decide**.
I**'d prefer** coffee.
I**'d rather take** the bus.

27 Capitalization and Punctuation Rules

	USE FOR . . .	EXAMPLES
capital letter	• the pronoun *I* • proper nouns • the first word of a sentence	• Tomorrow **I** will be here at 2:00. • His name is **Karl**. He lives in **Germany**. • **When** does the train leave? **At** 2:00.
apostrophe (')	• possessive nouns • contractions	• Is that **Marta's** coat? • **That's** not hers. **It's** mine.
comma (,)	• after items in a list • before sentence connectors *and*, *but*, *or*, and *so* • after the first part of a sentence that begins with *because* • after the first part of a sentence that begins with a preposition • after the first part of a sentence that begins with a time clause or an *if* clause	• He bought **apples, pears, oranges,** and **bananas**. • They watched TV, **and** she played video games. • *Because* it's raining, we're not walking to the office. • *Across from* the post office, there's a good restaurant. • *After he arrived*, we ate dinner. • *If it rains*, we won't go.
exclamation mark (!)	• at the end of a sentence to show surprise or a strong feeling	• You're here! That's great! • Stop! A car is coming!
period (.)	• at the end of a statement	• Today is Wednesday.
question mark (?)	• at the end of a question	• What day is today?

28 Pronunciation Table

These are the pronunciation symbols used in this text. Listen to the pronunciation of the key words.

VOWELS				CONSONANTS			
Symbol	Key Word	Symbol	Key Word	Symbol	Key Word	Symbol	Key Word
i	beat, feed	ə	banana, among	p	pack, happy	ʃ	ship, machine, station,
ɪ	bit, did	ɚ	shirt, murder	b	back, rubber		special, discussion
eɪ	date, paid	aɪ	bite, cry, buy, eye	t	tie	ʒ	measure, vision
ɛ	bet, bed	aʊ	about, how	d	die	h	hot, who
æ	bat, bad	ɔɪ	voice, boy	k	came, key, quick	m	men
ɑ	box, odd, father	ɪr	beer	g	game, guest	n	sun, know, pneumonia
ɔ	bought, dog	ɛr	bare	tʃ	church, nature, watch	ŋ	sung, ringing
oʊ	boat, road	ɑr	bar	dʒ	judge, general, major	w	wet, white
ʊ	book, good	ɔr	door	f	fan, photograph	l	light, long
u	boot, food, student	ʊr	tour	v	van	r	right, wrong
ʌ	but, mud, mother			θ	thing, breath	y	yes, use, music
				ð	then, breathe	t̬	butter, bottle
				s	sip, city, psychology		
				z	zip, please, goes		

29 Pronunciation Rules for the Simple Present: Third-Person Singular (He, She, It)

1. The third-person singular in the simple present always ends in the letter -s. There are, however, three different pronunciations for the final sound of the third-person singular.

/s/	/z/	/ɪz/
talks	loves	dances

2. The final sound is pronounced /s/ after the voiceless sounds /p/, /t/, /k/, and /f/.

top	tops
get	gets
take	takes
laugh	laughs

3. The final sound is pronounced /z/ after the voiced sounds /b/, /d/, /g/, /v/, /m/, /n/, /ŋ/, /l/, /r/, and /ð/.

describe	describes
spend	spends
hug	hugs
live	lives
seem	seems
remain	remains
sing	sings
tell	tells
lower	lowers
bathe	bathes

4. The final sound is pronounced /z/ after all vowel sounds.

agree	agrees
try	tries
stay	stays
know	knows

5. The final sound is pronounced /ɪz/ after the sounds /s/, /z/, /ʃ/, /ʒ/, /tʃ/, and /dʒ/. /ɪz/ adds a syllable to the verb.

miss	misses
freeze	freezes
rush	rushes
massage	massages
watch	watches
judge	judges

6. Do and say have a change in vowel sound.

do	/du/	does	/dʌz/
say	/seɪ/	says	/sɛz/

30 Pronunciation Rules for the Simple Past and Past Participle of Regular Verbs

1. The regular simple past and past participle always end in the letter -d. There are three different pronunciations for the final sound of the regular simple past and past participle.

/t/	/d/	/ɪd/
raced	lived	attended

2. The final sound is pronounced /t/ after the voiceless sounds /p/, /k/, /f/, /s/, /ʃ/, and /tʃ/.

hop	hopped
work	worked
laugh	laughed
address	addressed
publish	published
watch	watched

3. The final sound is pronounced /d/ after the voiced sounds /b/, /g/, /v/, /z/, /ʒ/, /dʒ/, /m/, /n/, /ŋ/, /l/, /r/, and /ð/.

rub	rubbed
hug	hugged
live	lived
surprise	surprised
massage	massaged
change	changed
rhyme	rhymed
return	returned
bang	banged
enroll	enrolled
appear	appeared
bathe	bathed

4. The final sound is pronounced /d/ after all **vowel sounds**.

agree	agreed
die	died
play	played
enjoy	enjoyed
snow	snowed

5. The final sound is pronounced /ɪd/ after /t/ and /d/. /ɪd/ adds a syllable to the verb.

start	started
decide	decided

GLOSSARY OF GRAMMAR TERMS

action verb   A verb that describes an action.
- *Alicia **ran** home.*

adjective   A word that describes a noun or pronoun.
- *That's a **great** idea.*
- *It's **wonderful**.*

adverb   A word that describes a verb, an adjective, or another adverb.
- *She drives **carefully**.*
- *She's a **very** good driver.*
- *She drives **really** well.*

adverb of frequency   An adverb that describes how often something happens.
- *We **always** watch that program.*

adverb of manner   An adverb that describes how someone does something or how something happens. It usually ends in *-ly*.
- *He sings **beautifully**.*

adverb of time   An adverb that describes when something happens.
- *We'll see you **soon**.*

affirmative   A statement or answer meaning *Yes*.
- *He **works**. (affirmative statement)*
- ***Yes**, he **does**. (affirmative short answer)*

article   A word that goes before a noun. The indefinite articles are *a* and *an*.
- *I ate **a** sandwich and **an** apple.*

The definite article is *the*.
- *I didn't like **the** sandwich. **The** apple was good.*

auxiliary verb   (also called **helping verb**) A verb used with a main verb. *Be*, *do*, and *have* are often auxiliary verbs. Modals (*can, should, may . . .*) are also auxiliary verbs.
- *I **am** exercising right now.*
- ***Does** he exercise every day?*
- *She **should** exercise every day.*
- *They**'ve** learned how to swim.*
- *They **can** swim very well.*
- *We **may** go to the pool tomorrow.*

base form   The simple form of a verb without any endings (*-s, -ed, -ing*) or other changes.
- ***be, have, go, drive***

capital letter   The large form of a letter. The capital letters are: *A, B, C, D, . . .*
- ***A**licia lives in the **U**nited **S**tates.*

clause   A group of words that has a subject and a verb. A sentence can have one or more clauses.
- ***We are leaving now.** (one clause)*
- ***When he calls, we'll leave.** (two clauses)*

common noun   A word for a person, place, or thing (but not the name of the person, place, or thing).
- *Teresa lives in a **house** near the **beach**.*

comparative   The form of an adjective or adverb that shows the difference between two people, places, or things.
- *Alain is **shorter** than Brendan. (adjective)*
- *Brendan runs **faster** than Alain. (adverb)*

comparison   A statement that shows the difference between two people, places, or things. A comparison can use comparative adjectives and comparative adverbs. It can also use *as . . . as*.
- *Alain is **shorter than** Brendan.*
- *Alain isn't **as tall as** Brendan.*
- *He runs **faster than** Brendan.*

consonant   A letter of the alphabet. The consonants are:
- ***b, c, d, f, g, h, j, k, l, m, n, p, q, r, s, t, v, w, x, y, z***

continuous   See **progressive**.

contraction   A short form of a word or words. An apostrophe (') replaces the missing letter or letters.
- ***she's** = she is*
- ***hasn't** = has not*
- ***can't** = cannot*
- ***won't** = will not*

count noun   A noun that you can count. It has a singular and a plural form.
- *one **book**, two **books***

definite article   *the*
This article goes before a noun that refers to a specific person, place, or thing.
- *Please bring me **the book** on the table. I'm almost finished reading it.*

dependent clause   (also called **subordinate clause**) A clause that needs a main clause for its meaning.
- ***When I get home**, I'll call you.*

direct object   A noun or pronoun that receives the action of a verb.
- *Marta kicked **the ball**. I saw **her**.*

formal   Language used in business situations or with adults you do not know.
- *Good afternoon, Mr. Rivera. Please have a seat.*

gerund   A noun formed with verb + *-ing*. It can be the subject or object of a sentence.
- ***Swimming** is great exercise.*
- *I enjoy **swimming**.*

helping verb   See **auxiliary verb**.

imperative   A sentence that gives a command or instructions.
- ***Hurry!***
- ***Don't touch that!***

indefinite article   *a* or *an*
These articles go before a noun that does not refer to a specific person, place, or thing.
- *Can you bring me **a book**? I'm looking for something to read.*

indefinite past   Past time, but not a specific time. It is often used with the present perfect.
- *I'**ve** already **seen** that movie.*

indefinite pronoun   A pronoun such as *someone, something, anyone, anything, anywhere, no one, nothing, nowhere, everyone,* and *everything.* An indefinite pronoun does not refer to a specific person, place, or thing.
- ***Someone** called you last night.*
- *Did **anything** happen?*

indirect object   A noun or pronoun (often a person) that receives something as the result of the action of the verb.
- *I told **John** the story.*
- *He gave **me** some good advice.*

infinitive   *to* + base form of the verb
- *I want **to leave** now.*

infinitive of purpose   *(in order) to* + base form
This form gives the reason for an action.
- *I go to school **(in order) to learn** English.*

informal   Language used with family, friends, and children.
- *Hi, Pete. Sit down.*

information question   See **wh- question**.

inseparable phrasal verb   A phrasal verb whose parts must stay together.
- *We **ran into** Tomás at the supermarket.*

intransitive verb   A verb that does not have an object.
- *We **fell**.*

irregular   A word that does not change its form in the usual way.
- ***good → well***
- ***bad → worse***

irregular verb   A verb that does not form its past with *-ed*.
- ***leave → left***

main clause   A clause that can stand alone as a sentence.
- *When I get home, **I'll call you**.*

main verb   A verb that describes an action or state. It is often used with an auxiliary verb.
- *She **calls** every day.*
- *Jared is **calling**.*
- *He'll **call** again later.*
- *Does he **call** every day?*

modal   A type of auxiliary verb. It goes before a main verb or stands alone as a short answer. It expresses ideas such as ability, advice, obligation, permission, and possibility. *Can, could, will, would, may, might, should, ought to,* and *must* are modals.
- ***Can** you swim?*
- *Yes, I **can**.*
- *You really **should** learn to swim.*

negative   A statement or answer meaning *No*.
- *He **doesn't** work. (negative statement)*
- ***No**, he **doesn't**. (negative short answer)*

non-action verb (also called **stative verb**) A verb that does not describe an action. It describes such things as thoughts, feelings, and senses.

- I **remember** that word.
- Chris **loves** ice cream.
- It **tastes** great.

non-count noun A noun that you usually do not count (air, water, rice, love, . . .). It has only a singular form.

- The **rice** is delicious.

noun A word for a person, place, or thing.

- My **sister**, **Anne**, works in an **office**.
- She uses a **computer**.

object A noun or pronoun that receives the action of a verb. Sometimes a verb has two objects.

- She wrote **a letter to Tom**.
- She wrote **him a letter**.

object pronoun A pronoun (me, you, him, her, it, us, them) that receives the action of a verb.

- I gave **her** a book.
- I gave **it** to **her**.

paragraph A group of sentences, usually about one topic.

participial adjective An adjective that ends in -ing or -ed. It comes from a verb.

- That's an **interesting** book.
- She's **interested** in the book.

particle A word that looks like a preposition and combines with a main verb to form a phrasal verb. It often changes the meaning of the main verb.

- He looked the word **up**.
  (He looked for the meaning in the dictionary.)
- I ran **into** my teacher.
  (I met my teacher accidentally.)

past participle A verb form (verb + -ed). It can also be irregular. It is used to form the present perfect. It can also be an adjective.

- We've **lived** here since April.
- She's **interested** in math.

phrasal verb (also called **two-word verb**) A verb that has two parts (verb + particle). The meaning is often different from the meaning of its separate parts.

- He **grew up** in Texas. (became an adult)
- His parents **brought** him **up** to be honest. (raised)

phrase A group of words that forms a unit but does not have a main verb. Many phrases give information about time or place.

- **Last year**, we were living **in Canada**.

plural A form that means two or more.

- There **are** three **people** in the restaurant.
- **They are** eating dinner.
- **We** saw **them**.

possessive Nouns, pronouns, or adjectives that show a relationship or show that someone owns something.

- Zach is **Megan's** brother. (possessive noun)
- Is that car **his**? (possessive pronoun)
- That's **his** car. (possessive adjective)

predicate The part of a sentence that has the main verb. It tells what the subject is doing or describes the subject.

- My sister **works for a travel agency**.

preposition A word that goes before a noun or a pronoun to show time, place, or direction.

- I went **to** the bank **on** Monday. It's **next to** my office.
- I told him **about** it.

Prepositions also go before nouns, pronouns, and gerunds in expressions with verbs and adjectives.

- We rely **on** him.
- She's accustomed **to** getting up early.

progressive (also called **continuous**) The verb form be + verb + -ing. It focuses on the continuation (not the completion) of an action.

- She**'s reading** the paper.
- We **were watching** TV when you called.

pronoun A word used in place of a noun.

- That's my brother. You met **him** at my party.

proper noun A noun that is the name of a person, place, or thing. It begins with a capital letter.

- **Maria** goes to **Central High School**.
- It's on **High Street**.

punctuation Marks used in writing (period, comma, . . .). They make the meaning clear. For example, a period (**.**) shows the end of a sentence. It also shows that the sentence is a statement, not a question.

quantifier A word or phrase that shows an amount (but not an exact amount). It often comes before a noun.

- *Josh bought **a lot of** books last year, but he only read **a few**.*
- *He doesn't have **much** time.*

question See **yes/no question** and **wh- question**.

question word See **wh- word**.

reciprocal pronoun A pronoun *(each other or one another)* that shows that the subject and object of a sentence refer to the same people and that these people have a two-way relationship.

- *Megan and Jason have known **each other** since high school.*
- *All the students worked with **one another** on the project.*

reflexive pronoun A pronoun *(myself, yourself, himself, herself, itself, ourselves, yourselves, themselves)* that shows that the subject and the object of the sentence refer to the same people or things.

- *He looked at **himself** in the mirror.*
- *They enjoyed **themselves** at the party.*

regular A word that changes its form in the usual way.

- ***play** —> play**ed***
- ***fast** —> fast**er***
- ***quick** —> quick**ly***

sentence A group of words that has a subject and a main verb. It begins with a capital letter and ends with a period (**.**), question mark (**?**), or exclamation point (**!**).

- ***Computers are** very useful.*

EXCEPTION: In imperative sentences, the subject is *you*. We do not usually say or write the subject in imperative sentences.

- ***Call** her now!*

separable phrasal verb A phrasal verb whose parts can separate.

- *Tom **looked** the word **up** in a dictionary.*
- *He **looked** it **up**.*

short answer An answer to a yes/no question.

- **A:** *Did you call me last night?*
  B: *No, I didn't.* OR ***No.***

singular one

- *They have **a sister**.*
- *She works in **a hospital**.*

statement A sentence that gives information. In writing, it ends in a period.

- *Today is Monday.*

stative verb See **non-action verb**.

subject The person, place, or thing that the sentence is about.

- ***Ms. Chen** teaches English.*
- ***Her class** is interesting.*

subject pronoun A pronoun that shows the person or thing *(I, you, he, she, it, we, they)* that the sentence is about.

- ***I** read a lot.*
- ***She** reads a lot too.*

subordinate clause See **dependent clause**.

superlative The form of an adjective or adverb that is used to compare a person, place, or thing to a group of people, places, or things.

- *Cindi is **the best** dancer in the group.* (adjective)
- *She dances **the most gracefully**.* (adverb)

tense The form of a verb that shows the time of the action.

- **simple present:** *Fabio **talks** to his friend every day.*
- **simple past:** *Fabio **talked** to his teacher yesterday.*

third-person singular The pronouns *he, she,* and *it* or a singular noun. In the simple present, the third-person-singular verb ends in -s.

- ***Tomás works** in an office.* (Tomás = he)

time clause A clause that begins with a time word such as *when, before, after, while,* or *as soon as*.

- *I'll call you **when I get home**.*

time expression A phrase that describes when something happened or will happen.

- *We saw Tomás **last week**.*
- *He'll graduate **next year**.*

transitive verb A verb that has an object.

- *She **paints** beautiful pictures.*

two-word verb See **phrasal verb**.

verb   A word that describes what the subject of the sentence does, thinks, feels, senses, or owns.

- They **run** two miles every day.
- I **agree** with you.
- She **loved** that movie.
- We **smell** smoke.
- He **has** a new camera.

vowel   A letter of the alphabet. The vowels are:

- **a, e, i, o, u**.

wh- question   (also called **information question**) A question that begins with a *wh-* word. You answer a *wh-* question with information.

- **A:** **Where** are you going?
  B: *To the store.*

wh- word   (also called **question word**) A word such as *who, what, when, where, which, why, how,* and *how much*. It often begins a *wh-* question.

- **Who** is that?
- **What** did you see?
- **When** does the movie usually start?
- **How** long is it?

yes/no question   A question that begins with a form of *be* or an auxiliary verb. You can answer a *yes/no* question with *yes* or *no.*

- **A:** **Are** you a student?
  B: **Yes**, I am. OR **No**, I'm not.
- **A:** **Do** you come here often?
  B: **Yes**, I do. OR **No**, I don't.

UNIT REVIEW ANSWER KEY

Note: In this answer key, where a short or contracted form is given, the full or long form is also correct (unless the purpose of the exercise is to practice the short or contracted forms).

UNIT 1

A
1. are you taking
2. don't
3. often speak
4. 's talking
5. Do

B
1. are . . . doing
2. 'm . . . playing
3. Do . . . want
4. don't eat
5. 'm feeling OR feel
6. looks
7. doesn't taste
8. are . . . shouting
9. Are
10. talk

C I live in Qatar, but right now I ~~stay~~ *'m staying* in Wisconsin. I'm studying English here. I ~~have~~ *'m having* a good time this summer, but in some ways it's a pretty strange experience. Summer in Wisconsin ~~feel~~ *feels* like winter in Qatar! Every weekend, I go to the beach with some classmates, but I ~~go never~~ *never go* into the water—it's too cold! I'm ~~enjoy~~ *enjoying* my time here though, and my culture shock is going away fast.

UNIT 2

A
1. b
2. c
3. a
4. c
5. a
6. c

B
1. Did . . . go
2. called
3. didn't answer
4. Yes . . . did
5. went
6. did . . . see
7. saw
8. didn't like

C The poet Elizabeth Alexander was born in New York City, but she didn't ~~grew~~ *grow* up there. Her father ~~taked~~ *took* a job with the government, and her family moved to Washington, D.C. As a child, she ~~have~~ *had* a loving family. Her parents were active in the civil rights movement, and Elizabeth ~~gots~~ *got* interested in African-American history. In her first book, she wrote about important African leaders. She met Barack Obama at the University of Chicago. They both ~~teached~~ *taught* there in the 1990s. On January 20, 2009, she ~~reads~~ *read* a poem at President Obama's inauguration.

UNIT 3

A
1. Did . . . hear
2. saw
3. turned
4. Were . . . driving OR Did . . . drive
5. was working
6. was raining
7. was finishing
8. was leaving OR left
9. stopped
10. looked

B
1. . . . Danielle was watching TV, I was studying.
2. I closed my book . . . the show *Dr. Davis* came on.
3. Dr. Davis was talking to his patient when the electricity went off.
4. . . . the electricity went off, we lit some candles.
5. We were talking (OR We talked) about a lot of things . . . we were waiting for the lights to come on.

C When I turned on the TV for the first episode of *Dr. Davis*, I ~~unpacked~~ *was unpacking* boxes in my freshman dorm room. I stopped and watched for an hour. After that, I ~~wasn't missing~~ *didn't miss* a single show while I was attending school. While I was solving math problems, Dr. Davis was solving medical mysteries. And *just* ~~while~~ *when* my dumb boyfriend broke up with me, the beautiful Dr. Grace left Davis for the third time. I even watched the show from the hospital when I ~~was breaking~~ *broke* my leg. The show just ended. I was sad when I ~~see~~ *saw* the last episode, but I think it's time for some real life!

UNIT 4

A
1. did
2. used to
3. Did
4. play
5. used to
6. used to

B
1. used to look
2. used to have
3. used to let OR would let
4. wouldn't get
5. used to play
6. used to practice OR would practice
7. Did . . . use to go
8. used to love

C Celine Dion was born in Quebec, Canada. When she ~~used to be~~ *was* five, her family opened a club, and Celine used to ~~sang~~ *sing* there. People from the community ~~would to come~~ *would come* to hear her perform.

At the age of 12, Celine wrote her first songs. Her
family used to record *recorded* one and sent it to a manager.
At first Celine used to singing *sing* only in French. After
she learned English, she became known in more
countries. As a child, Celine Dion would be *was* poor, but
she had a dream—to be a singer. Today she is one
of the most successful singers in the history of pop
music.

UNIT 5

A 1. h   3. f   5. g   7. c
   2. d   4. a   6. e   8. b

B 1. work   4. did she leave   6. is her boss
   2. did she   5. start   7. does
   3. told

C **A:** What did you did *do* with my math book? I can't
find it.

B: Nothing. Where you saw *did you see* it last?

A: In the living room. I was watching *Lost* on TV.
What *What's* Zack's phone number?

B: I'm not sure. Why you *Why do you* want to know?

A: He took the class last year. I'll call him. Maybe
he still has his book.

B: Good idea. What time does he gets *get* out of
work?

UNIT 6

A 1. 're going   3. is going to   5. is giving
   2. 'll   4. 's going to

B 1. are . . . going to do OR are . . . doing
   2. 're going to feel OR you'll feel
   3. is going to arrive OR will arrive
   4. is going to get
   5. 'll see
   6. 's going to cry
   7. does . . . start OR will . . . start OR is . . . starting
   8. Is . . . going to call OR Will . . . call OR Is . . .
calling
   9. won't forget OR isn't going to forget
   10. 'll speak

C 1. When will Ed gets *get* home tomorrow?
   2. The movie starts at 7:30, so I think I go. *'ll go* OR *'m going to go*
   3. Do you want to go with me, or are you study *studying* OR *going to study*
tonight?
   4. What you are *are you* going to do next weekend?
   5. I'm going *to* be home all day.

UNIT 7

A 1. graduate   4. Will   6. until
   2. finish   5. learning   7. Are you
   3. When

B 1. works OR 's working
   2. won't register OR isn't going to register
   3. 'll spend OR 's going to spend
   4. studies OR is studying
   5. won't look OR isn't going to look
   6. graduates
   7. 'll take OR 's going to take

C **A:** Are you going to call Phil when we'll *we* finish
dinner?

B: No, I'm too tired. I'm just going to watch TV
after *before* I go to sleep.

A: Before I wash the dishes, I'm going ^ *to* answer
some emails.

B: I'll help you, as soon as I'll drink *I drink* my coffee.

A: No rush. I have a lot of emails. I won't be ready
to clean up until you'll *you* finish.

UNIT 8

A 1. for   4. for   6. For
   2. since   5. Since   7. Since
   3. for

B 1. 've been   4. 've competed
   2. haven't had   5. 's won
   3. has loved   6. haven't seen

C 1. Marta and Tomás lived *have lived* here since they got
married in 1998.
   2. Tomás has been a professional tennis player
since he has come *came* to this country.
   3. He has won several competitions for *since* then.
   4. Since I have known Tomás, he had *has had* three
different coaches.
   5. I haven't see *seen* Marta for several weeks.
   6. She have *has* been in Brazil since April 1.
   7. I've wanted to visit Brazil since *for* years, but I
haven't had any vacation time since I got this
new job.

UNIT 9

A 1. already   3. yet   5. told
    2. still   4. Has   6. yet

B 1. has already graduated OR has graduated already
    2. still haven't had
    3. Have . . . delivered . . . yet
    4. still hasn't set
    5. 's already started OR 's started already
    6. still haven't arrived
    7. has arrived yet
    8. have . . . met . . . yet

C **A:** I can't believe it's the 10th already. And we still *haven't* ~~didn't~~ finished planning.

    B: We haven't checked the guest list for a while. Who hasn't *replied* ~~replies~~ yet?

    A: Sally hasn't called about the invitation ~~already~~ *yet*. I wonder if she's coming.

    B: Maybe she just forgot. Have you called ~~yet her~~ *her yet*?

    A: I've already ~~call~~ *called* her a couple of times. She *still hasn't* ~~hasn't still~~ called back.

UNIT 10

A 1. ever   3. been   5. lately
    2. just   4. Has   6. has

B 1. Have . . . seen   5. 've . . . wanted
    2. 've . . . been   6. has taken
    3. has . . . read   7. 's . . . shown
    4. 's given

C 1. I've ~~lately~~ traveled a lot *lately*.
    2. We've ~~returned just~~ *just returned* from an African safari.
    3. I've never ~~have~~ *had* so much fun before.
    4. Have you ~~been ever~~ *ever been* on a safari?
    5. No, but I've recently ~~went~~ *been* OR *gone* hot-air ballooning.
    6. My wife and I ~~has~~ *have* decided to go next summer.
    7. I've ~~saw~~ *seen* a lot of great photos on a hot-air ballooning website.

UNIT 11

A 1. When did you move to Vancouver?
    2. How long have you been an engineer?
    3. Did you work in Vancouver for a long time?
    4. When did you get married?
    5. How many years have you lived in Singapore?
    6. Has your wife lived in Singapore long?

B 1. 've been   6. was
    2. saw   7. has learned
    3. 've crossed   8. ordered
    4. haven't seen   9. didn't learn
    5. took

C Tina and Ken lived apart for a while, but then Tina found a job in Singapore. She ~~has moved~~ *moved* there last month. Here are some of their thoughts:

KEN: I'm so glad Tina is finally here. Last year ~~has been~~ *was* the hardest time of my life.

TINA: Before I got here, I didn't ~~understood~~ *understand* Ken's experiences. But I ~~was~~ *'ve been* in culture shock since I ~~arrive~~ *arrived*, and I'm learning a new job too! Now I know what a rough time Ken had at first.

UNIT 12

A 1. has written   4. has read
    2. has chosen   5. 've had
    3. 've been reading   6. 've taken

B 1. have . . . lived (OR been living)
    2. 've been
    3. 've been enjoying
    4. Have . . . read
    5. has . . . written
    6. 've been trying
    7. 've been studying
    8. has . . . been
    9. Has . . . chosen

C 1. Janet ~~hasn't been writing~~ *hasn't written* a word since she sat down at her computer.
    2. Since I've known Dan, he's ~~been having~~ *'s had* five different jobs.
    3. I've ~~drunk~~ *been drinking* coffee all morning. I think I've ~~been having~~ *had* at least 10 cups!
    4. We've been ~~lived~~ *living* here for several years, but we're moving next month.

UNIT 13

A 1. a 2. c 3. b 4. c 5. b

B 1. couldn't stay 6. can jump
2. could kick 7. can stay
3. couldn't keep 8. can't perform
4. was able to win 9. can start
5. can . . . dance 10. can raise

C A: I can't ~~no~~ see the stage. The man in front of me is very tall.

B: Let's change seats. You ^'ll be able to see from this seat.

A: Thanks. I don't want to miss anything. I ~~no can~~ *can't* believe what a great dancer Acosta is.

B: I know. He was so good as a kid that he ~~could~~ *was able to* win a breakdancing contest before he was nine.

A: I didn't know he was a street dancer! Well, I'm glad you were ~~abled~~ *able* to get tickets.

UNIT 14

A 1. come 3. borrow 5. please shut
2. Do 4. if

B 1. I borrow a pen
2. my sister leave
3. if I open a window
4. my friend and I (OR me and a friend OR we) come early
5. I ask a question

C 1. A: Do you mind if I ~~changed~~ *change* the date of our next meeting?
Not at all. OR *No, I don't.* OR *No problem.*
B: ~~Yes, I do.~~ When would you like to meet?

2. A: Could I ~~calling~~ *call* you tonight?
B: Sorry, but you ~~couldn't~~ *can't*. I won't be home.

3. A: Mom, ~~I may~~ *may I* have some more ice cream?
B: No you ~~mayn't~~ *may not*. You've already had a lot. You'll get sick.

4. A: Do you mind if my son ~~turn~~ *turns* on the TV?
B: ~~Not at all.~~ *Sorry, (but)* I can't study with the TV on.

5. A: Can my sister ~~borrows~~ *borrow* your bike?
B: Could I ~~letting~~ *let* you know tomorrow?
A: Sure. No problem.

UNIT 15

A 1. turning off 4. No problem
2. I'm sorry, I can't 5. pick
3. please text 6. I'd be glad to

B 1. lending me five dollars
2. you drive me to school
3. you (please) explain this sentence to me (please)
4. you carry this suitcase for me
5. you (please) distribute the report (please)
6. walking the dog tonight

C

JASON: Hi Tessa. It's Jason. Could you ~~taking~~ *take* some photos of the game today?

TESSA: Sorry, Jason, but I ~~couldn't~~ *can't*. My camera is broken. Maybe Jeri can help.

JASON: Hi Jeri. Would you ~~came~~ *come* to the game today? I need someone to take photos.

JERI: Jason, ~~can~~ *would* you mind calling me back in a few minutes? I'm busy right now.

JASON: Sorry, Jeri, I can't, but I'll email you. Would you ~~give me please~~ *please give me* your email address?

JERI: *Sure* OR *No problem* OR *Of course* OR *Certainly* ~~Not at all.~~ It's Rainbows@local.net.

JERI: Hi Jason, it's Jeri. I'm sending you those photos. ~~You could~~ *Could you* call me when you get them?

JASON: Thanks, Jeri. The photos are great. Now will ^*you* teach me how to put them on Facebook?

UNIT 16

A 1. a 2. c 3. a 4. b 5. a

B 1. Should . . . call 6. Yes . . . should
2. 'd better do 7. Should . . . do
3. should . . . contact 8. No . . . shouldn't
4. ought to call 9. 'd better wait
5. Should . . . ask

C 1. Vanessa should ~~gets~~ *get* a new computer. She should ~~no~~ *not* keep her old one.

2. She'd better not ~~buying~~ *buy* the first one she sees.

3. She ought ^*to* read reviews before she decides on one.

4. ~~Ought~~ *Should* she get one online or should she ~~goes~~ *go* to a store?

UNIT 17

A 1. a 2. b 3. c 4. c 5. a

B 1. Music is 4. Clothing shows
2. photographs show 5. Food goes
3. Money makes

C One night in ~~june~~ *June* 1,400 ~~Years~~ *years* ago, a volcano erupted in today's El Salvador and buried a village of the great Mayan civilization. Archeologists have already found many large ~~building~~ *buildings* from this time, but only a ~~little~~ *few* homes of farmers and workers. The village of El Ceren contains perfect examples of ~~a great deal of~~ *many* OR *a lot of* everyday objects. The archeologists have found some knives (with ~~foods~~ *food* still on them), ~~much~~ *many* OR *a lot of* pots made of ~~clays~~ *clay*, a lot ~~of~~ garden tools, a little fabric, and a book. On the wall of one room, they found a few ~~word~~ *words* in an unknown language. There is still a lot to learn from this time capsule, called "the Pompeii of Latin America."

UNIT 18

A 1. a 3. Ø 5. Some 7. the
2. a 4. an 6. Ø 8. the

B 1. the 2. the 3. a 4. a 5. an

C Yesterday I downloaded ~~the~~ *some* movies. We watched ~~a~~ comedy and ~~a~~ *an* Argentinian thriller. ~~A~~ *The* comedy was very funny. I really enjoyed it. The thriller wasn't that good. There wasn't enough action in it. Tonight I think I'd rather read ~~the~~ *a* book than watch a movie. I recently bought ~~the~~ *a* book of fables and a mystery. I think I'll read ~~a~~ *the* mystery before I go to bed.

UNIT 19

A 1. annoying 4. hard
2. late 5. surprisingly
3. perfect

B 1. interesting old house
2. big cheerful yellow kitchen OR cheerful big yellow kitchen
3. peaceful residential street
4. nice young international students
5. didn't seem friendly at all (OR at all friendly)
6. cute little Greek restaurant
7. really beautiful garden
8. wonderful old round wooden table
9. decide pretty quickly
10. rent awfully fast

C The conditions in Parker Dorm are pretty ~~shocked~~ *shocking*. The rooms are ~~terrible~~ *terribly* small, and the furniture is incredibly ugly. The locks on the doors don't work ~~good~~ *well*, so your stuff is never ~~safely~~ *safe*. The dorm counselors are great—they're all really nice, friendly people—but they can't make up for the ~~badly~~ *bad* conditions.

UNIT 20

A 1. as 4. less
2. better 5. longer
3. more 6. the more impatient

B 1. more expensive than 4. more convenient
2. bigger 5. farther
3. larger than

C Last night, I had dinner at the new Pasta Place on the corner of Main Street and Grove. This new Pasta Place is just as good ~~than~~ *as* the others, and it has just as many sauces to choose from. No one makes a ~~more good~~ *better* traditional tomato sauce ~~them~~ *than*. But there are much ~~interestinger~~ *more interesting* choices. Their mushroom cream sauce, for example, is as ~~better~~ *good* as I've ever had. Try the mushroom and tomato sauce for a healthier ~~than~~ meal. It's just as delicious. The new branch is already popular. The later it is, *the* longer the lines. My recommendation: Go early for a ~~more short~~ *shorter* wait. And go soon. This place will only get more ~~popular~~ and more popular!

UNIT 21

A 1. shortest 4. rainiest
2. biggest 5. most expensive
3. driest 6. cheapest

B 1. the coldest 5. the least fun
2. the most fantastic 6. the best
3. the most popular 7. the funniest
4. the most crowded

C Small towns aren't *the* most dynamic places to visit, and that's just why we love to vacation on Tangier Island. This tiny island is probably the ~~less~~ *least* popular vacation spot in the United States. Almost no one comes here. But it's also one of the ~~most~~ safest places to visit. And you'll find some of the ~~goodest~~ *best* seafood and the *most* beautiful beaches here. It's one of the easiest ~~place~~ *places* to get around (there are no cars on the island). If you get bored, just hop on the ferry. You're only a few hours from Washington, D.C., and a few more hours from New York and the ~~excitingest~~ *most exciting* nightlife ever.

A 1. well
2. doesn't run
3. more accurately
4. of
5. as well as
6. the more tired he gets
7. harder
8. better

B 1. well
2. faster
3. the most accurately
4. the hardest
5. the worst

C Last night's game was a very exciting one. The Globes played the best they've played all season. But they still didn't play as ~~good~~ *well* as the Stars. The Stars hit the ball more ~~frequent~~ *frequently* and ran ~~more fast~~ *faster* than the Globes, and their pitcher, Kevin Rodriguez, threw the ball more accurately. Their catcher, Scott Harris, handled ~~better the ball~~ *the ball better* than the Globes' catcher. The Globes are good, but they are ~~less good than~~ *not as good as* the Stars. All in all, the Stars just keep playing ~~good~~ *better* and better. And the better they play, the ~~hardest~~ *harder* it is for their fans to get tickets! These games sell out quicker than hotcakes, so go early if you want to get a chance to see the Stars.

A 1. not liking
2. smoking
3. feeling
4. joining
5. swimming
6. not eating
7. improving

B 1. Laughing is
2. suggests OR suggested watching
3. Telling . . . helps OR will help
4. advises OR advised against drinking
5. enjoy taking
6. think about smoking

C 1. You look great. Buying these bikes ~~were~~ *was* a good idea.
2. I know. I'm happy about ~~lose~~ *losing* weight too. ~~Didn't~~ *Not* exercising was a bad idea.
3. It always is. Hey, I'm thinking of ~~rent~~ *renting* a movie. What do you suggest ~~to see~~ *seeing*?
4. I've been looking forward to ~~see~~ *seeing* *Grown Ups*. Have you seen it yet?
5. Not yet. Do you recommend it? You're so good at ~~choose~~ *choosing* movies.

A 1. to get
2. to meet
3. to finish
4. to go
5. to play
6. to call

B 1. invited Mary to visit us
2. agreed to come
3. wants to make new friends
4. told her to come early
5. decided not to invite Tom
6. needs to finish his project

C 1. A: I want ^*to* invite you to my party.
B: Thanks. I'd love ~~coming~~ *to come*.
2. A: I plan ~~to not~~ *not to* get there before 8:00.
B: Remember ~~getting~~ *to get* the soda. Don't forget!
3. A: Sara asked ~~I~~ *me* to help her.
B: I agreed ~~helping~~ *to help* her too.
4. A: I promised ^*to* pick up some ice cream.
B: OK. But let's do it early. I prefer ~~don't~~ *not to* arrive late.

A 1. get
2. in order not
3. to take
4. too
5. clearly enough

B 1. easy enough to figure out
2. too hard for me to use
3. too fast for me to understand
4. too far for us to walk
5. in order not to be late
6. early enough for us to walk
7. too heavy for us to cross
8. my phone to get directions
9. clearly enough for it to work
10. a taxi to save time

C Is 16 too young ~~for~~ *to* drive? It's really hard to ~~saying~~ *say*. Some kids are mature enough to drive at 16, but some aren't. I think most 16 year-olds are still too immature ^*to* drive with friends in the car, though. It's ~~for them easy~~ *easy for them* to forget to pay attention with a lot of kids in the car. In order ~~preventing~~ *to prevent* accidents, some families have a "no friends" rule for the first year. I think that's a reasonable idea.

UNIT 26

A
1. starting
2. to finish
3. trying
4. to join
5. seeing
6. to call
7. Studying

B
1. doing
2. to take
3. working OR to work
4. sitting
5. taking
6. to get
7. studying

C It's difficult to study in a foreign country, so

students need ~~preparing~~ *to prepare* for the experience. Most people look forward to living abroad, but they

worry about ~~don't feel~~ *not feeling* at home. They're afraid of not understanding the culture, and they don't want

~~making~~ *to make* mistakes. It's impossible to avoid ~~to have~~ *having* some problems at the beginning. No one escapes from feeling some culture shock, and it's important

~~realizing~~ *to realize* this fact. But soon most people stop ~~to feel~~ *feeling* uncomfortable and start to feel more at home in the new culture.

UNIT 27

A
1. each other
2. himself
3. one another
4. herself
5. myself
6. ourselves
7. yourselves
8. itself

B
1. talk to each other
2. greet each other
3. help yourself
4. enjoying themselves
5. drove herself

C When I first met Nicole, I told myself, "I'm not

going to like working with ~~herself~~ *her*." I was really

wrong. Nicole has helped ~~myself~~ *me* out with so many

things. When she ~~oneself~~ *herself* didn't know something, she

always found out for me. That way, both of ~~ourselves~~ *us* learned something. After I learned the job better, we

helped ~~each other's~~ *each other* OR *one another* out. Now the job ~~themselves~~ *itself* isn't that challenging, but I'm really enjoying myself.

Everyone here likes ~~each another~~ *one another* OR *each other*. That makes it a great place to work. I feel lucky to be here.

UNIT 28

A
1. out
2. up
3. on
4. out
5. up
6. over

B
1. Joe gets up early.
2. He turns on the TV OR He turns the TV on.
3. He sits down with Ana.
4. They get along well.
5. They look over his schedule OR They look his schedule over.
6. They talk it over.
7. They put it away.
8. They put on their coats OR They put their coats on.

C As soon as Ina wakes up, she finds Abby's leash

and puts it ~~away~~ *on* her. Then the two of them set for^ *out*

their morning walk ~~out~~. They keep ~~up~~ *on* walking until they get to the park, where there are a lot of other dogs and their owners. Abby is a very friendly animal,

and she gets ~~well along~~ *along well* with other dogs. Ina loves dogs and always had one when she was growing

~~over~~ *up*. There is a saying that "A dog is a man's best friend," but Ina knows it's a woman's best friend too. "I enjoy playing with Abby," she says, "and just being

with her cheers ~~up me~~ *me up*." Abby obviously enjoys being with Ina too. The two have become really good friends and have improved each other's lives a lot.

UNIT 29

A
1. don't have to
2. Does
3. can't
4. 've got to
5. had
6. have

B
1. don't have to do
2. have to pick up
3. 've . . . had to stand
4. don't have to wait OR won't have to wait
5. can't smoke
6. has to move OR will have to move
7. can't sit
8. have to have OR 'll have to have
9. had to eat OR 'll have to eat

C
1. He can't ~~boards~~ *board* the plane yet.
2. Passengers ~~must not~~ *don't have to* stay in their seats when the seat belt light is off.
3. Passengers: Please note that you ~~gotta~~ *have to* OR *must* pay extra for luggage over 50 pounds.
4. You don't ~~have got to~~ *have to* show your passport right now, but please have it ready.
5. Paul ~~will has~~ *will have* OR *has* to unpack some of his stuff. His suitcase is much too heavy.

A 1. a   2. b   3. c   4. a   5. c

B 1. 're supposed to be

2. isn't supposed to start

3. are . . . supposed to sit

4. 're supposed to go

5. Was (OR Am) . . . supposed to wear

6. 're (OR were) supposed to wear

7. isn't (OR wasn't) supposed to rain

8. was (OR is) supposed to be

C 1. Dahlia was ~~suppose~~ *supposed* to drive. She was ~~supposed not~~ *not supposed* to fly.

2. She ~~is~~ *was* going to wear her blue dress, but she changed her mind.

3. What are we supposed to ~~doing~~ *do* after the ceremony?

4. My parents ~~will~~ *were* supposed to fly home tomorrow, but they're staying another day.

5. It was ~~no~~ *not* supposed to be this cold, and it ~~didn't suppose~~ *wasn't supposed* to rain.

A 1. Will   5. get
2. might   6. could
3. going to   7. Maybe
4. may

B 1. Are . . . going to go

2. may OR might OR could

3. Is . . . going to be

4. may not OR might not

5. are . . . going to

6. may OR might OR could stay

7. may not OR might not open

8. may OR might OR could open

C Suddenly, weather forecasts all over the world are predicting terrible storms. Climatologist Jack Hall understands weather trends, and he thinks that a new ice age could ~~to~~ begin very quickly. His son Sam is in New York with his high school class. One student is sick and ~~mayn't~~ *may not* live without medicine. ~~May~~ *Will* those kids survive by themselves? They ~~maybe~~ *may* OR *might* not. Jack bundles up and starts walking to New York to save them. There ~~might could~~ *may* OR *might* OR *could* be a happy ending. Or the world could end. You'll have to watch to find out!

A 1. must   4. can't
2. has got to   5. Could
3. could   6. could

B 1. couldn't be   5. can't be
2. could be   6. Could . . . lead
3. could . . . want 7. might know
4. Could . . . be

C 1. Jason has been coughing all morning. He might ~~having~~ *have* a cold.

2. Diana must not ~~likes~~ *like* fish. She left most of it on her plate.

3. ~~May~~ *Could* OR *Can* the package be from your parents?

4. That's impossible! It ~~might not~~ *couldn't* OR *can't* be true.

5. Is the bank still open? That's a good question. I don't know. It might. *be*

6. She ~~could~~ *couldn't* OR *can't* be a thief! I trust her completely!

7. It's got *to* be a joke. I don't believe it's serious.

CREDITS

PHOTO CREDITS:

Page 231 (left) Shutterstock.com, (middle) SuperStock/SuperStock, (right) Ralf-Finn Hestoft/Index Stock Imagery; **p. 237** Shutterstock.com; **p. 252** SuperStock/SuperStock; **p. 253** Alinari/Art Resource, NY; **p. 255** Ralf-Finn Hestoft/Index Stock Imagery; **p. 265** (left) Ariel Skelley/Corbis, (middle) Shutterstock.com, (right) Andrew Gunners/Getty Images; **p. 266** (top) Ariel Skelley/Corbis, (left) Shutterstock.com, (middle) Shutterstock.com, (right) Shutterstock.com; **p. 272** Ariel Skelley/Corbis; **p. 273** Shutterstock.com; **p. 276** Shutterstock.com; **p. 278** Shutterstock.com; **p. 282** Shutterstock.com; **p. 296** Andrew Gunners/Getty Images; **p. 307** AP Images/ Andre Penner; **p. 313** Glyn Kirk/Getty Images; **p. 314** Fotosearch/Digital Vision; **p. 316** AP Images/Kyodo; **p. 321** (right) Shutterstock.com; **p. 322** www.CartoonStock.com; **p. 328** RubberBall Productions; **p. 334** RubberBall Productions; **p. 342** Nancy Ney/Getty Images; **p. 344** Shutterstock.com; **p. 348** Shutterstock.com; **p. 349** (1) Shutterstock.com, (2) Shutterstock.com, (3) David Allan Brandt/Getty Images, (4) Shutterstock.com, (5) Shutterstock.com, (6) Shutterstock.com, (7) Jon Arnold Images Ltd/Alamy, (8) Shutterstock.com; **p. 354** Marisa Acocella Marchetto/The New Yorker Collection/www.cartoonbank.com; **p. 368** Dreamstime.com; **p. 375** (middle) Shutterstock.com, (right) Rick Friedman/Corbis; **p. 376** (left) holbox/Shutterstock, (right) Lou Chardonnay/Corbis; **p. 380** Shutterstock.com; **p. 391** Douglas Kirkland/Corbis; **p. 397** Rick Friedman/Corbis; **p. 398** Photolibrary.com; **p. 407** (left) Fotosearch/Corbis; **p. 408** Fotosearch/Image Club; **p. 413** Shutterstock.com; **p. 422** Fotosearch/ Corbis; **p. 429** Corbis; **p. 432** Shutterstock.com; **p. 443** (left) Shutterstock.com, (right) Shutterstock.com; **p. 457** (woman) Shutterstock.com, (plate) Joseph Sohm/Visions of America/Corbis, (paint) Shutterstock.com, (toys) Dreamstime.com, (shoes) Shutterstock.com.

ILLUSTRATION CREDITS:

Steve Attoe – page 357; **Chi Chung** – pages 246, 247; **ElectraGraphics** – page 354; **Paul Hampson** – page 232; **Jock MacRae** – page 387; **Tom Newsom** – pages 382, 383; **Dusan Petricic** – page 254; **Steve Schulman** – pages 367, 370, 452 (left); **Gary Torrisi** – pages 258, 260, 303, 452 (right)

INDEX

This index is for the full and split editions. All entries are in the full book. Entries for Volume A of the split edition are in black. Entries for Volume B are in red.

Adj. order

Opinion + Size + Age + Shape + Color + Origin
+ Material + Purpose + Noun

Opinion + Size + Age + Shape + Color + Origin
+ Material + Purpose + Noun